Reflections from the Audience

Sixty Years Attending
Thousands of Performances
—and Writing About Each

Les Epstein

YBK Publishers   New York

Reflections from the Audience: Sixty Years of Attending Thousands of Performances —and Writing About Each

Copyright © 2023 by Les Epstein

All rights reserved including
the right of reproduction
in whole or in part in any form.

YBK Publishers, Inc.
39 Crosby Street
New York, NY 10013

ISBN: 978-1-936411-87-0

Library of Congress Cataloging:in:Publication Data
Names: Epstein, Les, author.
Title: Reflections from the audience : sixty years of attending thousands of performances --and writing about each / Les Epstein.
Description: New York : YBK Publishers, 2024. | Summary: "Containing ample quotes from his reviews, the book details performances and performers; most of them world-famous; others obscure but deserving of greater fame. Some, the author admires deeply; a few, not so much. These are not just verbal descriptions. Epstein provides URLs of videos and audio recordings that enable you to click along to see and hear what he saw and heard. Going back in real time to as far as his elementary school days and the pop music of that era, he even tells you about that period in time-about Captain Video on TV and about serials at Saturday morning movie-theater kiddie shows"-- Provided by publisher.
Identifiers: LCCN 2023047447 (print) | LCCN 2023047448 (ebook) | ISBN 9781936411870 (paperback) | ISBN 9781936411887 (kindle edition)
Subjects: LCSH: Musical criticism. | Music videos--Catalogs. | Epstein, Les--Anecdotes. | Music fans--United States--Anecdotes. | Popular music fans--United States--Anecdotes. | LCGFT: Catalogs. | Autobiographies.
Classification: LCC ML3785 .E67 2024 (print) | LCC ML3785 (ebook) | DDC 070.4/4978--dc23/eng/20231020
LC record available at https://lccn.loc.gov/2023047447
LC ebook record available at https://lccn.loc.gov/2023047448

Manufactured in the United States of America
for distribution in North and South America
or in the United Kingdom or Australia
when distributed elsewhere.

For more information, visit
www.ybkpublishers.com

Contents

Preface   v

BACKGROUND   2
Popular Music as a Reflection of Its Time   2
Musical Influences   4
Martin Block and the *Make Believe Ballroom*   6
Classical Music Makes Its Entry   8
Mario Lanza   12
My Early Days as an Opera Lover   13
Richie, "Uncle Ray," and My Introduction to Franco Corelli   15

OPERA AND OPERA SINGERS   17
The Old Met   17
My Early Met Performances   19
Early *Memorable* Opera Performances   20
Tenors and Italian Opera at the Old Met   22
Lois Kirschenbaum   24
Two Legendary Divas   26
A Tale of Two *Toscas*   29
Tito Gobbi   32
Franco Corelli   37
My Introduction to German Opera at the Old Met   49
Böhm and Strauss at the New Met   51
Placido Domingo   52
The Elephant in the Room   58
Sherrill Milnes   60
The New York City Opera, Norman Treigle, and Beverly Sills   61
The Summer of 1969 in Washington D.C.— Ellington, Schwarzkopf, and Stilwell   68

OPERA PRESERVED   77
Opera and Record Companies   77
Broadcasts and Tapes   79
Edward J. Smith & Giovanni Martinelli   82
Lauritz Melchior, Others, and Pirated Recordings   86
Classical Music Stations in New York in the 1960s and Now   97

CONDUCTORS   100
Arturo Toscanini and My Toscanini Legacy   100
Toscanini's Rivals   103
The Golden Age of Conductors   104
Leopold Stokowski   106
Leonard Bernstein   111
James Levine   115

MUSICALS AND MUSICAL THEATER PERFORMERS   119
My First Broadway Musical   119
A Listing of Great Musicals   120
Sondheim and the Post-1970 Musicals   122
Encores! and the City Center   130
Broadway Bootlegs   132
Ethel Merman, Patti LuPone, Sutton Foster, and More   133
Judy Garland   152
Barbra Streisand   156
Julie Andrews   157
Happy End   161
Male Musical Theater Performers   162
Homage To My Favorite Musical Theater Performer   167
Returning Stars   175
More Returning Stars   180
Comden and Green   184
The 1971 "Tony Awards" Show   186

PLAYS AND ACTORS   187
The Summer of 1964 and Hamlet/John Barrymore   187
Eugene O'Neill, Tennessee Williams, Arthur Miller, and Jason Robards   195
More Great American Plays   206
Shaw, *Man and Superman*— Paul Sparer, Harris Laskawy,
    and Philip Bosco   209
Shakespeare in the Park   223
The Two Funniest Shows I've Seen on Broadway   226
Two Seminal Solo Shows   228

POTPOURRI   231
Tony Bennett   231
My Vote for the Most Overrated Popular Singer   234
The Age of the Singer/Songwriter   235
Performing Arts on the Cheap   239
Reflections *on* the Audience   245
Hamilton, Diversity, and the Future   246

Dedication

*This book is dedicated to my wife, Victoria.
You may have heard of football widows.
My wife was very often an opera widow,
but she has managed to put up with that,
and me, for over forty-five years now.*

Also, to our son, Drew, and daughter, Elizabeth.

Dear Print Edition Reader

The audio/video Internet links found herein cannot be "played" from the printed book, but we can quickly and easily get you set up to do this, at no cost to you by providing you with an additional medium.

Simply send an email to the publisher at ybkpublishers@gmail.com, inserting the code REFLECTIONS into the subject line, and we will send you a "clickable" PDF of the links in the book that can be downloaded to any "smart" device you own.

The PDF contains live links that, when clicked, will connect you to the Internet and let you listen to and see the subject material being discussed in the text.

Devices on which the PDF can be mounted are the MacBook, your PC desktop or laptop, a Fire tablet, Kindles that support Internet connection, and any other type of smart device onto which PDFs can be loaded, *including your smartphone*, a very convenient way to listen to and see the links as you encounter them.

There are many different ways to mount a PDF. A Google-search will reveal the easiest way to get it onto your device. Among the easier ways is to email the PDF to yourself as an attachment and then double-click the PDF where it is stored on the device.

The Internet is flexible and fluid, changing from moment to moment. It is inevitable that some links will become broken as time goes by—that, occasionally, a link will not open when it is clicked on. Because these links are created by others, they can be withdrawn by their creators at any time. We will comb all of the links from time to time to keep them up to date by deleting or replacing broken links. If you would like to report a broken link, please tell us just the final several characters (six or eight, say) of the broken link in an email to info@ybkpublishers.com and we will see to its quick repair.

There may be occasions when clicking on a link fails to make the connection from the PDF. In such cases, try copying the link to your clipboard and pasting it into your browser.

Preface

I saw my first live professional performance of any kind at New York City's Lewisohn Stadium in July of 1960, at the age of fourteen. Lewisohn Stadium was built in 1915 and demolished in 1973. It was the athletic field of the City College of New York. It was also the outdoor summer performance home of the New York Philharmonic for many years. Seven years later, I would graduate from City College. Little did I know on that pleasant summer night in 1960 that that concert was to be the first of several thousand performances I would attend over the next sixty years. I had recently become interested in opera and that first performance, billed as "Italian Night," was a concert of opera selections sung by Mary Curtis-Verna, Jan Peerce, and Robert Merrill.

The next day I wrote a short critique, a "review," of that concert. I have been writing *and keeping* reviews of every performance I've ever seen of music and theater of any kind, from 1960 right up until the Covid-19 pandemic that closed down live performances of any kind, pretty much everywhere in the world, in February, 2020.

Having seen thousands of performances in all arenas of the performing arts, that's a lot of writing! Most of it is in handwritten form and was stored in my basement in a multitude of loose-leaf binders. When I was writing these reviews, I never much thought about why I wrote them. It simply seemed like a very good thing to me to go ahead and write about every performance I saw.

No one but I has ever read them, and I have rarely looked back at what I wrote. At some point during that dark Covid period, I had the realization that I had seen and written about some truly memorable, and some even historic performances that might very well be of interest to others to hear about; maybe, and perhaps, especially, people who were not around to witness those performances.

Don't worry, I'm not going to include all the reviews, not even remotely close. There will be just an easily digested comprehensive

> Live Performances I Have Seen
>
> I. (1960 Season)
>
> 1. July 21, 1960 Thursday 8:30 P.M. at Lewisohn Stadium in New York City: **Italian Night**
>   Conductor: Alfredo Antonini, Stadium Symphony Orchestra
>   Soloists: Mary Curtis-Verna, Soprano
>   Robert Merrill, Baritone
>   Jan Peerce, Tenor
>
>   With this concert I decided to start this list. Since January I have been interested in opera and because of this I really enjoyed this concert, which contained many excerpts from operas. Another reason was the famous soloists. Enjoyed Jan Peerce most because I like and am more familiar with tenors. He sang E lucevan le stelle beautifully. Others were also good and so was the orchestra.
>
> 2. (1960 - Season)
>
> 2. August 1, 1960 Monday 8:30 P.M. at the Mall in Central Park in New York City: **Operatic Favorites**
>   Featuring: The Goldman Band
>   Conductor: Richard Franko Goldman
>
>   A good free concert, but no where near the above concert. The main reason behind my enjoyment of this concert is my interest in opera. The selections as played by the band were satisfactory, but an orchestra would have played them better.

From the basement archives: My first two "reviews." I was fourteen.

distillation of the more interesting ones; many of them about performances not well-documented elsewhere. It would be much too lengthy (and boring) to quote them all, (especially the earlier stuff, from my teen-age years, that is ill-formed). So, instead, I will sometimes just give you the impressions they revived in me as I re-read them.

I sometimes trace back to periods before my time to identify performers I did not see in live performance, but who left an indelible impression on me through their recordings and movies. In other entries, I will provide an overview of my thoughts on various aspects of the performing arts, its works, and the artists. On occasion I may tell a personal story related to what is being discussed. Also, I will provide occasional tidbits of opera or theatrical trivia.

What scholastic qualifications do I have that "permit" me to review professional performances or to write at large about the performing arts? None. I have no special education in music nor any qualification that makes my opinion more valid than yours. I was simply a member of the audience who was there to be entertained, uplifted, or otherwise moved or challenged by the performance. I then took pen to paper shortly after every time I was in an audience. If there were a doctorate for viewers of the performing arts, this would be my dissertation.

The 1960s was the dawn of a new consumer technology era during which live performances could be recorded, not just by professional record companies, movie, and radio and television studios, but illicitly by audience members, using equipment that came to be within their economic reach at that time. Opera lovers were among the forefront of this, as many of them would sneak their new portable tape recorders into opera houses and record those performances that were not broadcast over the radio.

It took another two or three decades for the technology to reach a point that an audience member could record not just the audio of a performance, but the visual element as well. This was a boon to lovers of musicals. People began, unobserved, to record Broadway musicals.

Perhaps, at first, those illicit recordings stayed in the collection of the individual who recorded them, but opera lovers soon began trading tapes among themselves. Soon enough, a cottage industry of pirated opera records sprang up. And, following that, a couple of decades later, people were selling bootleged Broadway videos through an even newer medium, the Internet.

With the advent of YouTube and similar Internet sites, a little over a decade ago (after YouTube ended its policy of limiting the maximum play length of posted videos), full length operas and videos of Broadway musicals began to appear. Operas and musicals were available to watch for free, along with radio and television broadcasts of all kinds.

Thus, as I began writing this book, YouTube had already become a vast resource for performing arts videos of all description. What started out as a book of essays of my thoughts on certain of the performing arts—put forth from the perspective of my sixty years in the audience—became something more. With the insertion of URL hyperlinks to various resources, readers can now both see and hear for themselves what I have written about.

With the use of links to videos, I can illustrate various points, and readers can see and hear for themselves what is discussed. These are my personal opinions. You will find you sometimes disagree. Of course! The clips will enable you to make your own determination.

There are both brief sampling links and links to full length performances. Obviously, the full-length links are not necessarily meant to be viewed at that point in the text at which they are placed, although one might want to view a couple of minutes to get an idea of the context. They are there for future reference. The shorter clips usually illustrate a specific point in that part of the text and will enhance what you are reading by viewing or listening to them *as* you are reading the book.

The bulk of the links are to YouTube. That could end up being problematic as these links are sometimes deleted by their creators. Of course, nothing prevents the reader from doing one's own Internet search, which might even uncover a video I missed or one that was posted after the book was published.

Opinions don't arise out of thin air. They are formed by the multiplicity and variety of the life experiences of the person who holds them. Thus, I will start the book with how I came to be led to opera, to then devote a good portion of the discussion to opera and classical music.

I am aware that opera does not have the larger following that some of the other art forms do, such as theater musicals. For readers who may not care for opera, or have not been exposed to it at length, if you listen to some of the clips provided, you might come to see opera in a more positive light. If this book actually creates a new opera lover, terrific, but that is not its specific intention.

I start with pop music, the music of the 1950's that led me to opera. Indeed, the second chapter has many links to songs that were the formative music experience of my youth. Many readers will already be familiar with some of these songs. Still, listening to them, whether for the first or umpteenth time, should give you a better understanding of how my opinions were formed. It may also be an enjoyable, uplifting listen. And, it might prompt you to think about how your own (probably very different) opinions were formed.

Background

Popular Music as a Reflection of Its Time

It has been said that popular music is a reflection of its time. The music of the 1950s was certainly that.

"The Greatest Generation," those who had fought World War II, had seen battlefield horrors, atrocities, and genocide. They came home wanting a peaceful life. And for the most part, for at least the following decade, they got it. Postwar America was booming, and the middle class was, too. Big bands and swing music gave way to crooners, girl singers, and vocal groups with soothing harmonies. A form called "Easy Listening" music became a thing. All was good. The forces of freedom had beaten the forces of evil and it was simply time to enjoy the fruits of victory.

Of course, all was not good. There were segments of American society who did not share in the prosperity and its availability. As Thurgood Marshall and the NAACP Legal Defense Fund were laying the groundwork for the fight for equality, Martin Luther King, Jr. emerged as the leader of the Civil Rights Movement. More militant Black leaders like Malcolm X and the Black Panthers were to emerge during the next decade.

It was a revolution sparked by the civil rights movement to be later further fueled by the opposition to the Vietnam War, by the Women's Movement, and by Gay Right's activists. By the late 1960s, it became an era of peace, love, drugs, and hippies, that was carried out by the "Baby Boomers," the sons and daughters of "The Greatest Generation," who were now often in conflict with their parents.

By the mid-1950s, the oldest of the baby boomers realized that pop music, the music their parents were listening to, did not do it for them. Rock and Roll began slowly with Bill Haley, taking a giant step with Elvis, and it kept on going with Little Richard, Jerry Lee Lewis,

Chuck Berry, and so on. The harmonies and lyrics of vocal groups became somewhat less soothing as the do wop groups came along.

Then, as the late fifties progressed and the sixties commenced, even more boomers were coming of age. So began the "folk revival:" The Kingston Trio; Peter, Paul and Mary; Joan Baez; Judy Collins, and others were followed by Bob Dylan (beginning the age of the singer-songwriter), the Beatles, and the "British invasion" (by music, of course).

The music of boomer parents, singers backed by lush orchestral arrangements, was replaced by a different, rawer music influenced by rhythm and blues and soul, the music created by those segments of American society marginalized during the 1950s and before. One can only wonder if this younger generation's appreciation for, and co-opting of, that music helped that generation also to identify with and become more involved in the fight for equality. Meanwhile, this now mainstream music would become even rawer as the decades progressed and rock and roll evolved into hard rock; continuing to stray even more greatly from the music of the fifties, engaging such variations as heavy metal, punk rock and the even-later phenomenon, hip-hop.

By the early 1960s, one might wonder whether pop music was a reflection of its time or was beginning to define its time. When Dylan wrote and sang *The Times They are a-Changin,'* he wasn't simply expressing what was going on around him, he was helping to move that change along.

[https://www.youtube.com/watch?v=s3qndXvBmr0]

Music became an integral part of the life of that period's listener in a way that had never happened before. Their parents (then called bobby soxers) may have swooned for the youthful Frankie, but Sinatra wasn't an integral part of a social and political revolution. In the sixties, music wasn't there just to dance to, or to relax and sooth you after a long and bitter war, it was egging you on to a different type of struggle going on in the U.S.A.

I began to listen to pop music in 1950 at the age of five, right in the middle of that booming post-war era. It was the era between the fall of the big bands at the end of World War II and the dawn of rock and roll that came to great popularity in the mid-1950s; and it hasn't stopped yet. Would I have become an opera lover had I "gotten into" pop music at a later age—in my teens, at the time most of my generation got into pop music? That would have been the dawn of the rock era, and too late to provide me with the earlier formative exposure to the individual singing voice that ultimately led me to opera.

Musical Influences

Pop music of the 1950s is often looked down upon and ridiculed, perhaps unfairly. It was the era of solo singers, many of whom had been lead band-singers in the years before: Perry Como, Frank Sinatra, Jo Stafford, Doris Day, and Kitty Kallen. There were those who didn't start out as band-singers such as Nat (King) Cole (who started out as a jazz pianist), Theresa Brewer, Frankie Laine, Eddie Fisher, Dean Martin, Patti Page, Johnny Ray, Guy Mitchell, Vic Damone, and Tony Bennett, to list a few.

One of the first songs I can remember was Jo Stafford's *Shrimp Boats*. [https://www.youtube.com/watch?v=Sbd8s98FrWw] Okay, it plays almost like a children's song, but it was a big hit in 1951.

Among my favorite songs from that period were Patti Page's Tennessee Waltz
[https://www.youtube.com/watch?v=cQjSnHQLPTk],
Eddie Fisher's *Lady of Spain*
[https://www.youtube.com/watch?v=eHUR4Q-5rew],
Johnny Ray's Walking *My Baby Back Home*
[https://www.youtube.com/watch?v=IPYq_wjzjwk],
Frankie Laine's *Do Not Forsake Me*
[https://www.youtube.com/watch?v=9wmq5FLz5ss] (When I saw *High Noon*, the movie in which that song was introduced, it was, disappointingly, not Frankie Laine who sang it),
Doris Day's *Secret Love*
[https://www.youtube.com/watch?v=aiueIiFJdN8],
Kay Starr's *Wheel of Fortune*
[https://www.youtube.com/watch?v=b3iamUsIsic],
Theresa Brewer's *Till I Waltz Again With You*
[https://www.youtube.com/watch?v=WZkTC0YmfVY],
Frank Sinatra's *Young at Heart*
[https://www.youtube.com/watch?v=L0ivcZYilsE],
Perry Como's *Wanted*
[https://www.youtube.com/watch?v=cMVDQi16d4s],
Dean Martin's *That's Amore*
[https://www.youtube.com/watch?v=L6GRPGSUvFA],
Tony Martin's *Stranger in Paradise*

[https://www.youtube.com/watch?v=HXSp7kP2-4A],
Kitty Kallen's *Little Things Mean a Lot*
[https://www.youtube.com/watch?v=H3J5lzCr1n0],
Nat Cole's *Haji Baba*
[https://www.youtube.com/watch?v=jp59Pln_Jw4],
Rosemary Clooney's *Hey There*
[https://www.youtube.com/watch?v=8LBzeKRZhuY],
Don Cornell's *No Man is an Island*
[https://www.youtube.com/watch?v=wNfUY4xglN4],
Al Hibbler's *Unchained Melody*
[https://www.youtube.com/watch?v=GbT9fNJGpEo],
Vic Damone's *On the Street Where You Live*
[https://www.youtube.com/watch?v=0vuJW35IK6w],
Guy Mitchell's *Singing the Blues*
[https://www.youtube.com/watch?v=eGgTdJeCzLE],
Sonny James's *Young Love*
[https://www.youtube.com/watch?v=pU_8D5jBqd0],
Jerry Vale's *You Don't Know Me*
[https://www.youtube.com/watch?v=gybMh2Vob00],
Johnny Mathis's *Chances Are*
[https://www.youtube.com/watch?v=1CieoQeLqcU],
Della Reese's *Don't You Know*
[https://www.youtube.com/watch?v=N86nxxZW6UY] (Little did I know I was listening to Puccini's *La Boheme*.)

And, let's not leave out the hits of Tony Bennett throughout that decade.

Even the granddaddy of the band singers who became solo stars, Bing Crosby, had his last hit in the mid-50s with *True Love*
[https://www.youtube.com/watch?v=bra5o8RC9zo]
(which proved that even the ultra-sophisticated Cole Porter could write a sappy love song).

Most of the singers listed had multiple hits during this period, but there were also the one-hit wonders of the time like Texas golfer Don Cherry's *Band of Gold,*
[https://www.youtube.com/watch?v=TUXOIP6zcjc]
a Brit named David Whitfield who sang the very operatic-sounding *Cara Mia,*
[https://www.youtube.com/watch?v=LE9pRwVYo5k]
and Gogi Grant's *The Wayward Wind*
[https://www.youtube.com/watch?v=bW52i3iHQzg].

While I enjoyed many of the vocal groups of that period, it was the very distinctive, unique, and beautiful solo voices that captured my heart and imagination during those early formative years.

Martin Block and the *Make Believe Ballroom*

The radio program I most listened to during the 1950's and into the 1960's was Martin Block's the *Make Believe Ballroom.* The program began in 1935, its initial premise being to sound as though it was being broadcast from an actual ballroom with big name bands performing live; but, of course, it was simply Martin Block playing recordings in a radio studio somewhere in Manhattan. It was heard on station WNEW. In 1954, Block switched to WABC, and, finally, to WOR; all broadcast from New York City.

Block had been one of the most famous disk jockeys during the Big Band era. Indeed, some believe the term "disc jockey" was coined to describe what he did. To get an idea of how popular he was, the theme song for the program, "Make Believe Ballroom Time," for which he wrote the lyrics, was recorded by Glenn Miller in 1940, when Miller was at the height of his popularity.
[https://www.youtube.com/watch?v=7sqoFqc91kc]

In 1948, Block appeared in a movie short, *Martin Block's Musical-Go-Round* [https://www.youtube.com/watch?v=icl4xICJgcA], and in the next year there followed a Make Believe Ballroom feature film. You can see him hosting and doing commercials (at 5:45, 20:10 and 23:44), in the days bfore the dangers of cigarette smoking were widely known to the general public on *The Chesterfield Supper Club Starring Perry Como*, with guests that included Patti Page and Victor Borge. But don't watch just to see Block and the now-banned commercials, watch Perry and Patti to hear additional examples of the mainstream pop music being played at about the time that I started to get into to pop music—and to see Victor Borge before his great success on Broadway, which I report on later.
[https://www.youtube.com/watch?v=mTCiKVC7rBU&list=PLHWNRn9JB2ARUOrcQLGUMsWAKpd9ylo-r]

The main vocalist you see in *Martin Block's Musical-Go-Round* is Buddy Clark, a singer little remembered today. Toward the end of that short, he sings a very charming song called *Linda*. It was Clark's biggest hit, rising to number one in the charts in 1946. Sadly, Clark's life was cut short by a plane crash in 1949. You wouldn't suspect a connection between that 1946 song and the Beatles, but there is one.

Linda was written by Jack Lawrence who, when he got the idea for the song was visiting at his attorney's home. His attorney's infant daughter was named Linda. Lawrence took her name as the name for the song. His attorney was famed entertainment attorney Lee Eastman. That daughter, Linda, more than twenty years later, married Paul McCartney.

Back to Martin Block. In 1954, when Block left WNEW to move to WABC, he continued to use the Miller recording of *Make Believe Ballroom Time* to start his program, despite the fact that a *Make Believe Ballroom* program continued to be broadcast by WNEW—except that their program was now hosted by William B. Williams and no longer opened with the Miller recording.

Make Believe Ballroom continues still to be broadcast on public broadcasting stations (without Martin Block, of course).

[https://www.youtube.com/watch?v=I5WU4kEOK3Y&t=563s]

I began listening to Martin Block's *Make Believe Ballroom* around 1951, after he had abandoned the initial concept of the program, possibly because the Big Band era had ended and the era of the solo singer didn't lend itself to the concept of dancing to the music, ballroom-style.

Occasionally, Block would tell the story about a skinny eighteen-year-old kid from Hoboken who came to his studio one day with his girlfriend Nancy, telling Block that he was going to be a singing star. After hearing him sing, Block introduced him to Tommy Dorsey. The rest is Sinatra history.

During weekdays in the 1950s, Block would be on for several hours, usually playing a single artist (generally a singer) during each fifteen-minute slot. On Saturday mornings he would play that week's "hit parade" popularity list, starting with around number forty, counting down to number one.

[https://www.youtube.com/watch?v=ZBfXQq7qKm0]

He had strong views on artists, and he was something of a prude. Tony Bennett was one of Block's favorites, but on one occasion I remember Block going into a rant about how disappointed he was that Bennett had recorded *Love for Sale,* a song he found morally objectionable. (It's about a prostitute.) Block vowed that he would never play that song on his program!

[https://www.youtube.com/watch?v=Tone-1pksxY]

Block's signature sign-off at the end of each *Make Believe Ballroom* program was to say: "So long to you—and you—*and especially to you."* He can be heard signing off at the end (13:22) of this extended clip from one of his mid-1960s shows.

[https://www.youtube.com/watch?v=fwcoJspFv50&t=102s]

By the early 1960s, I had mostly abandoned listening to pop music on the radio and was spending more and more time listening to opera recordings and going to the opera. There is clearly a reason I drifted toward opera. It was because the popular music of the mid and late 1950s began moving toward rock and roll with its rawer vocals, less melodic content, and sparer instrumentation. Opera was much closer to the music I had been listening to, highlighting the singing voice, backed by large orchestras. It wasn't until my first year in law school in 1967, and my first toke, that I rejoined my generation, musically speaking, by now listening to, understanding, and appreciating its music.

Classical Music Makes Its Entry

As a very young boy I listened to and watched shows geared to my demographic. In those days, there were lots of westerns for kids featuring Roy Rogers, Gene Autry, Hopalong Cassidy, Wild Bill Hickock, and, of course, The Lone Ranger.

I first heard *The Lone Ranger* on the radio, as the radio version was still broadcast during the early 1950s. There was also the radio version of *Gunsmoke* with William Conrad. I was hugely disappointed when the TV show made its debut, because I found James Arness's voice disappointing; it was so ordinary when compared to Conrad's. I felt better several years later when Conrad was given his due to star in his own TV show, *Cannon.*

The Lone Ranger theme was the first operatic music I'd ever heard. The famous fanfare that started each show was, of course, the finale from Rossini's *William Tell Overture.*

[https://www.youtube.com/watch?v=p9lf76xOA5k]

It took me a long time to process that this *Lone Ranger* music was actually from a nineteenth-century French opera written by an Italian, about a Swiss folk hero!

[https://www.youtube.com/watch?v=YIbYCOiETx0]

Still, I, and perhaps most of my generation, will always associate the *William Tell Overture* with "Hi Ho Silver, away!"

I watched TV science fiction shows of the time: George Reeves as

Superman [https://www.youtube.com/watch?v=Q2l4bz1FT8U] and, occasionally, *Tom Corbett Space Cadet* [https://www.youtube.com/watch?v=CNZ8n1ovcbw].

There was also *Captain Video and his Video Rangers.* [https://www.youtube.com/watch?v=-0bVqbAJHKQ].

The latter two were broadcast live, with very primitive special effects. These shows soon disappeared, so I found a worthy substitute among the old 1930s movie serials being broadcast then, especially Buster Crabbe's *Flash Gordon* serials.

[https://www.youtube.com/watch?v=fgHKEaGbyDo&list=PLESDrGLwFOLXT0jfvQVzzvQzEaV-3F13u]

Flash Gordon began as a comic strip in 1934 and was turned into three different serial films in 1936, 1938, and 1940.

Single fifteen-minute episodes of such serial films, made in the 1930s and 1940s, were originally often shown in movie theaters during Saturday morning children's movie-theater "specials" when three or four cartoons, a newsreel, and a serial episode were shown between the regular double-feature presentations that were normal for the time. By the 1950s these serials were mostly relegated to being shown on TV.

In the mid-1950's, TV's channel five in New York, (WABD until 1958; WNEW-TV after), had been the flagship station of the by-then defunct DuMont network which had broadcast the *Captain Video* show, resurrected it, *sort of.* Al Hodge, who had played Captain Video, became the host of a half-hour-daily *Captain Video Show,* where, in full Captain Video regalia, he would introduce many of the old 1930s movie serials, including *Flash Gordon*. During one show, Hodge mentioned that they had received many letters asking about the show's music. He explained that the *Captain Video* theme was Wagner's *The Flying Dutchman* overture. Here's an episode of the original *Captain Video* show complete with commercials, its primitive special effects, and sometimes-corny acting. You may wish only to listen to the two-minute introduction. The second link is to a concert performance of *The Flying Dutchman* overture.

[https://www.youtube.com/watch?v=GLN-j5PXRbc&t=672s]]
[https://www.youtube.com/watch?v=Ezqen5-UxlQ]

Captain Video's explanation continued that the music heard in the *Flash Gordon* serial he was showing used Liszt's *Les Preludes.*

[https://www.youtube.com/watch?v=Yj66TCxu21I]
[https://www.youtube.com/watch?v=IywXC0KsEWQ]

I later wondered whether Stanley Kubrick got the idea to use a nineteenth-century orchestral tone poem in a sci-fi movie because he watched *Flash Gordon*. (Kubrick famously used the opening of Richard Struass's *Also Sprach Zaruahustra* for his 1968 film, *2001: A Space Odyssey*.)

In the summer of 1970, I had just graduated law school, gotten a job with the Legal Aid Society in New York, and was looking for an apartment in Manhattan. This was not an easy thing on my budget, even then. So I looked at the ads in *The New York Times* and went to various real estate agencies.

One agency, on 42nd Street, was so low-budget that they didn't even accompany you to the apartment. They gave you a key and you looked at it on your own. When I returned to give back the key, the agent I had been dealing with gave me his card and said I should call him if I wanted to look at more apartments. I looked at the card and everything came together—his face, his voice, and the memory of what I'd read in the *Times* metro section several years earlier.

A *Times* writer had reported that Al Hodge, Captain Video, the show having ended, had reported that he was "in real estate."

The name on the card I had been handed said, "Albert E. Hodge."

"You were Captain Video!"

"No, you're mistaken."

I was shocked!

I knew that this person was *the* Al Hodge of Captain Video fame.

If he didn't want to admit it, I wasn't going to challenge him, but it was apparent who he was.

His hair was grey, his face a little craggier than when I last saw him on TV a dozen years before, but his voice was the same. Actors who started out in radio (he had been radio's "Green Hornet" before he became TV's Captain Video), had the kind of resonant voice that commands attention.

I said, "Sorry," and I left.

I was puzzled, but I guessed that he probably felt a bit embarrassed, having once been a well-known television actor who now worked in a third-rate real estate agency. While I was initially proud of myself for recognizing him, I now felt a little sad to have put him in an embarrassing position. Perhaps his co-workers didn't know he had been famous.

About a week later, still looking for an apartment, I called the agency and asked for Mr. Hodge. I was told he was no longer employed there. I hung up and never went back to that agency. When he died, in 1979, the local TV stations (especially his old channel 5) did obituaries on Captain Video's passing. He had died penniless, in an SRO, a single room occupancy hotel, one step above a flophouse, in midtown Manhattan, an alcoholic.

I never did find an apartment in Manhattan. Instead, I shared a railroad flat in downtown Newark with some friends. Having just graduated Rutgers Law School in Newark, it was a short commute to lower Manhattan where I worked. Living in New Jersey, where I met my wife, turned out to be the best decision of my life, but that's a whole other story.

Mario Lanza

At the age of ten, I began to collect records. My first was Harry Belafonte's *Calypso* around 1956, followed soon thereafter by Tony Bennett's second LP, *Tony*, and a slew of greatest hits albums of many of my favorite singers. Oh!—and because I loved Vic Damone's hit recording of *On the Street Where You Live*, which is from *My Fair Lady*, I had to get original cast album of *My Fair Lady*.

I think it was sometime in 1959, that, always looking for a bargain, I picked up a copy of a budget-priced RCA Camden Mario Lanza LP titled after the Cole Porter song, *You Do Something to Me*. Previously

Mario Lanza around 1950.

I had only heard Lanza's signature pop recording, *Be My Love*.
[https://www.youtube.com/watch?v=EQz1McBv0fw]

A hit in 1949, *Be My Love* was just before I began listening to pop music. Be that as it may, the Lanza album contained a variety of songs and a few arias. As I listened, I realized that I was hearing one of the most beautiful voices I had ever heard. Among the recording's cuts was *Beloved* from the movie version of *The Student Prince*, in which Lanza was supposed to star, but provided only the singing voice. *Beloved* was not in the original Romberg score; it was written for the film version especially for Lanza.

[https://www.youtube.com/watch?v=WS9V61nH-lw]

To my ears this recording is even more beautiful than Lanza's signature *Be My Love*. Indeed, *Beloved* is my all-time favorite Lanza recording. The music for both those songs was written by Nicholas Brodszky.

That the Lanza album also included a gorgeous rendition of *The Song of India* was a bonus.

[https://www.youtube.com/watch?v=b80muNCsfkc]

Among the recorded arias in that album, I found that *Che Gelida Manina* from Pucinni's *La Boheme* was as beautiful as any of the other more popular and popular-sounding tracks on the album.

[https://www.youtube.com/watch?v=y2awXYZKGl0]

I was hooked. The second Lanza album I bought was, to my thinking, the finest of Lanza's original LPs. It was a 1954 release entitled, *A Kiss and Other Love Songs,* In addition to the title song [https://www.youtube.com/watch?v=Bh4luaF1IwY], there were glorious renditions of *Long Ago and Far Away*

[https://www.youtube.com/watch?v=YSOFj8W19jo],
My Romance.
[https://www.youtube.com/watch?v=JkOCyXrZf_U]
and *The Night is Young and You're So Beautiful.*

I bought more Lanza albums, including *The Great Caruso,* containing only opera arias. I loved what I heard, so the next step was to listen to complete opera recordings—recordings made by "real" opera singers who made opera a career. This statement is not meant to denigrate Lanza. Except for less than a handful of performances before he became a movie star, he never again appeared in a complete opera performance.

In my opinion, Lanza certainly was the greatest tenor who sang English without an accent. Listen to Lanza sing any popular song, show tune, or operetta song in English and listen to how utterly

natural it sounds. Take for instance, *The Night is Young and You're So Beautiful.*
 [https://www.youtube.com/watch?v=V_yHf_0HVyg]
How perfectly he enunciated the English language and phrased the lyrics. Listen to how liquid his voice gets at the end of the word "kiss*able*" and "permiss*ible*," how he stretches the word "fool" and "do" and follows it all up by virtually caressing the word "love." Add the magnificence of his voice and his utter passion and you have a truly great artist.

I do not lament that Lanza abandoned opera. There are many great renditions of *Che Gelida Manina,* but no other tenor can touch Lanza at making even second-rate American pop songs sound like great art. If Lanza's career had been primarily in opera, he might have recorded some songs in English, but it is unlikely that we would have the huge legacy of his magnificent recordings in English that we do.

After listening to Lanza and the other opera singers he led me to, I was ready to *actually go* to the opera!

My Early Days as an Opera Lover

Having been introduced to opera through Mario Lanza recordings, tenor singing became my favorite voice category. Lanza introduced me to Caruso, ultimately bringing me to have four favorite operatic tenors: Beniamino Gigli, Jussi Björling, Franco Corelli, and Lauritz Melchior. Caruso didn't make the list because I found it difficult to determine the actual tonal quality of his voice from his acoustic recordings.

I remember some of the earliest recordings of Gigli and Björling that I immediately fell in love with. My first Gigli album contained the four duets he recorded with baritone Giuseppe DeLuca in 1927. While they were all wonderful, the duet with De Luca from Bizet's *The Pearlfishers,* with its glorious melody that ends with a magnificent *mezza voce,* stands out. (*Mezza voce* translates as "half voice." Its definition is, "using about half the singer's vocal power.") Listen to the last notes of the duet beginning at [4:16]. It sounds not like they are reducing the vocal power, but actually halving the voice!
 [https://www.youtube.com/watch?v=FsQJ6_XEJNc]
As I began listening to more opera recordings, this version of that duet remained my gold standard. There are two other recorded versions often lauded by opera lovers. Listen to the 1907 version with

Caruso and Mario Ancona. Even the great Caruso couldn't match Gigli in those final notes [3:09].

[https://www.youtube.com/watch?v=6lGVEZAsrgE]

The 1951 recording by Jussi Bjorling and Robert Merrill is in the original French, as opposed to the Italian translation heard in the Caruso and Gigli versions. But here, too, the ending is anticlimactic [4:10] compared to the Gigli/DeLuca version.

[https://www.youtube.com/watch?v=hVpCumaT028]

Of course, all three versions are beautifully sung and separately worthy of their reputation.

If you think that the *mezza voce* ending by Gigli was a fluke, think again. While, as far as I'm aware, Gigli never appeared in a complete performance of *The Pearlfishers*, the big first-act aria from that opera was a specialty of his. Listen to his 1931 recording of the aria. He duplicates that stunning *mezza voce* [at 3:10].

[https://www.youtube.com/watch?v=Pn5XnM5Fg9E]

Amazingly, twenty years later, the then-sixty-plus-year-old Gigli could still wow the audience with that *mezza voce*. Listen to this version from a 1951 recital [at 3:10].

[https://www.youtube.com/watch?v=srtzLdEZKhg]

Having gone overboard discussing Gigli, I will just note the two arias that made me a Bjorling fan forever. In my first Björling album, it was the vocally gorgeous and immensely passionate, "Ah! Foyez, douce image" from Massanet's *Manon*

[https://www.youtube.com/watch?v=E12bfCTKets]

and Lenski's aria from Tchaikovsky's *Eugene Onegin* (sung in Swedish) that most impressed me.

[https://www.youtube.com/watch?v=P_WcfmOZ5qU]

Having just become a Björling fan, I had hoped to get to see him at the Met, only to read of his death in September, 1960. When I finally did get to the Met to see my first opera performance in January 1961, it was *Manon Lescaut* with Licia Albanese and Richard Tucker. I'm guessing that this may have been a performance for which Björling was originally scheduled, as he had recorded the complete opera five years earlier with Albenese and, that same year, had sung it with her at the Met. Tucker was a poor substitute for Björling, and although I saw him many times between 1961 and his death in 1974, I could not warm to his voice. Listen to the first act aria from *Manon Lescaut*, first as sung by Tucker, then by Björling.

[https://www.youtube.com/watch?v=yEanJlO8Jko]

[https://www.youtube.com/watch?v=6W3OJe_VGB0]
   Tucker became the first tenor I designated as "overrated," a term I choose to use to avoid being overly negative. I am not suggesting those I call overrated are not fine artists, but I believe their popularity over other artists that may be as good or even better than they are, is greater than it should be. For instance, I don't call Carlo Bergonzi, Nicolai Gedda or Jon Vickers, three other beloved tenors of the period, who are not among my favorites, overrated, because they did not achieve the kind of adulation among the non-opera-loving masses that Tucker (and later, Luciano Pavarotti) had.

Richie, "Uncle Ray," and My Introduction to Franco Corelli

I had a childhood friend, Richard Fornuto, who grew up on the same block in the Bronx as I. Long before *Happy Days* and "Fonzie" Fonzarelli, we nicknamed him "Footsie." After a while of being called Footsie, he put his foot down. He didn't like that name. Because he was athletic and had a reputation for being the best fighter in the neighborhood, no one argued with him and we quickly resumed calling him Richie.
   Despite that I was into books and music, and not at all athletic (in other words, a nerd), Richie and I were good friends and talked about lots of different things. He was a big Tony Bennett fan, although we differed on our favorite Tony Bennett album. I liked the *Greatest Hits* album, and he liked the concept album, *Hometown, My Town*.
   [https://www.youtube.com/watch?v=CAOq8_YHZpg]
   When I began to become an opera fan, I told him about my favorite tenors, Björling and Gigli. He told me that he had an uncle who was a big opera fan who, too, was a Gigli fan.
   Sometime later (around the fall of 1960) Richie introduced me to his uncle, who was visiting. I don't remember his name. I think it was Ray, so I'll call him Uncle Ray. Uncle Ray told me that he had attended Gigli's farewell recital at Carnegie Hall in 1955. He waited at the stage door to see Gigli, hoping to take his picture. When Gigli appeared, he had his camera ready, but, in a not-uncommon occurrence in those days, instead of it firing, the flashbulb sprang out of the flash gun, almost striking Gigli. Gigli thought he was being attacked. He may have been a little skittish. It being the first time he was in the U.S. since the War, he may have thought that there were

those who might want to harm him because of his earlier wartime support of the fascists.

Since we both loved Gigli's voice—and he also indicated that he didn't care for Tucker's voice—I figured we had similar tastes and I asked Uncle Ray who he thought was the best living tenor. (It was shortly after Björling had died, so Björling was not considered.) He responded Franco Corelli, a young tenor who would be making his Metropolitan debut that season. It was the first time I heard that name, so I made sure to remember it to later see what I thought of him. Franco Corelli has his own section later in this book, so you'll hear more about him then, but I was able to follow up on Uncle Ray's recommendation soon after our discussion.

Opera and Opera Singers

The Old Met

When I saw my first-ever opera performance in 1961 at the old Metropolitan Opera House on Broadway and 39th Street, I thought it might be the only performance I would ever see there. It was scheduled to close at the end of that season to be replaced by a new structure at Lincoln Center, which is why I was determined to see at least one performance that season. Of course, as it ended up, there were construction delays at its proposed new home. The Old Met (as it came to be known) continued to operate until the spring of 1966. It turns out that I saw about a hundred performances there (more than ninety operas and a handful of ballets).

The Old Met on Broadway between 39th and 40th Streets in New York City

Old Met interior

It was a lovely venue, although terribly outmoded as it was performing a different opera every night (except Sunday), plus two on Saturday. Sets had to be stored on the street under a canvas. But, inside, the red and gold auditorium was splendid, while its exterior was often compared to an ugly brewery. We plebeians, who had only Family Circle seats (the cheapest seats; farthest from the stage and at the highest level), had a separate entrance, on the 40th Street side of the building, that allowed no mixing with the patrons who held the more expensive seats. Adding insult to injury, we were provided an elevator that looked like the kind that carries cattle! Even so, most opera lovers wanted the Old Met to be saved, as Carnegie Hall had been, but the Metropolitan Opera wanted the money it would get from a sale or lease of the land. Despite a campaign to save the Old Met, it failed to obtain landmark status from the newly created New York City Landmarks Preservation Commission and was ultimately sold in 1967 and demolished to make way for a drab office building.

My Early Met Performances

The 1960–61 season was the first season I began to regularly listen to Metropolitan Opera radio broadcasts and attended my first opera performance—as mentioned, *Manon Lescaut* with Richard Tucker. It was the only Met performance I saw that season. However, I was able to follow up on Franco Corelli by listening to the three Metropolitan Opera radio broadcast appearances he made that season: Verdi's *Il Trovatore*, his debut role, sung alongside Leontyne Price, *Don Carlo*, and the new production of Puccini's *Turandot*, an opera that hadn't been performed at the Met in over thirty years. By the time the next season came around, I was definitely a Corelli fan, and I knew I had to see him on stage. Oddly, the first performance I saw that season included Tucker! This time a *Tosca*, with Dorothy Kirsten and George London.

I wanted to see a performance of *Tosca*, so I went to that Tucker performance. I didn't have a season schedule, so I was not aware that Corelli would be singing in his first *Tosca* at the Met later that same season. When I did find out that Corelli was singing in *Tosca* I didn't care that I had recently seen it. I wanted to see Corelli in *Tosca*. That January 27, 1962 performance of *Tosca* became the first of more than two hundred opera performances in which I would see Corelli sing. Listen to recordings of the first act aria from Tosca; first Tucker, then Corelli.

[https://www.youtube.com/watch?v=wAUosBr8ohk]
[https://www.youtube.com/watch?v=csuxsEO3Xw8]

Early *Memorable* Opera Performances

The first truly memorable performance I saw of any opera occurred exactly two weeks before Corelli's first Met *Tosca*, on January 13, 1962, when I saw *L'elisir d'amore* with Anna Moffo, Ferruccio Tagliavini, Frank Guarrera, and Salvatore Baccaloni. Ferruccio Tagliavini (1913–1995) was an Italian tenor who was very popular in the 1940s and 50s. This performance marked Tagliavini's return to the Met after an absence of several seasons, and it ended up being his last Met season. If I didn't think Tagliavini was in the same league as Gigli, Björling, and Corelli, I did think he had an exceptionally beautiful voice that was Gigli-like. Indeed, many felt that their voices were very similar.

I remember a radio interview I heard with Tagliavini shortly after that January, 1962 performance. He told the story about how, one day in the 1940s, he was in a cafe with Gigli and Maria Caniglia (a leading soprano of that period) when the cafe played a recording of a tenor aria. Caniglia turned to Gigli and complimented him on how well he sounded. Tagliavini turned to Gigli and said, "but that's *my* recording," to which Gigli responded—"Shush!" I don't know whether this story is true, but Tagliavini told it, and he was clearly proud that Gigli would take credit for one of *his* recordings.

Nemorino in *L'elisir d'amore* was one of Tagliavini's best roles; and he was wonderful, singing beautifully throughout, even that late in his career. Although Nemorino in *L'elisir* was one of Tagliavini's greatest roles, he never recorded it commercially. There is a complete performance video of him (small portions of the video image, but not the audio, were lost) as Nemorino recorded in Tokyo in 1959, that, unfortunately, is not currently on You Tube, (however, a DVD was issued by VAI [Video Artists International] an independent label). Here is a clip that *is* on YouTube.

[https://www.youtube.com/watch?v=74WWddo19j0].

There is a 1949 Metropolitan Opera broadcast of *L'elisir* with Tagliavini, soprano Bidú Sayão, and bass Italo Tajo.

[https://www.youtube.com/watch?v=pZXd43gtYIA].

Finally here's Tagliavini in some "Voice of Firestone" TV appearances. You can view him singing Nemorino's famous aria *Una Furtiva Lagrima* at 31:30.

Anna Moffo was excellent, but to get to see the great basso-buffo, Salvatore Baccaloni (1900–1969), in one of his finest roles, Dr. Malatesta, was a joy. He was past his vocal prime, but about Baccaloni, it was his comic antics that made the performance so memorable. Also memorable in that Met production, Dr. Malatesta entered, not in a horse drawn vehicle as in most productions, but from the sky in a hot air balloon! (Of course, it was actually held up by wires.) Here's Baccaloni singing Malatesta's famous aria.

[https://www.youtube.com/watch?v=d8fFgvcgg4c]

I was to see Ferruccio Tagliavini perform three more times: a tepid *La Bohème* a month later (although *he* was vocally quite fine), a Carnegie Hall concert performance of Mascagni's *L'Amico Fritz* in the 1970s (singing nicely for a man in his sixties), and, lastly, at a concert in Newark, in April, 1981.

That April 1981 concert featured several well-known opera singers, each doing a set of songs and/or arias. One of those artists was Franco Corelli in his first public appearance in nearly six years. It was Corelli's appearance that drew people from all over to Newark's Symphony Hall that day and it would be his next-to-last public performance. It was the last time I was to see him.

I remember being in the crowded lobby after the concert (there's no stage door in Newark's Symphony Hall) seeing Tagliavini walk out alone, virtually unnoticed. It was sad to see one of the most popular tenors of the '40s and '50s being ignored by a throng of fans of the upstart, Franco Corelli. I guess I was complicit.

The first truly memorable Corelli performance I saw was later in the 1961–62 season when I saw his first Enzo in *La Gioconda* on March 9, 1962. It was memorable not only for Franco's magnificent singing, but because the Gioconda was sung by Zinka Milanov (1906–1989), in what would be her next-to-last performance of one of her signature roles. Of course, in 1962 she was past her vocal prime. There's a Met broadcast of *Gioconda* that she sang with Giovanni Martinelli that dates back to 1939!

[https://www.youtube.com/watch?v=zAsi6bQMn7A]

Even as late as 1962, Milanov could still spin out a glorious *pianissimo* (she was famous for her *pianissimi*)—and her *Suicidio* in the last act of *Gioconda* was thrilling.

The cast included Robert Merrill and Giorgio Tozzi. Here's more than an hour of highlights from a non-broadcast performance that,

two weeks later, would be her final performance of the role. It had the same cast I saw two weeks earlier, but as these highlights concentrate on Milanov; Corelli, Merrill, and Tozzi get short shrift .
[https://www.youtube.com/watch?v=RKoW84YJbEE&t=69s]

I would later see Corelli do numerous *Giocondas* with Renata Tebaldi, but the one with Milanov sticks in my memory as special.

During that 1961–62 season, I saw my first *Turandot*, which had, by then, become my favorite opera. Unfortunately, the season after its premiere, Corelli sang Calaf only on the radio broadcast with Birgit Nilsson on February 24, 1962 (which I stayed at home to tape) and one later performance with Mary Curtis Verna, but, as with the *Tosca* earlier that season, I was anxious to see *Turandot*, so I had sat through a performance with Tucker earlier that season, on November 4, 1961. Happily, Birgit Nilsson was the Turandot in that performance, and she was marvelous.

It wasn't until the following season, on January 17, 1963, that I finally got to see Corelli and Nilsson do a performance of *Turandot* together. For the next decade, Nilsson and Corelli were very often paired in *Turandot* at the Met. As I was, by then, going to most Corelli performances, I got to see them together in *Turandot* numerous times. Their *Turandot* performances together are now the stuff of legend, and rightly so, as I can attest. I count myself very lucky to have seen so many of those now-legendary performances. Although there are several radio broadcasts of them together in *Turandot* (including three from the Met), as well as their studio recording, here's the only visual footage of the two together in *Turandot*, containing Turandot's fiendishly difficult aria, *In Questa Reggia,* at the end of which Corelli challenges her dramatically and vocally. I believe the video was shot in 1971 with the audio dubbed from their 1966 studio recording.
[https://www.youtube.com/watch?v=S-GV5t5XLjg]

Tenors and Italian Opera at the Old Met

During the 1961–62 season, I saw eight Met performances. The next season I saw nine, including, most memorably, Franco Corelli, Eileen Farrell, and Robert Merrill in Giordano's *Andrea Chenier* and Franco Corelli, Leontyne Price, Cornell MacNeil, and Jerome Hines in Verdi's *Ernani*. By the 1963–64 season I had attended twenty Met performances (as well as a miscellany of classical orchestral performances, plays, and other presentations). It was in the 1964–65 season that I began attending virtually every performance Corelli sang at the Met, skipping only those performances that were broadcast so I could stay at home to tape them. In the last two seasons of the existence of the old Met, I saw about sixty operas there. Obviously, not all were with Corelli.

No matter how hard I tried, I could not get away from Richard Tucker. For instance, I had no desire to see his *Andrea Chenier*, especially after seeing Corelli do it several times, but I did want to see Zinka Milanov in her farewell performance, so I was again stuck with Tucker.

[https://www.youtube.com/watch?v=pY_qx-XJ3J0&t=21s]

Also, since I wanted to see Renata Tebaldi in *Simon Boccanegra*, I was stuck with Tucker singing Gabriele. I'm sure that some of you reading this are thinking, how can he say "stuck with," when Tucker was such a fabulous tenor? Well, simply, I found his voice harsh, guttural, and not at all pleasing to my ear. While he did have a ringing top and, at times could give a passionate performance—sorry, Tucker fans, it just wasn't enough for me.

There were other tenors I admired, most notably Sándor Kónya (1923–2002) and Flaviano Labò (1927–1991). I saw Labò in several operas, including *Don Carlo, Tosca* (with Leonie Rysanek), and *Un Ballo in Maschera* (with Birgit Nilsson).

[https://www.youtube.com/watch?v=x5frU69BWWc]
[https://www.youtube.com/watch?v=wCvCz0LdG6w]

I found his voice to be ingratiating and charming, but he never became the big time tenor I thought he could have been. I saw Kónya in a number of Italian operas. He was mostly fine in these, but, as his Italian repertoire pretty much duplicated Corelli's, he was overshadowed by Corelli. In the light German repertoire, however, he was often magnificent.

[https://www.youtube.com/watch?v=68ycYrR2Ic0]
[https://www.youtube.com/watch?v=PKh9XN4OY3I]

I was not able to warm to the other big time Italian tenor of that period, Carlo Bergonzi (1924–2014), but I did see a few of his performances over the years.

[https://www.youtube.com/watch?v=Ewg1XZd-bdw&t=65s]

Famed tenor, Mario Del Monaco (1915–1982) left the Met before I began attending, allegedly because Franco Corelli, who hadn't even debuted there yet, had been given the new production of *Turandot* over Del Monaco, a veteran of a decade at the Met, so I never got to see Del Monaco.

[https://www.youtube.com/watch?v=SDmLxPJZVi4]
[https://www.youtube.com/watch?v=ltYi5CIQPJ4]

Another well-regarded tenor in those days was Nicolai Gedda (1925–2017), the Swedish tenor who was a fine artist, but in my opinion lacked his Swedish compatriot, Jussi Björling's shimmering vocal beauty. First a clip of Gedda followed by Björling singing "Salut! demeure chaste et pure" from Gounod's *Faust*.

[https://www.youtube.com/watch?v=LBz-jnt-8To]
[https://www.youtube.com/watch?v=AFfr7SxWuXw]

I saw Giuseppe Di Stefano (1921–2008) in January, 1965, in his return to the Met after an eight-season absence not in an Italian, but a French opera, *The Tales of Hoffmann*. I thought he sounded fine, his voice quite beautiful. Evidently, the critics disagreed. After just that one performance, even though he was scheduled for more, he cancelled his remaining performances and never appeared at the Met again. I did get to see him again, however, in *La Boheme*, in Newark, as well as in a concert at Carnegie Hall with soprano Licia Albanese (1909–2014). And, of course, again at the Maria Callas farewell concert at Carnegie Hall.

[https://www.youtube.com/watch?v=RvN70d4nJfk]

I shouldn't leave out Jon Vickers (1926–2015). I didn't think much of him in Italian operas and almost never went to see him in those, but I did see him regularly in German operas, as well as in Britten's *Peter Grimes*.

[https://www.youtube.com/watch?v=OWT0jsCbl28]

Lois Kirschenbaum

If one went to the opera or ballet in New York during the period from the late 1950s through the early 2000s, one might have come across, and perhaps even become friendly with, Lois Kirschenbaum. That I attended thousands of performances may seem remarkable, but Lois's record well surpassed mine. The number of opera, ballet, and theater performances that she attended makes my number puny. She was at some performance or other virtually every night of the week for more than six decades—most often opera. She would almost always go backstage after a performance. She became acquainted with and befriended countless artists. I first met Lois in the early 1960s, just after I began going to the opera.

Lois died at age eighty-eight on March 27, 2021, just before I began

to write this book. The headline of her rather lengthy obituary in the April 7, 2021 edition of The New York Times accurately read, "Lois Kirschenbaum, the Ultimate Opera Superfan."
[https://www.nytimes.com/2021/04/07/arts/music/lois-kirschenbaum-dead.html]

Lois loved most singers, but her all-time favorite was Renata Tebaldi. It was Tebaldi who got Kirschenbaum started on her love of opera. Although she rarely had a bad thing to say about any singer, I would say Franco Corelli may have been among her least favorite tenors. We were friends for decades and mostly avoided talking about tenors, except for Björling, whom we both loved.

I probably would have attended a lot fewer performances had I not known Lois. It was she who introduced me to the ticket-taker who accepted dollar bribes to let one in. (That was a last resort.) Us poor folk, or so I thought we were, would often wait outside before the performance, hoping to get a free ticket from a patron who had an extra ticket not being used. Lois was absolutely great at this, asking almost everyone walking in if they had an extra ticket; and was almost always successful. Sometimes she would get two and give the extra to a friend. Often, even after she had obtained one free ticket for herself, she continued asking to ensure getting a ticket for a friend. I was often the beneficiary of her largesse.

Being less outgoing than Lois, my method was to size up an incoming patron and ask only those who I thought looked like they might have a ticket. Though not nearly as successful as Lois, I did obtain a goodly number of tickets that way—and maybe, once or twice, was able to reciprocate, but not anywhere near able to balance out the number of tickets Lois had provided to me over the years.

I remember a time in 1966, when we had gotten seats together for a performance of *Fidelio* with Leonie Rysanek and Jon Vickers, conducted by Joseph Rosenstock. The production had made its debut earlier that season with Birgit Nilsson and James King. The dramatic commitment and the vocal intensity of Rysanek and Vickers was so great, it made this one of the most exciting performances I'd ever seen. I remember that Lois had audibly gasped when Rysanek, as Leonore, posing as the lad Fidelio, opened her jacket to reveal her true identity. Yes, sometimes there's more to opera than mere vocal splendor.

In later years, due to family and work obligations, I went to the opera less frequently. Still, it was always a joy, and my expectation, to find Lois at the Met during intermission, seated in the chair outside of the doors to the dress circle, surrounded by a coterie of opera lovers, discussing the performance, and various other opera topics.

For years Lois would compile a list of the next season's Met performances (complete with casts, derived, in part, from her conversations with the artists themselves), long before the Met's official schedule came out. She would make numerous copies, carrying them in the huge bag she toted to all performances, and, during intermission, would hand them out to whoever asked. That big bag she carried was always overstuffed.

When James Levine "ran" the Met, he arranged at the beginning of each season, for Lois to get a season's-worth of score desk tickets (seats on the side of the Family Circle, the highest tier, that have a desk on which to place the written score, enabling one to follow the music). Score desk tickets were her backup, but she would still hang out in front of the house before performances, hoping to get a better seat. As far as I know, she almost never paid for a ticket. Thus, I was shocked by a *New York Times* article printed two weeks after her obituary, "Opera's Biggest Fan Leaves Behind a Sprawling Time Capsule."

The article reported that she had two-and-a-half million dollars in savings!

https://www.nytimes.com/2021/04/23/arts/music/lois-kirschenbaum-metropolitan-opera.html?searchResultPosition=1

Considering the huge number of performances she had attended across more than six decades, the thought came to me that, had she actually paid for her seats, she *would* have died penniless! Joking aside, Lois Kirschenbaum was a great friend, and among the most selfless people I have ever met. Going to the opera knowing that Lois will not be in the audience is not the same.

In the picture at the top of the next page, Lois is the one pointing. I'm on the far right. The gentleman next to me is a friend, Lewis Levenson, the other is a friend with whom I've lost touch over the years. The photograph was taken during the winter of 1966, the last few months before "the old Met" was demolished in 1967. I believe Lois was pointing to the name of her favorite tenor, Jon Vickers, in the poster announcing the performance of *Fidelio* that I talked about.

Two Legendary Divas

Two of the leading sopranos of the 1950s were Maria Callas (1924–1977) and Renata Tebaldi (1922–2004). They had something of a

Lois Kirschenbaum and others

rivalry, and much has been written about both of them, especially Callas, whose fame transcended the world of opera. They had some things in common. They were born within two years of each other in the early 1920s, they both became known in the mid-1940s, and, in both cases, their vocal resources declined by the early sixties. However, there were many differences.

Like Enrico Caruso before her, and Luciano Pavarotti after her, Maria Callas became an international celebrity while maintaining a professional career almost wholly within the operatic sphere. Ezio Pinza gained his greater fame outside the world of opera when he starred on Broadway, as did Lauritz Melchior when he appeared in several MGM musicals, but Caruso, Callas, and Pavarotti stayed mostly within their operatic roots, achieving their iconic status in opera. Part of Callas's fame beyond the world of opera, was attributable to her famous tabloid-exploited affair with one of the then-richest men in the world, Aristotle Onassis. It is unlikely that the tabloids would have been interested in Callas had she been a run-of-the-mill operatic soprano. She was certainly not that!

What set Callas apart from the other sopranos of her era—and perhaps *any* era—was a voice having extraordinary range and expressiveness. Hers may not have been *the* most beautiful soprano voice, but it was a very distinct voice, made charismatic because she was something rare in opera: *a great actress*. She was one of just a few operatic artists whose commitment to her art was such that she would seek truly to *become* each character that she portrayed—and she almost always succeeded, so much so that many of her performances became legendary.

It was even more than that. She had a wide repertoire. Early in her career, she sang Wagner, but it was in *bel canto* operas (late seventeenth-century and early nineteenth-century operas in which coloratura pyrotechnics were the norm) that made her a star in the early 1950s. She also excelled in Verdi and the later verismo operas (opera drawing its themes from real life and emphasizing naturalistic elements), especially Puccini's.

Callas may well have been the most influential singer in the history of opera. As she was arriving on the scene, many bel canto operas had gone out of favor. With a few exceptions, like Donizetti's *Lucia di Lammermoor*, Rossini's *The Barber of Seville*, and Bellini's *Norma*, others were rarely, if ever, revived. Callas had so much a success in this repertoire that she had the box office clout to require some long-neglected bel canto operas to be revived. Once they were back out, that segment of opera gained new life that was further built upon by her successors: Joan Sutherland, Montserrat Caballé, and Beverley Sills. Today, many of those long-neglected operas have, more or less, become part of the standard repertoire.

As to the traditional standard repertoire, Callas's performances of many Verdi and Puccini operas are also legendary. Puccini's *Tosca* was one of her signature roles and her 1953 commercial recording of that opera with Giuseppe Di Stefano and Tito Gobbi, conducted by Victor de Sabata, remains, after seventy years, the definitive recording of that opera—and the one that all others that came after must be judged against.

[https://www.youtube.com/watch?v=rkMx0CLWeRQ]

Unfortunately there is no video of Callas in a complete opera, but there are two full concerts; from Hamburg in 1959 and Paris in 1962.

[https://www.youtube.com/watch?v=_mkLcgZ3gXI]

Sadly, in the early 1960s, Callas' voice developed a wobble and lost much of its celebrated flexibility. Some thought her massive loss of weight during the mid-fifties, and, later, Aristotle Onassis's marriage (he having been her long-time lover) to Jackie Kennedy contributed to her vocal decline and abandonment of the stage. She continued to perform, now and then, mostly in *Tosca*, for the first half of the decade, including recording a stereophonic remake of her classic *Tosca* (again with Gobbi) in 1964, which was unfavorably compared to the earlier set. She stopped performing after 1965, except for a world concert tour with Giuseppe Di Stefano in 1972 showing very little voice to be left, but maintaining a continuing charismatic presence. She died five years later in Paris, at the age of fifty-three, a virtual recluse.

To go from a multi-paragraph abridgement of Maria Callas's colorful and tumultuous life to write ever-so-very briefly about the much less cinematic life of Renata Tebaldi would seem anti-climactic and even somewhat of a slight. Unlike Callas, Tebaldi rarely strayed far from the standard repertoire. Her voice was not that of a coloratura soprano, so her meat-and-potatoes roles were Verdi, Puccini, and other verismo operas. She was a decent, but not-inspired actress. What she brought to her performances, however, was one of the single-most-beautiful soprano voices ever to grace the operatic stage. If opera is about beauty-of-voice, Tebaldi reigns supreme.

Tebaldi had a vocal crisis in the early 1960s, but took some time off to rehabilitate her voice. After her return in 1964, her voice sometimes had an edge and steely sound, but the basic timbre remained, and, by further limiting her repertoire to roles congenial to her now-somewhat-reduced vocal capabilities, she was able to extend her career another decade.

Like Callas, Tebaldi's glory years were the 1950s, so it is not surprising, because they were in a "sort of" competition during that period, that there were verbal clashes between their respective partisans and, sometimes, between the performers themselves. I stayed above the fray. While I am passionate about tenors, I could remain neutral about sopranos. I appreciated both Callas and Tebaldi for their differing contributions to the vocal art.

As an example of these two diva's art, and to lead us into the next segment, here are videos of Tosca's big aria *Vissi d'arte*. First, Tebaldi in 1959 in glorious voice with minimalist acting; then Callas in a 1956 emotionally compelling version.

[https://www.youtube.com/watch?v=XOnF_bsm1hQ&t=21s]
[https://www.youtube.com/watch?v=ggywso5O9zw]

A Tale of Two Toscas

The first of many times I would see Renata Tebaldi was on March 22, 1964. It was the first performance of *Tosca* for that Metropolitan

Opera season, and marked the return of Tito Gobbi, who previously had appeared at the Met for only five performances over two seasons between 1956 and 1958. As I had never before seen Tebaldi or Gobbi, I got a ticket to the opening performance, even though the tenor was scheduled to be Barry Morell, a not-favorite of mine.

I will first quote from my review of that *Tosca* of March 22, 1964 and follow it with a review of the *Tosca* performance almost exactly a year later on March 19, 1965; the two principals were the same as the year before, but the title role was sung by Maria Callas in her return to the Met, six years after her infamous firing by General Manager Rudolf Bing for refusing to perform *Macbeth* and *La Traviata* too close together as they varied so widely in style.

Met Performance of Tosca, **March 22, 1964 (Written 3/23/64)**

I am trying to figure out how to describe this performance. In the four seasons I've been going to the opera, I don't believe I have seen as great a performance as last night's "Tosca." It was honestly and unequivocally the finest opera performance I have ever seen. Even when opera is just mediocre, I enjoy it, but this performance showed what opera can be when it's at its greatest.

Renata Tebaldi's Tosca is a beautiful creation. She did have that same edge to her high notes I noticed in last week's broadcast of "Boheme." She also veered off her note course once or twice, but, with Tebaldi, who cares about a few flaws? Perhaps she'll never have the warmth in her voice that characterized it six or seven years ago, yet, what a beautiful voice Tebaldi has; in my humble opinion, the most beautiful soprano voice at the Met today. Her Tosca is still one of the great Tosca's of our era.

I had heard that Tebaldi's acting wasn't very good. Last night, however, I found her conception of Tosca excellent. Her nervousness about taking the knife in Act II seemed just what I'd want an opera singer to be like when about to murder someone. Her entire performance was exciting, an excitement no other opera singer around today, except for Callas, can match.

Speaking of excitement, the most all-around satisfactory performance of the evening came from that great veteran, Tito Gobbi. Probably no Scarpia ever received as much applause as Gobbi did as he strode onto the Met stage for the first time in seven years. Gobbi did a beautiful job. Of course, he couldn't do everything he once did, but what he did in acting made up for what no making up was needed. I have never seen acting on an opera stage like Gobbi's. His facial expressions said everything and his actions showed Scarpia's character. And in his second act duet with

Tebaldi, he sang and acted as no other baritone alive can. What a powerful performance he gave, and even powerful is too weak a word.

Barry Morrell was originally scheduled to sing Cavaradossi. In the house there was no "indisposed" sign, but rumors get around fast and people were saying and asking, "Corelli's singing"—"Is Corelli singing?" At 7:55, the general manager, Rudolph Bing, came out in person to make the welcomed announcement that he probably thought would be a pleasant surprise. It was anticlimactic, but Corelli's name elicited handsome applause, of which I was, of course, a part.

It should be noted that if Morell were replacing Corelli, Bing would have sent out his assistant, Ossie Hawkins, to give the audience the *bad* news. When inferior singers were to replace a well-known singer, Hawkins came out to make those announcements and bear the audience groans. But, this time, a star tenor was to replace a less-regarded house tenor, so Bing, himself, came out to hear the cheers.

Vocally, Corelli was the most brilliant of the trio. He was the only one of the principals still in his prime (and what a prime). I have heard Gigli, Bjorling, etc. do Cavaradossi on records, yet never have I heard such a strikingly beautiful Cavaradossi as Corelli's. I doubt if even Caruso could equal it. In every act he pulled and held high notes. Purists may scoff, but for my ears nothing could be more beautiful. Corelli even outdistanced his performance of two seasons before. [*His first Met Cavaradossi that I referred to earlier.*].

This was the most powerful and beautiful performance of any opera I've seen. It's as good as anything in "The Golden Age." In fact, this was "The Golden Age.

You, too, can listen to that "Golden Age' performance: [https://www.youtube.com/watch?v=PCkeF80Y-BA&t=2207s]

I should mention here that I *did* see the second performance of *Tosca* that same trio did a week later, but I will now move a whole year ahead to Callas.

Met Performance of Tosca, March 19, 1965 (Written 3/20/65)

In the late 1950s, Callas's voice developed a wobble. This wobble became progressively worse, so much so, that in 1962, she abandoned staged opera altogether to retrain her voice. She made a triumphant return to opera at Covent Garden in 1964. However, as one familiar with a tape of that performance, I know the wobble was still there.

When the chords sounded and Callas sang out, "Mario, Mario," a gasp went out through the house. Then she came out. The audience cheered and cheered, and only after many minutes was the music able to continue. Her voice was quite low, much less powerful than I expected, but, at times, it was beautiful. Also, at times, it was wobbly, especially in the last act, when she let out one cranky wobble that made the whole audience audibly shudder. There were times she was vocally insecure.

With all her vocal problems, her performance was great. One may ask how an opera singer with vocal problems can give a great performance? It is simple. Her conception of the role sweeps away every consideration. In act I, during the Cavaradossi–Tosca duet, she smiled just like a coy, designing teenager. Her facial expressions captured me. She has electricity in that face.

Tito Gobbi, like Callas, by the sheer magnitude of his portrayal, puts to shame all other baritones. His eyes just shine, and when he sings the *Te Deum*, vocally, he was as thrilling as ever. He is, without a doubt, one of the greatest singers of all time.

As Cavaradossi, Franco Corelli was vocally splendid. On this occasion he was kind of overshadowed in the first two acts, but his best work came in the last act, wherein he sang one of the best *E Lucevans* I've ever heard from him, as well as an exquisite *O dolci mani.*

Thus, on the first anniversary of what I thought was the *Tosca* to end all *Tosca*s, I saw another *Tosca* I can't conceive of being duplicated again."

For the record, I was also present at Callas's next, and final, Met performance a week later, this time with Richard Tucker's blustery Cavaradossi. The only other time I saw Callas was with Di Stefano in their farewell concert tour in the early '70s. It should be noted that in-house audio recordings of both of Callas's March, 1965 Met *Tosca* performances can be found on YouTube; this one with Corelli [https://www.youtube.com/watch?v=ftWYz1m4FIU&t=106s] and this one with Tucker.
[https://www.youtube.com/watch?v=2M1McWkkKqk&t=425s].

Tito Gobbi

I first became aware of Italian baritone Tito Gobbi (1913–1984) soon after I became an opera lover. While in those early days I didn't get to the opera house very often, a local New York TV station, WOR (channel 9), had a regularly shown program called *Foreign Film Festival*. This was a misnomer as they showed only Italian movies. This was probably because it was sponsored by Progresso, the Italian soup company. (To this day I remember the announcer intoning, "Brought to you by Progresso Instant Italian Espresso Coffee.") Among the films they showed were a number of Italian opera films made in the 1940s. In most of them, the baritone lead was Tito Gobbi. I remember seeing him in movies of *L'elisir d'amore,, La forza del destino, Rigoletto, Il Barbiere di Siviglia,* and *Pagliacci*; there were others. I also remember seeing Gobbi in a non-opera film, wherein he played a singing truck driver who sent coded messages to the allies in song—over the radio! It should be noted that the films often abridged the operas and they were further cut by the station, having to be shown in a ninety-minute time slot that included commercials. In addition to seeing him sing among the soup commercials, I also listened to Gobbi on recordings, especially the ones he made with Callas. You can now watch many of those movies uncut, without commercials, on YouTube:

Rigoletto (1946):
[https://www.youtube.com/watch?v=xJfTOKEJRy8];
Il barbiere di Siviglia (1946)
[https://www.youtube.com/watch?v=AuubQMj4oGE] with Ferruccio Tagliavini:
Pagliacci (1946):
[https://www.youtube.com/watch?v=yhdZeqiCuVk].

In this film, Gobbi is the only performer who provides his own singing voice. All the others' voices are dubbed, thus giving Gina Lollobrigida one of her early starring roles as the onscreen Nedda. Gobbi not only acts and sings the lead baritone role of Tonio, he also portrays the secondary baritone role of Silvio!

L'Elisir d'amore (1947):
[https://www.youtube.com/watch?v=JMgwvx2CMkE].

A little opera trivia here. In the relatively small role (called *comprimario* roles in opera) of Giannetta in the film is Loretta Di Lelio. Several years later she married Franco Corelli.

La forza del destino (1949):
[https://www.youtube.com/watch?v=Evj_DlJn5_8&t=3059s].

Based on those films and recordings, I thought very highly of Gobbi, already thinking of him as the foremost baritone of his era, but, in 1964, I didn't know whether it fittingly continued to be "his era." The movies in which I had seen him were made in the 1940s, which at my age then, seemed like eons before. It is why I commented in my 1964 *Tosca* review that everybody (meaning me) was waiting to see if he had anything left when he returned to the Met in 1964. It turns out he had a lot left. His voice might not have been as agile as it had been, but it was still an imposing instrument and, together with his command of characterization and compelling stage presence, it made him a joy to see.

I was fortunate to see Gobbi often during the last decade of the major portion of his career, as it was during a period in which he came to the Met frequently. I saw his Scarpia in *Tosca* more than dozen times, Falstaff about a half-dozen times, Iago in Verdi's *Otello* several times, and the Count in Mozart's *Le Nozze di Figaro* twice (plus a dress rehearsal). The *Le Nozze* performances were in June, 1968 with the Rome Opera, then on tour at the Metropolitan Opera House.

[https://www.youtube.com/watch?v=97Ze3cqPvoI]

After Gobbi's signature role of Scarpia, his Falstaff was the second-finest role I saw him in. Here's what I wrote the day after first seeing his Falstaff, which was his first *Falstaff* at the Met, on March 5, 1966:

"Had I not loved the opera to start with, I still should have loved this performance, as in the title role was my favorite baritone and one of the great Falstaffs of all time, Tito Gobbi. What a brilliant portrayal his is. His little comic actions roused the audience, but it was his sense of the part, and the music, that really gave it its breadth. His sense of fun permeated to the very end when he pointed not only to the audience, but to the prompter's box. True, his voice was a little dry,

With Tito Gobbi backstage at the New Met in 1968

Opera and Opera Singers

but I have come to love that voice."

Here's a complete Gobbi *Falstaff* video done in Paris in 1970. [https://www.youtube.com/watch?v=F9ZU0CloETU].

In 1956, Gobbi made a classic studio recording of Falstaff for EMI, conducted by Herbert von Karajan.

[https://www.youtube.com/watch?v=JDZlOY-IoXs]

Among the many radio broadcasts of Falstaff with Gobbi, the most famous is from the Chicago Lyric Opera in 1958. Its star-studded supporting cast boasts Reanata Tebaldi, Anna Moffo, Giuletta Simionato, and Cornell MacNeil, splendid in the other baritone role of Ford.

[https://www.youtube.com/watch?v=Aw5VdDCjExl]

The most famous Falstaff of the generation before Gobbi, was probably Mariano Stabile (1888–1968), who sang the role under Toscanini at the 1937 Salzburg Festival. Here is a 1941 Falstaff broadcast with Stabile in the title role. The supporting cast includes the young Ferruccio Tagliavini as Fenton and, as Ford, *the young Tito Gobbi.*

[https://www.youtube.com/watch?v=POt5FK8A6Ik]

To a large extent, Gobbi was the baritone equivalent of Callas. Like Callas, he was a charismatic actor as well as a singer, who mined every role to its depths. That they both recorded for EMI/Angel and thus made many complete-opera recordings together, is a great gift to posterity. One regrets that there are no *complete* opera videos of them together; Callas never made a complete opera video. The closest we have is Act II of *Tosca* in which there are two examples, one from Paris in 1958, and another from London in 1964. Both of these show Gobbi's definitive Scarpia. Here's an excerpt from the 1958 Paris video [https://www.youtube.com/watch?v=S1PnVd1YXvc] followed by the complete Act II from the 1964 London performance.

[https://www.youtube.com/watch?v=xnFlg1z1hPc&t=412s]

Upon his return to the Met, Gobbi appeared on the same radio opera-interview program that Tagliavini had been on two years earlier. He told a story about his first Scarpia in Rome in 1940. After the performance, Gobbi recalled, an opera fan named Gino, who came to most of his performances, had come backstage to see him as usual. Gobbi asked Gino what he had thought of the performance. Gino said something nice, but it was not the high praise he regularly heard from Gino. He pressed Gino to tell him what was wrong. Gino finally asked, "How old do you think Scarpia is?" Gobbi responded, "about fifty." Gino then remarked, "you walked like a twenty-five-year-old," which, of course, was about Gobbi's age at the time. "So," Gobbi continued, "that weekend I was visiting my parents in the country, and I sat and studied the way my father, who *was* fifty, walked and moved, and at the next performance I walked and moved like my father." I've related this story because it demonstrates Gobbi's dedication to creating the character. Some years later, I read Gobbi's autobiography and I was surprised to find that he had not retold that story there. Of course, by the time *I* first saw his Scarpia, Gobbi, himself, was fifty!

Here's a 1956 Chicago radio interview with Gobbi, followed by a 1979 British television interview.

[https://www.youtube.com/watch?v=YcyIN9GLvI4]
[https://www.youtube.com/watch?v=lzt6w1WecLw]

Perhaps you are thinking: "He's simply a dedicated fan of Gobbi's, and going well overboard in his praise, as fans often do. Professional critics, more educated in music than he, wouldn't gush about their subjects as he does." The following is part of a review of Tito Gobbi's Metropolitan Opera debut on January 13, 1956 that was published in the defunct-since-1966 *New York Herald Tribune*.

Be assured that this will be only one of two times in this book that I will quote from a review that I didn't write. As I read this review, I realized it was exactly what I would have written about Gobbi's performance as Scarpia when I first saw it eight years later—if at eighteen I could write that well. The reviewer was Jay S. Harrison.

> Let it be recorded directly at the outset that Mr. Gobbi's Scarpia is without doubt, hesitation or question, the finest this writer has ever seen. And, in a sense, the emphasis on "seen" is not to be taken lightly. From the top of his forehead to the soles of his feet, Tito Gobbi is an actor, a rousing, imperious man of the theater. He has only to walk on stage, furrow his brow, smile cynically, and take in the scene for one to know that a master dramatic craftsman had come among us. And once arrived, Mr. Gobbi quite frankly took over.
>
> To begin with, the baritone's Scarpia is the more insidious for being entirely regal. His elegance, his ease, his off-hand manner makes every sinister deed, every monstrous plot, a thing of ghoulish horror. Gobbi is no menacing upstart, no Johnny-come-lately on the Roman police force— he is a Baron trained to evil and brilliantly wise in its ways. Indeed, every vicious word of his text was accompanied by a gesture or an expression that faithfully translated and underlined the dark meaning of his words. In short, his Scarpia is a macabre fiend, an aristocratic one who prefers the

rapier to the meat-ax. It was a harrowing portrayal. And a great one.

Given these circumstances it was quite simple to fall so completely under Mr. Gobbi's dramatic witchery as to overlook his voice. And that is a pity, for his baritone is a grand one—ringing, lofty, extravagantly virile. Myself, I found a slight tendency to monochrome, and I fancied his tones a mite dry and sapless, though it is certainly possible his interpretation of the role inclined him in this direction. At any rate, Mr. Gobbi is possessed of rare vocal skills. He can thunder, he can croon; he can rage, he can plea. All of which is no more than another way of saying that Tito Gobbi is an artist.

Okay, if I had been the one who wrote that, I would have put the word "great" before artist . . . You should know that although Baron Scarpia in *Tosca* was Gobbi's signature role, performing it hundreds of times (he claimed it to be nearly a thousand) and commercially recording it twice, he performed nearly a hundred other roles over his forty-year career, including the title role in the Italian premiere of Alban Berg's seminal 12-tone opera *Wozzeck*, performed in an Italian translation.

[https://www.youtube.com/watch?v=2GHCND4rTz4]

Franco Corelli

In his day, Franco Corelli rarely, if ever, got the laudatory reviews that Tito Gobbi got. Yes, most critics acknowledged Corelli's magnificent voice, but then the nitpicking began. He held high notes too long. He scooped too much. He sobbed too much. He acted indifferently. His French (in French opera) was terrible—and on and on they continued. But, no matter how hard they hammered, none of this mattered to his ardent fans; of which, I, of course, was one.

I have already indicated how I first became aware of Corelli. That, perhaps, because it was Mario Lanza who introduced me to opera, the tenor voice is my favorite vocal classification and, as such, I am more passionate—and more opinionated—about tenors. So, while I can remain neutral in the Tebaldi versus Callas debate, when it comes to tenors, I make my choice and I make no apologies for it.

About tenors, it's the timbre (what I sometimes call tonal beauty) of the voice that is my most important criterion. If I don't like the basic sound of the voice a tenor has, I am unable to think of him as a great tenor, no matter what other merits he may have. Conversely, I can forgive the faults of a tenor whose voice I find beautiful. There can be many vocal and musical sins heard, so long as the sound of his voice overwhelms me. So it is with me and Corelli.

Corelli had many detractors in his time (I think fewer now) because of what some considered to be his artistic lapses. I guess my directive would be, "If you have it, flaunt it." Corelli had it and often flaunted it.

[https://www.youtube.com/watch?v=05Rj0NZFoaI]
[https://www.youtube.com/watch?v=FaGt4952Cro]
[https://www.youtube.com/watch?v=A-n_4ys8TiQ]
[https://www.youtube.com/watch?v=fQN8Y5EouHw]
[https://www.youtube.com/watch?v=5dzZ3YKEsIM&t=326s]
[https://www.youtube.com/watch?v=WDaUN7E-L6k]

If you're a purist who cannot accept an artist going beyond the letter of the sacred score, Corelli is not for you. If you luxuriate in the sound of beautiful singing, Corelli is your man.

I'd like to describe what it is in the voices of my favorite tenors that attracts me to them, but I don't think language has adjectives enough to accurately describe the timbre of the human singing voice—but I guess I'll try anyway. Corelli's voice was very different from the honeyed sweetness of Gigli or the crystal clear, silvery

Backstage with Franco in 1966

sound of Björling's. Of course, Corelli was a dramatic tenor, so his voice was fuller, with a bright and rich, sensuous sound. As I said, the words alone probably don't reveal very much; one really must listen for oneself. Suffice that all of my favorite tenors have, or had, a unique quality to their voice that makes them stand out. So, listen for yourself. Mario Cavaradossi in *Tosca* is one of many roles they had in common. Listen to each in *Cavardossi*'s first act aria *Recondita Armonia*.

Gigli [https://www.youtube.com/watch?v=pllSPDNGNUU]
Björling [https://www.youtube.com/watch?v=m4dtdp43VZk]
Corelli.
[https://www.youtube.com/watch?v=csuxsEO3Xw8]

If you wonder how each compares to other tenors, listen to this comparison clip. It includes these three, plus seventeen other famous tenors singing a portion of this aria.

[https://www.youtube.com/watch?v=hQsmZqhzIys]

Corelli's career was relatively brief in comparison to my other favorite tenors. Gigli (1890–1957), who died at age sixty-seven, had a forty-three-year career from 1912 to 1955. Björling (1911–1960) was forty-nine when he died (approximately the same age as Caruso was when *he* died), but his career went from 1930 to his death, thirty years later. Corelli (1921–2003) lived to eight-two, but was a late bloomer. His debut occurred in 1951 at the Teatro Nuovo in Spoleto and he sang his last operatic performance in 1976. (The 1981 concert performance I referred to previously on page 21 was one of only two public performances Corelli gave after 1976. The other was later that year, also a concert and also in New Jersey.)

Corelli's rise to operatic stardom in his native Italy was rapid. Despite performing for barely two years, Corelli had two very prestigious engagements in 1953. In May of that year, he created the role of Pierre in the world premiere of Prokofiev's *War and Peace* in Florence. By 1953, Corelli had already appeared in several performances of *Norma* opposite Maria Callas. She was to become instrumental in getting him his first La Scala engagement. In December, 1954, Callas and Corelli opened the La Scala season in Spontint's rarely heard *La Vestale*.

[https://www.youtube.com/watch?v=Y98tDTVD-JQ&t=70s]

Corelli did not make his Metropolitan Opera debut until 1961. This was due, in part, to his fear of flying. Once he overcame that, he appeared at the Met for fourteen consecutive seasons, where he sang nearly four hundred performances. Indeed, he came to love New York so much that, even after he retired from singing, he kept an apartment in New York, spending a good part of each year there for the next quarter-century.

For some reason, unfathomable to me, the aria *Nessun Dorma* from *Turandot* has become closely associated with Luciano Pavarotti. I find it strange because Pavarotti only sang five performances of *Turandot* at the Met, compared with Corelli who sang it fifty-seven times, thus owning the role at the Met for the length of his Met tenure. Corelli sang it at the premiere of the Met's new production in February, 1961, only a month after his debut, and his final performance at the Metropolitan Opera House was in *Turandot* on a Saturday matinee broadcast in December, 1974. On the other hand, Jussi Björling never sang the role onstage, but his 1944 recording of *Nessun Dorma* is rightly a classic and his 1958 complete recording of the opera with Birgit Nilsson and Renata Tebaldi is equally treasured. Listen to these three tenors sing *Nessun Dorma*. First Björling , then Pavarotti, and finally, Corelli. You make up your own mind, but I put Pavarotti in the middle because I believe his version is dwarfed by the other two giants.

[https://www.youtube.com/watch?v=wPEG914GATk]
[https://www.youtube.com/watch?v=1so8si-8oxw]
[https://www.youtube.com/watch?v=yBr9TZDWNuM]

For a direct comparison between Corelli and Pavarotti in this aria:
[https://www.youtube.com/watch?v=ds_PGBe_pf0]

Here's an interview with Pavarotti during which he speaks of his admiration for Corelli.
[https://www.youtube.com/watch?v=1GTsoK2QMF8&t=63s]

Corelli's Met debut, on January 27, 1961, in *Il Trovatore*, opposite Leontyne Price, who was also making her Met debut, is the stuff of legends.
[https://www.youtube.com/watch?v=EMOwlLLcgEc]

I regret I did not get to see that historic performance, but as I stated earlier, I tried to make up for this by attending most of his Met performances after 1963 (and a few before). I therefore have more than two hundred (perhaps more than three hundred—I haven't actually tried to count them) reviews that I could choose from to reproduce here. I respectfully decline to do so. I'm a devoted fan. As such, those reviews all will repeatedly say pretty much the same laudatory things. Although I might quibble about this or that about a given performance, I don't think anything in those reviews will give you any greater insight than what has already been presented about his voice and art.

I have been asked what is my favorite Franco role? How can I choose between Calaf (in *Turandot*), Andrea Chenier, Manrico (in *Il trovatore*), Don Carlo, Radamès (in *Aida*), or Cavaradossi (in *Tosca*)? Impossible. But his Dick Johnson in Puccini's *"La fanciulla del West* holds a special place in my heart. He only did six performances at the Met (December 1, 7, 17, and 23, 1965, January 8 matinee broadcast, and March 18, 1966) of which I saw five, (staying home on January 8 to tape the Saturday matinee broadcast).

The famous tenor aria, *Ch'ella mi creda* from *La fanciulla del West*, occurs in the third act, but I prefer the lesser-known second act aria, *Or son sei mesi*. Perhaps this is because the first time I heard it was on Corelli's 1955 Cetra recording, on which he takes the phrase toward the end of the aria, *la mia vergogna! Ahimè! Ahimè!*, in one breath, to magnificent effect.

[https://www.youtube.com/watch?v=BRejM5CwuQ8]

I've subsequently heard many recordings of that aria and rarely heard it sung without a pause for breath in the middle of that phrase. But, when Corelli performed it a decade later at the Met, he did not sing those words together. Was it because he was no longer able to?

I usually went backstage to see Corelli after a performance. There were many Corelli fans there. His wife, Loretta, made certain none of us had more than a few seconds to talk to him. After the second *"fanciulla"* performance, (December 7, 1965) I went backstage and used my few seconds to ask him why he hadn't sung the phrase in *Or son sei mesi* in one breath as he did in the recording. His answer was that he sings ten or fourteen performances over a short span of time and didn't want to tire his voice. "Furthermore," he added, "Puccini wrote it with those pauses." This comment was commendable, but strange coming from a singer notorious for often being more interested in showing off his vocal abilities than adhering to the composer's intentions. Nevertheless, this is what I wrote of Corelli's final *"fanciulla"* at the Met (on March 18, 1966):

> Franco Corelli was superb as Dick Johnson. His acting was greatly improved and his vocal resources are perfect for this role. He even took

the words "la mia vergogna! Ahimè! Ahimè!" in one breath, as he had done in his recording."

That's the kind of minutiae you'll find in my Corelli reviews.

For much of his Met tenure, Corelli continued to perform regularly in Italy as well. Between 1960 and 1964 he performed at La Scala's prestigious opening night (which always occurs on December 7) five consecutive times. In the first of those opening night's, paired with Callas again, they performed another rarely heard piece, Donizetti's *"Poliuto."*

[https://www.youtube.com/watch?v=UCm8ZdZ9cTY]

May 28, 1962 was a legendary opera night of the twentieth century—the first performance in decades at La Scala of Giacomo Meyerbeer's *Les Huguenots*. As it is a long opera, it was cut and performed in an Italian translation as *gli ugonotti*. Maria Callas was originally scheduled to sing Valentine opposite Franco's Raoul, but by this time, her vocal resources were so limited that she had to cancel. The great Italian mezzo-soprano, Giulietta Simionato took over the *soprano* role of Valentine and triumphed. But, there's more—this was a star-studded evening as everyone in the cast was an opera superstar. The others were: soprano Joan Sutherland as Queen Marguerite (there are two major soprano roles in this opera), bass Nicolai Ghiuarov as Marcel, mezzo-soprano Fiorenza Cossotto as Urbain, and bass Giorgio Tozzi as St. Bris. The lengthy duet between Simionato and Franco is legendary, and rightly so. The two are vocally resplendent and dramatically thrilling. If there is any performance that Franco did that I did not see, and wished I could have seen, it is this one. The first link is to the magnificent duet with Franco and Simionato, the second is the complete performance.

[https://www.youtube.com/watch?v=9FTRRtBzT04]
[https://www.youtube.com/watch?v=W_xlg4VI8Ac]

Corelli performed sporadically in Parma, Italy during the sixties. There was one performance he did there that has become legendary. It was neither a rare opera, nor a star-studded one. Indeed, Corelli was the only star in this performance of *"Tosca"* in 1967, as the names Virginia Gordoni (as Tosca) and Attilio D' Orazi (as Scarpia) are somewhat obscure. In this singular performance of Cavaradossi, Corelli pulled out all the stops. He flaunted more in this one performance than in ten other *Tosca*'s. The audience went wild. At the end of the performance, the applause was so persistent and so loud that Corelli came back on stage, with the conductor at the piano, and sang *Core 'ngrato*! This performance was all the more amazing as Parma audiences are notoriously hard to please. Legend has it that both Caruso and Gigli were booed there.

I'd like to contrast three artists in their recordings of the third act aria from *Tosca, E lucevan le stelle*. First, Jussi Björling's beautifully sung and stylish version, without too many embellishments,

[https://www.youtube.com/watch?v=oKAcKaaVq90]

then Caruso's 1904 recording.

[https://www.youtube.com/watch?v=3TjEoAXzJ9E]

Note Caruso's tendency to milk the high notes and his sobs at the end. Somehow, when it comes to Caruso, his tendency to sob is glossed over by critics. Finally, listen to Corelli's 1967 Parma performance [https://www.youtube.com/watch?v=T-RrG4sfdis]; no sobs, but he does milk the high notes even more than Caruso. He also produces a very long, absolutely magnificent, *diminuendo* (voice diminishing in loudness) the middle of the aria. These were just some of the vocal treats Corelli gave the Parma audience that night. If this whets your appetite, you can find the complete 1967 Parma *Tosca* on YouTube, including the audience's explosive reactions and the *Core 'ngrato* encore after the performance.

[https://www.youtube.com/watch?v=O4z9LGNgWBQ&t=3900s]

(Or, you can obtain a copy of one of the many pirated CDs that are available.)

Tosca was not the only opera in which Corelli used his *diminuendo* to stunning effect. Here's a short clip (of poor video quality) of the very end of *Celeste Aida* from *Aida*.

[https://www.youtube.com/watch?v=7KRpbHq3pVc]

We can further sample Corelli on video (happily, the video quality here is superb).

[https://www.youtube.com/watch?v=W_XzSVDsU0g&t=645s]

You can also view a complete concert in Tokyo in 1971.

[https://www.youtube.com/watch?v=xZu4jbcr-Fk]

Two years later, again in Tokyo, Corelli appeared in a joint concert with Renata Tebaldi. While both of them are in the twilight of their careers they are still magnificent.

[https://www.youtube.com/watch?v=CL0aDjcx2nY&t=1076s]

For capsule reviews of some of Corelli's finest recordings, both live and in-studio:

[https://www.csmusic.net/content/articles/what-you-can-learn-from-corellis-best-recordings/]

Here is a personal Corelli story I can relate. As I've said, I often went backstage to see Corelli after his performances. He was always gracious, but seemed somewhat aloof, perhaps because his wife, Loretta, was very protective and kept the line of admirers moving by making certain no one spoke to Corelli for more than a few seconds. As was noted earlier, I would regularly say a few nice words about his performance and move on. Though he knew me by sight, I'm sure he didn't know my name.

One September day in 1968, I had gone to see a movie at the Museum of Modern Art, one of the few places one could see rare vintage films, uncut, and without commercials in the days before DVDs, cable, Turner Classic Movies, YouTube, and streaming services.

Leaving the museum just after dark, I noted an individual walking toward me. As he got closer, I realized it was Franco. I was so shocked that, when he got closer, I simply blurted out: "HELLO, FRANCO!" I expected him to say "Hello" and continue on. To my surprise, he stopped, and we chatted for several minutes. All that I remember of the conversation was that he said that he was currently rehearsing *Adriana*; which he was doing opposite Tebaldi to open the Met that season. That memory provided me with the information I needed to place the year of this occurrence. It wasn't the content of the conversation that was important, it was just how (unexpectedly) friendly he was. (Was it because Loretta wasn't hovering over him?)

I have often re-told the story of this chance meeting with Franco, but I rarely speak of what happened right afterward. In light of the revelations that have appeared in books by Rene Seghars and Stefan Zucker, I now feel free to tell my little tale.

Movie presentations at the Museum of Modern Art began at 5:30 P.M. although the museum closed at 6:00 P.M. Therefore, when the screenings were over, the museum was closed, One entrance door near the cloakroom was kept unlocked so the movie audience could retrieve their belongings and exit. I happened to be acquainted with an attendant in the cloakroom who was working that day. She was a beautiful young woman who was an aspiring actress. I got to know her because she was a big Corelli fan and I would see her and her boyfriend at the Met, among the post-performance fans in Franco's dressing room.

After this encounter with Franco, I began to think. Could Corelli have been on his way to a rendezvous? As if I were a 1940s movie-screen detective, I crossed the street and tucked myself into a doorway where I could see the entrance to the museum. (I'm thinking Humphrey Bogart in *The Big Sleep* as he stakes out the bookshop.) Sure enough, Corelli walked into the museum through the one unlocked door. He clearly knew which door was unlocked! As the Museum was closed, there could only be one reason that he would be going in (while there could be another, that would be a big coincidence). I thought about waiting to see whether they came out together, but I didn't know how long I would have to wait, and I felt foolish enough already.

The next day, I accidentally-on-purpose bumped into the coat check person as she left work. I walked with her for a time, making small talk, before bringing up the subject. Her response was something like, "Yes, wasn't that a delightful surprise!" My plan, of course, was to find out more, but I chose to be a gentleman and refrained from further questioning.

It was pretty obvious what was going on. I don't recall seeing her again after that, but some time later (perhaps weeks or /months?), I saw her boyfriend, and, during the course of our short conversation, he told me they had broken up. I might have asked, "Was it because of Franco?" but, again, I demurred, possibly because there were other people around and/or perhaps there was a chance he actually didn't know.

Although my evidence was wholly circumstantial, I felt there was a good chance they were having an affair. Decades later I read in Rene Seghar's biography of Corelli (*Franco Corelli: Prince of Tenors*, Amadeus Press, 2008) that, in 1969, "... there was a crisis in his marriage, which would lead to a temporary separation between Franco and Loretta. Franco is said to have had a mistress for some time...." (p. 381). In a footnote to that statement, Seghers writes, "The lady wished to remain anonymous..." I, too, will be circumspect, despite Stefan Zucker's more recent revelations.

Stefan Zucker's three-volume series, *Franco Corelli and the Revolution in Singing* (Bel Canto Society, Volume 1, 2015, Volumes 2 and 3, 2018) is not a standard form biography, but uses Corelli as the linchpin for a sometimes scholarly but exceedingly technical—sometimes gossipy, sometimes opinionated—discussion of tenors throughout history. There's a lot about Corelli in it, including copious excerpts from Zucker's numerous interviews with Corelli. Volume two has an entire chapter that details Corelli's extra-marital sexual exploits—perhaps in greater detail than some of us would like to be aware of.

For some years, Zucker had a program on WKCR (Columbia University's radio station) called "Opera Fanatic." It ran for several hours on Saturday nights. During the program's run, he conducted several interviews with Corelli, each the length of the program. These interviews were in the early 1990's, some years after Corelli stopped singing.

It took me a long time to take Zucker seriously. The reason was because I actually once heard him sing. He is proud of the fact that he is in the *Guinness Book of World Records* as the world's highest tenor. I don't believe that, in his case, this is something to be proud of.

Sometime in the early 1970s I ventured to New York's Town Hall because there was to be a fully staged performance of a rare bel canto opera. Reading the program notes before the performance, it stated that the lead tenor, Stefan Zucker, would be singing in head voice, the way tenors sang in the eighteenth century until the chest voice came into vogue. Interesting I thought. . . . until he came out and sang.

I don't know how to describe the sounds that came from Zucker's mouth. I will just say it was painful to listen to, while comical at the same time. When he reached for a high note, it was absurd. Indeed, tittering soon began to be heard in the audience. I, too, was having a hard time restraining myself. At some point I realized I would not be able to control myself. If I didn't leave, I would soon be laughing out loud. I somehow made it through thirty to forty-five minutes of the performance before I really had to leave.

In the thousands of performances I've seen, there were only a handful I didn't see to the end. This was the most infamous of those. It is why I have no written review of this performance and must recount it to you from memory.

I believe that what I saw was the performance the Guinness book refers to. Whether the specific high note occurred during the portion I attended, I can't tell you. What I can be pretty sure of is that it is difficult for me to believe that there was any period in history during which audiences found this style of singing pleasurable. Perhaps Zucker's version of "head singing" is not exactly what those audiences heard. We have no recordings from the eighteenth century to verify the sound. Therfore, some years later, when his radio show began to be heard, I didn't listen to it, until he conducted the Corelli interviews.

If you think I'm exaggerating that he couldn't be that bad, here's an example. Evidently the person who posted this video was equally as incredulous as I, as you can see and hear in this clip. Be forewarned, if you are sensitive to vulgarity and bad or comical singing, you may want to skip this.

[https://www.youtube.com/watch?v=SfFAoU29q38]

Well, I did warn you. Perhaps you think he is putting us on, but he is dead serious.

[https://www.youtube.com/watch?v=SfFAoU29q38]

Zucker likes to point out that Franco Corelli came in first when he asked listeners to vote for their favorite tenors of the century, a poll he conducted for several weeks on his "Opera Fanatic" program (Björling, Caruso and Gigli followed, in that order). Only 600 voters created a not-very scientific poll that was further marred by the fact that, during the several weeks Zucker conducted this "poll," his guest for the entire several hours of his program, on at least two occasions, was Franco Corelli. For the record, I didn't vote.

Here's part of one of Zucker's lengthy radio interviews with Corelli. It's in two parts, it lasts two hours, and it isn't even the whole interview!

[https://www.youtube.com/watch?v=BxAU8f2PiC8]

[https://www.youtube.com/watch?v=hMm0sBSWaBA&t=59s]

For those who don't want to spend two hours listening to a Corelli interview, here is a link to a much shorter, much earlier, interview. It's a 1962 interview, probably Corelli's first in English, on a radio program called "Opera for You" hosted by William H. Wells.

[https://www.youtube.com/watch?v=NjihqC6ehDE]

Many years later, when I was working at New York City's Department of Housing Preservation and Development, I was at a meeting and was introduced to Bill Wells, a colleague in the department. As soon as he began to speak, I recognized his voice. When I asked, he confirmed that he was the William H. Wells who had hosted the radio program. Like me, being an opera lover was not his day job.

While there are numerous audio recordings of Corelli in complete opera performances, there are only a handful of video representations of his art. Unfortunately, the Metropolitan Opera did not begin telecasts until four years after Corelli's last performance at the Met. Being tall (6'2") and handsome, not to mention his miraculous voice, he would have been a shoo-in to become a worldwide sensation, even among the non-opera loving public. Thus, it was left to his immediate successors, Placido Domingo and Luciano Pavarotti, to parlay that additional exposure into the kind of fame few opera singers previously achieved. Still, that handful of Corelli opera videos are more than most of his tenor contemporaries made. Here's a complete list of Corelli's complete opera videos:

From a 1954 *Pagliacci* telecast produced by RAI (Radiotelevisione Italiana), in which he is joined by Tito Gobbi in Gobbi's second video recording as Tonio in *Pagliacci*.
[https://www.youtube.com/watch?v=IKpPGocnqLQ&t=1020s]

There are two video representations of Corelli's Cavaradossi in *Tosca*.

In 1955, Corelli appeared in an RAI TV production of *Tosca*. If only the soprano was Tebaldi or Callas, but Renata Heredia Capnist acquits herself well enough.
[https://www.youtube.com/watch?v=H8OtR6FkOYQ]

In the very next year (1956), he starred in a color film version of *Tosca*. In that film he was the only one of the three principals who appeared onscreen. The Tosca was portrayed onscreen by Franca Duval, while the voice was provided by veteran soprano Maria Caniglia (who eighteen years earlier had recorded the role commercially with Gigli as her Cavaradossi). Afro Poli, a well-known baritone portrayed Scarpia onscreen, but strangely, his singing voice was provided by another, younger, baritone, Giangiacomo Guelfi:
[https://www.youtube.com/watch?v=PC1p7daDig8]

In 1956 there is also a video of Corelli as Don Jose in Bizet's *Carmen* with Belen Amparan in the title role. Be forewarned, this French opera is performed in an Italian translation.
[https://www.youtube.com/watch?v=RnB3W9sXlCc&t=2223s]

In 1958, RAI produced *Turandot*. Corelli is magnificent as Calaf and Lucille Udavich is excellent in the title role, but, still, she's no Nilsson.
[https://www.youtube.com/watch?v=zCiJGYCFy90&t=85s]

Strangely, in 1969 RAI produced another *Turandot*, still in black and white, this time *with* Nilsson, but the tenor in that performance was Gianfranco Cecchele.
[https://www.youtube.com/watch?v=totuvUW7hJ8]

In 1958, a live performance from Teatro San Carlo in Naples was telecast, a complete performance of Verdi's *La Forza del Destino*, in which Corelli is joined by Renata Tebaldi (in her glorious vocal prime) and the great baritone and bass, respectively, Ettore Bastianini and Boris Christoff. A resplendently sung performance is marred by primitive black and white video and sound. Okay, so some of the acting is also a bit primitive.
[https://www.youtube.com/watch?v=k9sRRKNZULE]

Finally, in 1973, there is a RAI film, in color, of Giordano's *Andrea Chenier*. Alas, the synchronization of the prerecorded soundtrack leaves a lot to be desired, but two years before his retirement Corelli's voice still blazes forth—and at age fifty he remains extremely photogenic.

Act I [https://www.youtube.com/watch?v=EkTo4J0Q-HQ]

Acts II–IV [https://www.youtube.com/watch?v=cNfMOe8p3Pw&t=3s]

What is unfortunate is that the fifteen-year gap between the 1958 *Forza* and the 1973 *Chenier* encompassed Corelli's greatest years and there is no complete opera video with him from that period. Imagine what we might have had if the Met had begun regular telecasts two decades earlier!

My Introduction to German Opera at the Old Met

My introduction to opera was Italian opera. It took me a little while to come to love German opera. I think Italian (and, in general, most languages derived from Latin) are more singable. I believe this is because the majority of words in Italian start and/or end with a vowel. It's so much easier to connect the next word when there is a vowel at the beginning, end or, especially, both. And a good part of singing is connecting words. Also Wagner and Strauss are a little more difficult for the novice opera lover than Verdi and Puccini. Nevertheless, my first German opera performance at the Met came fairly early, in November, 1962. Wagner's *Die Meistersinger* with Sandor Konya, Otto Weiner, and Ingrid Bjoner. Of course, my impetus in seeing this performance was the tenor. The little I had heard of Konya before this had impressed me. I was even more impressed *after* the performance as he was an ideal Walther.

[https://www.youtube.com/watch?v=68ycYrR2Ic0]

My second Wagner opera was *Lohengrin*, in February of 1964, with Konya, again, and Regine Crespin. To quote from my nearly contemporaneous review:

> In his gold costume and wig, Konya was a sight to behold. Opening his mouth, a voice to challenge the best. His "Mein Lieber Schwann" and "In Fernam Land" were exquisitely done. His entire performance was on the highest level of voice and vocal artistry."

[https://www.youtube.com/watch?v=PKh9XN4OY3I&t=124s]

In March, 1966, I saw my first *Parsifal*, also with Konya and Crespin. Neither of them was anywhere near as good as in *Lohengrin*. In between, in March, 1965, I saw my first *Walkure* with Birgit

Nilsson, Jon Vickers, Leonie Rysanek, and George London. A very star-filled cast by today's standards, but my notes tell me I didn't think the principals were in their best voice.

My first non-Wagner German opera at the Met was *Fidelio* in March, 1963. It starred Birgit Nilsson and Jon Vickers with Karl Böhm conducting The performance was splendid with some wonderful singing. For the first time I have mentioned in a review, the conductor of the performance because, previously, I was interested mostly in the singers, and because it was the orchestral playing that had the biggest impact on me in that performance. I wrote then:

> I have never heard the Metropolitan Opera Orchestra play so heavenly as they did in Fidelio. Mr. Bohm brought out excellent quality tone and all-around sound. The minute the opening chords of the "Fidelio" Overture sounded I knew I was in for a treat. The sound was extraordinarily beautiful throughout, especially in the Leonore Overture No. 3, which was breathtaking.

[https://www.youtube.com/watch?v=OGq5Le12lr4]

In those days the Met would perform Beethoven's *Leonore Overture No. 3* between the two scenes of the last act, making the final scene somewhat anti-climactic, as, musically, the *Leonore* is so overwhelming it dwarfs what comes after.

In the 1960s, the Met Opera orchestra was a solid opera house orchestra, but could not match the standards of the great symphonic ensembles. Under the likes of the Met's regular roster of conductors such as Fausto Cleva, Joseph Rosenstock, George Schick, Francesco Molinai-Pradelli, Nello Santi, Silvio Varviso, Kurt Adler, Jan Behr, and others, it would mostly give workmanlike, rarely inspired, performances. The more-well-known conductors who appeared sporadically during this period—Leopold Stokowski (he conducted my first *Turandot*), Leonard Bernstein (my first *Falstaff* and, some years later, *Cavalleria*), Georg Solti (*Otello* and others), and the young Zubin Mehta (*Turandot* and *Aida* in 1966 and in several other operas for the five years he regularly conducted at the Met)—did somewhat better, but the orchestra still did not sound like a great ensemble. When Karl Böhm was on the podium it sounded like a completely different orchestra—a great one.

I wrote the last sentence of the previous paragraph before I had reread (in my reviews) what I wrote about a January, 1966 performance of the then-new production of *Fidelio* with Birgit Nilsson and, this time, James King, with Böhm again conducting. What it proved is that my memory is pretty good. What I wrote in 1966 sounds very similar to what I wrote in 2023 .

Again, the greatest triumph of the evening was Karl Bohm, who positively makes the Metropolitan Opera Orchestra sound like another instrument, like a first-class European symphony orchestra.

Yet, as great as Böhm's *Fidelio*'s were, even they didn't prepare me for his spectacular conducting of Strauss's operas.

Böhm and Strauss at the New Met

I ultimately saw Karl Böhm conduct five Richard Strauss operas at the Met: *Salome, Elektra, Ariadne auf Naxos, Der Rosenkavalier,* and *Die Frau ohne Schatten*. I attended all except *Salome* at the new Lincoln Center Metropolitan Opera House. Each one of them was a thrilling experience, with the orchestra in magnificent form. The pinnacle was reached with *Die Frau ohne Schatten,* which was premiered as one of the four new productions that opened the New Met .

Die Frau ohne Schatten, October 2, 1966, Metropolitan Opera House at Lincoln Center (Written 10/4/66)

This production easily ranks as one of the best productions ever mounted by the Metropolitan Opera. The scenery was absolutely sensational; there is no other word for it. If anything showed off the superlative stage facilities of the new House, it was this production's beautiful scenery, moving back, forth, down and in every which way. The spectacle on stage was a glittering array, colorful and splendid. [*Having so praised the set, it was remiss of me at that time to not have put the name of the set designer into the review. It was Robert O'Hearn.*]

In the music department, things were just as good. This opera impressed me more on first hearing than any other Strauss opera I've ever seen. There need not be any qualification in saying that the Metropolitan Opera Orchestra was at its ultimate best. Of course, the man in the pit was Karl Böhm. I don't know what magic Böhm has that he can make the orchestra play like that. His conducting made this performance one of the most glowing, as far as orchestral sound, that I've ever seen.

[*The star-filled cast included Leonie Rysenek, James King, Walter Berry (in his Met debut), Christa Ludwig, Irene Dalis and William*

Dooley. They were all outstanding, but I won't include my comments on all, just the one who deserves special mention.]

Christa Ludwig was returning to the Met after several seasons absence. I have already described the production and Böhm's conducting as sensational. The third sensational element of the performance was the singing of Christa Ludwig, which must rank as one of the greatest mezzo-soprano efforts at the Met in recent years. Ludwig has a wide range, embracing a soprano top, and she showed it here with high notes galore. She sang beautifully and excitingly so that, by the end of the performance, she had the audience eating out of her hands."
[https://www.youtube.com/watch?v=Ks00CJIRmV0]

There is another characteristic of the sound of the orchestra that I hadn't thought about until hearing a radio interview with bass Jerome Hines (on Stefan Zucker's *Opera Fanatic*), whose Metropolitan Opera career lasted over forty years and encompassed both the old and new Met. He opined that the Lincoln Center Met has livelier orchestra acoustics than the old Met. I think he was right. The sound of the orchestra in the new Met is much brighter. Still, no other conductor got the kind of sound from the Metropolitan Opera Orchestra that Böhm did—until the arrival of James Levine, who is discussed later.

Placido Domingo

This review conveys my first impression of Placido Domingo:

Cavalleria Rusticana and *Pagliacci*, concert performance by the Met, Lewisohn Stadium, August 9, 1966, (Written 8/10/66)

Opera's most famous double-bill are given interesting concert readings by members of the Metropolitan Opera. Probably the most notable novelty of the performance was Placido Domingo's singing of the top tenor role in each opera. Mr. Domingo has a rising reputation among young opera tenors, but is not exactly new to New York audiences, having sung with the New York City Opera in their new production this spring of Ginastera's "Don Rodrigo." Unfortunately, that is not exactly a role to judge tenors by, and I didn't see it, so this was really the first opportunity to judge his voice.

On the whole, Mr. Domingo made an extremely favorable impression on me. I'm even almost tempted to say an astounding impression on me. I really wasn't expecting much, knowing the level of quality of most new

tenors here is low, except for the golden rare ones (like Corelli in 1961). But, as soon as Mr. Domingo sang his off-stage "Siciliana," I realized that this tenor is no passing fad, but a tenor with a truly beautiful voice. The fact is that the voice is beautiful, and if I had to compare it to a tenor of the past, it would have to be Jussi Björling. The voice, though, is lyric, and singing two roles of this nature in one evening is even trying for dramatic tenors, so amends must be made for a little vocal tiring and lapses by the middle of "Pagliacci." The only thing Mr. Domingo must be sure to do, is stick to the lyric repertoire and not ruin his voice by singing too many operas like "Pagliacci" too often. Mr. Domingo, though appearing with the Met company at Lewisohn, has, as yet, no Met contract, but he is scheduled to sing Cavaradossi with the City Opera here in New York. If he were added to the Met roster today, he would easily rank among the top tenors at the Met."
[https://www.youtube.com/watch?v=AEq5wIPRWxw]

A little more than two years after I first saw Placido Domingo, and following numerous performances he gave with the New York City Opera, he made his Met debut in September, 1968, substituting for Franco Corelli in Cilea's *Adriana Lecouvreur*. This is the review I wrote:

Adriana Lecouvreur, **Metropolitan Opera House, September 28, 1968 (Written 10/5/68)**

Placido Domingo finally made his Metropolitan Opera debut, and under rather curious and unexpected circumstances. Originally, Mr. Domingo was supposed to make his Met debut October 2 in this season's fourth "Adriana Lecouvreur" while Franco Corelli was rehearsing "Tosca." But, at 7:55 PM Domingo was seen running backstage at the Met and at 8:00 PM Ossie Hawkins came out to make the announcement that Corelli found he was unable to sing and Placido Domingo was going to make his Met debut a few days early. At any rate at 8:20 PM the performance commenced, and Placido Domingo, as everyone who has heard him sing at the New York City Opera knew he would, went on to a great personal triumph. He sang gloriously, his voice easily filling the big house and coming through clear and beautiful, with high notes that are beginning to ring. He managed to create the best impression, despite memories of Corelli's gorgeous and exciting singing in the role."
[https://www.youtube.com/watch?v=VDDT3LgOIGQ]

The subsequent decades proved my initial impressions correct. Placido Domingo has had one of the most spectacular careers of any operatic tenor. More than fifty consecutive seasons at the Met, singing over forty roles, brought him a record that no other Metropolitan Opera principal singer can come near to matching. And there is more: a record number of Met opening nights, twenty-four, breaking Caruso's record of seventeen; an international career that took him all over the globe; and, I suspect, more audio and video recordings than any other tenor. Also, he conducted regularly at the Met and at other opera houses and was the general director of both the Washington and Los Angeles opera companies; all this while maintaining a full schedule singing. As approving as I thought of him that summer night in 1966, I didn't expect such a landmark kind of career. I was wrong—despite singing numerous demanding dramatic roles in operas such as *Trovatore* and *Aida* early in his career, he managed to keep the innate beauty of his voice secure for decades. That said, and although I am clearly a Domingo fan, I don't think he is in quite the same league as my four favorite tenors (Gigli, Björling, Corelli, and Melchior).

When I first became an opera lover, I had a youthful view that, in about every twenty years, a tenor would emerge who would become the greatest of that era. Thus, I could say that from 1900 to 1920 it was Enrico Caruso; from 1920 to 1940 it was Benjamino Gigli; from 1940 to 1960 it was Jussi Björling; and in 1960, Franco Corelli emerged. Very neat and tidy. I fully expected Corelli to be active through 1980 and a new great tenor to emerge for the last two decades of the twentieth century. But, of course, Corelli stopped singing in 1976, and no tenor emerged in 1980, or even 2000, to join the exalted list of "my greatest tenors." While I can't add Domingo to that list, he does come close in my opinion, and has filled most of the forty-five-year gap since Corelli's retirement.

Having seen Corelli in more than two hundred performances, Domingo comes in second. I have no idea how many times I've seen Domingo, but considering I've seen him in every one of the over forty roles he's done at the Met, many of them more than once, and, before that, seeing many of his performances with the City Opera, not to mention concert performances at Carnegie Hall and a few performances at the New Jersey State Opera, I would say it is something approaching two hundred. Unlike Corelli, who I tried to see in almost every performance at the Met after 1964, I went to see Domingo more sparingly. Yet, because of his prolific performing schedule and longevity, I saw him more than any tenor other than Corelli.

In Domingo's first few seasons at the Met he competed directly with Corelli and, in the several roles they sang in common, there was no comparison in my opinion. As good as Domingo was as Maurizio (*Adriana Lecouvreur*), Manrico (*Il Trvatore*), Cavaradossi (*Tosca*), and in title roles in *Ernani, Romeo,* and *Werther*—and he was quite good—it was Corelli's magnificent singing that won my heart. Domingo, however, sang many other roles that Corelli never sang, among them Riccardo in *Un Ballo in Maschera*, Rodolfo in *Luisa Miller*, Arrigo in *I Vespri Sicilliani,* and the title roles in *Faust* and *Tales of Hoffmann.* In those he was often terrific and far and away better than any other tenor then singing at the Met.

As the years progressed, Domingo matured into more dramatic roles. In 1979 he sang his first *Otello* at the Met, and in 1996 his first Sigmund in *Die Walküre.* And, yes, by the late '70s, I had changed my opinion about the dramatic roles I considered him unsuited for as I wrote in that first review. Giovanni Martinelli and Mario Del Monaco fans may cringe when I say Domingo was my favorite Otello ever, but I think he had the most beautiful voice to sing that role. It should be noted that Caruso, Gigli, Björling, and Corelli never sang the role— Melchior did, but never at the Met, and no recording exists of a complete performance of *Otello* with Melchior.

It wasn't just his voice. Domingo was a strong actor and his conception of the role of Otello was commanding. I think Domingo had a way with tortured characters. His performances in roles like Don Jose in *Carmen*, Canio in *Pagliacci, Tales of Hoffmann,* and, of course, *Otello,* were thrilling. To mollify Mario Del Monaco fans, these are two videos of Del Monaco as Otello.

RAI Milan, 1958:
[https://www.youtube.com/watch?v=4q8z-s9lSSY]
Tokyo, 1959 with Tito Gobbi as Iago:
[https://www.youtube.com/watch?v=f8_vhpF6YUQ&t=6s]

Based on these video links, I do find Del Monaco's singing and conception compelling. Perhaps if I had seen him sing live, I might think to place him above Domingo, but I find Domingo's voice more beautiful.

Domingo first sang Otello at the Met in 1979 and sang his last performance of that role there twenty years later. He sang virtually every performance the Met presented of that opera during that entire period, including three telecasts! None of those telecasts can be found on YouTube. (The Met is pretty scrupulous in keeping their opera telecasts off YouTube.) However, Domingo appears in numerous *Otello* telecasts sung at other opera houses. (He probably holds the record of the most *Otello* telecasts of any tenor.)

Here's one from La Scala
[https://www.youtube.com/watch?v=Sm_Usoo7LvY],
another from Mexico City
[https://www.youtube.com/watch?v=bqWzCwt2BX4]
and a third from Paris
[https://www.youtube.com/watch?v=YXRJb0vLAts].

Domingo also starred in a movie version of Otello. It's not on YouTube, but here's the theatre trailer:
[https://www.youtube.com/watch?v=kC0YJGmlwXk]

Domingo's Siegmund in Wagner's *Die Walkure* was something wonderful to see and hear. I had seen him in the two other Wagner operas he sang at the Met, the title roles in *Lohengrin* and *Parsifal,* and enjoyed his performances without being overwhelmed, but his Siegmund in *Die Walkure* (another tortured character) blew me away. From my review of Placido Domingo's first two complete Metropolitan Opera Siegmunds:

Die Walkure, Metropolitan Opera, April 15 and 23, 1996 (Written 4/28/96):

I have always felt that if I ever saw a tenor who approximated Melchior in my favorite Heldentenor role (Siegmund), I would see as many performances as I could. While I liked Domingo in his two prior Wagner forays at the Met as Lohengrin and Parsifal, his voice in those operas seemed a little too small-scale for Wagner, lovely as the sound was. But, as Siegmund, all my reservations were thrown away. Mr. Domingo is big and burly these days, just like Melchior, but more importantly, as Siegmund, his voice rang out with a burnished power that surprised even me (especially in the April 23 performance). His voice often had a clarion tone, sometimes possessing the bounce on the top that was a hallmark of what made Melchior so great. In both performances Domingo was magnificent, but in the April 23 performance he came as close to Melchior as I ever hoped to see on stage. Yes, he is not Melchior and on a couple of occasions one still missed the sheer beauty of Melchior's voice, but Domingo managed to come near to the pinnacle."

As with Otello, Domingo owned the role of Siegmund at the Met and sang it in virtually all Met performances of *Die Walküre* for the next several years. But, in 1996, when he first sang the role at the

Met, he was fifty-five years old, so his reign in that role was relatively short, only seven years. I saw virtually all his performances in the role (as usual, skipping the radio broadcast performances to tape them). He never disappointed, though I must say, by 2003, when he last essayed the role at the Met, he was slightly less spectacular. He could no longer hold the Valse's for fifteen seconds to rival Melchior.

The baritone colleague who Domingo appeared most frequently with in the first three decades of his career was Sherrill Milnes. They made their Metropolitan Opera debuts within two years of each other and went on to appear in numerous operas together at the Met and in other opera houses. They also appear together in many complete commercial opera recordings. Among their earliest recordings was an album of baritone/tenor duets for RCA Victor in 1971. In the following year, they recorded, again for RCA Victor, a unique LP. On one side were baritone arias sung by Milnes, with the orchestra conducted by Domingo; on the other were tenor arias sung by Domingo, with the orchestra conducted by Milnes! Domingo continued to conduct throughout his career, Milnes did not. After a three-decade career, Milnes retired. Domingo, on the other hand, continued singing and has usurped Milnes's baritone repertoire, extending his career into his eighties.

This last stage of Domingo's singing career is something of a trial for me. Unlike Ramon Vinay, who I understand retrained his voice when he switched from a tenor to a baritone, Domingo sings baritone roles as a tenor. I sometimes refer to him a baritenor. (Given that his personal motto [on placidodomingo.com/calendar] is "If I rest, I rust," I doubt whether he is constitutionally able to take time off!) As he aged, the sound of his voice in his middle register remained quite beautiful, and although it darkened a bit, it showed little sign of his age, an age at which many tenors seem to thin out and sound somewhat quavering.

Take, for example, the legendary lyric tenor, Tito Schipa (1888–1865), who sang into his seventies.
[https://www.youtube.com/watch?v=UjF8i8pTV6Y]
Admirable as his artistry remained into his mid-seventies, his is clearly heard to be the voice of an old man long past his vocal prime. In the next excerpt from Verdi's *Nabucco*, you *see* what clearly is an old man singing, but in this case Placido Domingo's voice belies the screen image, sounding strong and secure, his timbre intact despite that he is singing this on his eightieth birthday. If you listen to it

without the video image you might think you're hearing a singer half his age. Admittedly, unlike Schipa, he is not trying to reach those tenor high notes.

[https://www.youtube.com/watch?v=MK9o6fVkIEw]

Indeed, I can attest that Domingo's voice was still strong and secure the last time *I* saw him, which was as Gianni Schicchi in 2018, when he was seventy-seven. That said, both the *Nabucco* excerpt above and *Gianni Schicchi* are baritone roles and Domingo simply is not a baritone. In many of the baritone roles he has undertaken, his performance is underwhelming because the character seems to need more than just a darker voice, but a baritone timbre that Domingo just doesn't have. Thus, when I saw him in in a baritone role for the first time, the title role in Verdi's *Simon Boccanegra*, in January 2010, the performance seemed out of kilter. It was a relief when I next saw that opera sung by the late, great Dmitri Hvorostovsky.

[https://www.youtube.com/watch?v=QsD2-fYbB0A] Milnes
[https://www.youtube.com/watch?v=SEWsrUIc6kI] Domingo
[https://www.youtube.com/watch?v=eD1iXp0zm7A] Hvorostovsky

Okay, call me obsessive, but, whatever you think of the above clips, I must include one of the greatest interpreters of Simon Boccanegra, *Tito Gobbi.*

https://www.youtube.com/watch?v=YpuV9VcwGso]

So, it's time to tackle the elephant in the room. I will need a whole section to do that.

The Elephant in the Room

I realized it would be best to write this section early on, near to the time I discuss my admiration for Karl Böhm's conducting of the Metropolitan Opera Orchestra, but I knew I had to address it in reference to a number of artists, so I held off. Now, after my discussion of Placido Domingo's illustrious career, it's time to write about the elephant in the room.

I suppose one would start with Richard Wagner.

Many decades ago, during a Metropolitan Opera broadcast intermission, a musical scholar was opining that Wagner was a musical genius, but a miserable human being. Everyone knew he was a rabid antisemite who made his feelings known in print. Whether he would have approved of Naziism can be debated ad nauseam, but his widely publicized views could well have helped to forward the Nazi regime. There is also little question that much of the music he wrote is held to be among the greatest music of Western Civilization. Should we deny ourselves the pleasure and beauty of this music because the man who wrote it held and disseminated despicable views?

Moving on to Karl Böhm. Twenty years before I was first wowed by Karl Böhm's conducting, Böhm had conducted musical performances with Hitler in the audience. During the Nazi era, he reputedly began each concert by giving the Nazi salute. Descriptions put him forth as an enthusiastic Nazi.

In 1963, I was seventeen years old and I was not aware of his background; by the late 1960s, I was. Should I have revised my opinion of his music-making because of what I had learned? Should I have forsworn his performances? By not doing so, was I dishonoring the memory of six million Jews who died under Hitler's direction? These are questions I have been grappling with for over fifty years.

So, too, the question—how can a man with his background be able to provide us such a magnificent reading of Beethoven's great paean to freedom, *Fidelio*? I couldn't answer it then, and I can't answer it now. Can one divorce the music-making from the man making the music? In many cases I am able to, but is that the right thing to do? Is just posing the question enough? The question is not a singular one. It goes to other great conductors whose activities were Nazi-aligned such as Herbert von Karajan, Wilhelm Furtwängler, and Willem Mengelberg. (Then there's Benjamino Gigli, a supporter of the Italian fascist regime during World War II, whose voice melts my heart nonetheless.)

We presently have additional considerations that people decades ago didn't even think about. While not on the scale of Naziism's final solution, the recent #MeToo movement has brought to the fore sexual assault and sexual harassment, primarily against women, that had previously been ignored; or, even worse, accepted. It has rightly changed the mores of society, and in doing so, it has also ended the careers of some well-known performers. Two of my favorites, casualties of this movement, are James Levine and Placido Domingo.

In Levine's case he was ill and in the twilight of his career. His death came just three years after he was banished from the Met, his musical home for more than forty-five years. Domingo, while forced to leave the Met after a whopping fifty seasons, and being fired from the Los Angeles Opera, where he was its general director, even at the age of eighty and during a pandemic, he seems to be having less trouble finding work in Europe, which apparently has a weaker #MeToo movement.

Sherrill Milnes

While I admired Tito Gobbi in all of his performances, for voice and characterization, Sherrill Milnes had one of the most beautiful voices of any baritone I've ever seen perform. The first time I saw him was at the New York City Opera on September 22, 1965, in what was the last opening night at the City Center before their move to Lincoln Center. The opera was Prokofiev's *The Fiery Angel* (then billed as *The Flaming Angel*) in an English translation.

This is what I wrote about his singing, two days after the performance:

> Sherrill Milnes possesses a fine baritone voice with some excellent high notes. He...performed his part beautifully.

Exactly three months later, on December 22, 1965, Milnes made his Met debut during the same performance of Gounod's *Faust* in which the great Spanish soprano, Montserrat Caballé, made her Met debut. I wrote of Milnes two days after that performance:

> Sherrill Milnes, making his Met debut as Valentin, showed off a voice of merit. He sang Valentin's aria beautifully and got a thunderous ovation for it. However, the best part of his singing came after the aria, and it was exquisite. It's still much too early to tell, but he may be following in the steps of such other American baritones as Robert Merrill and Cornell MacNeil. At any rate, a welcome addition to the Met roster."
> [https://www.youtube.com/watch?v=Akujojgi4NI&t=41s]
> [https://www.youtube.com/watch?v=RjRVxWvx-MM]

Still, I wasn't all-in as a Milnes fan. That came about later, in a unique way.

On January 23, 1967, I went to see a working rehearsal of *Il Trovatore* at the Met. Working rehearsals were final dress rehearsals to which the Met gave tickets to Met Guild members to honor their financial contributions. The more you gave, the more tickets you were entitled to. The tickets were general admission, no reserved seats. I was usually able to score a free ticket in the lobby from a patron who had an extra ticket. As they never gave out more than a third of the seats in the house, I was often able to sit in what would have been very expensive seats had it been a regular performance. On this occasion I met a friend on my way in and we got seats together in the Grand Tier. The rehearsal was for the *Il Trovatore* season premiere with Martina Arroyo, Richard Tucker, Robert Merrill, and Biserka Cvejić. I wrote:

> Here lay the most interesting and best performance of the afternoon. When Count di Luna came in, I commented to my friend that Robert Merrill looked taller and was singing like he was ten years younger. [*This was a rehearsal, so there were moments when the performance stopped, giving me time to make comments, something I would never do during a performance.*] It seems that the Met management didn't feel it necessary to make an announcement about replacing Merrill until the beginning of Act II. At any rate, when I finally realized who was really singing, and as Milnes progressed from act to act, I realized how really fine he was at singing—and that, indeed, he was the best sounding di Luna I've ever seen. His very top notes may not have been as exquisite as Cornell MacNeil in his prime, and his acting needs working on (though he is already far ahead of Merrill in this respect), but his performance was little less than fabulous.

Although I had seen Milnes several times between the two performances described and this rehearsal—in such disparate roles as the Herald in *Lohengrin* and Amonasro in *Aida*—and continued to admire him, it was during this *Il Trovatore*, at first thinking I was seeing a rejuvenated Merrill, that made me an all-out Milnes fan.

[https://www.youtube.com/watch?v=Z021RrD3Yvo]

The New York City Opera, Norman Treigle, and Beverly Sills

New York is the performing arts center of the United States. On the stages of Broadway, Off-Broadway, Lincoln Center, Carnegie Hall, City Center, Town Hall, and many other venues, the number of live performances that go on in New York City on any given day may reach a hundred or more. With respect to opera, no opera company in the United States can match New York's Metropolitan Opera in the number of performances it presents, nor the quality of those performances. However, it does happens that a particular opera may get a better performance at another American company.

That the Metropolitan Opera is the largest opera organization in the United States goes without saying. When I began attending the opera in the 1960s, New York City had another opera company that may have been the second biggest opera company in the United

States, at least in terms of the number of performances it presented annually. That was the New York City Opera. In their peak period, they would perform six or seven performances a week; usually Tuesday or Wednesday through Sunday, with matinees on Saturday and Sunday. They had two seasons per year: the fall season from late August through November, and a spring season from late February to mid-May. In mid-winter and in late Spring, The New York City Ballet would take over the stage at the New York City Opera's original home, the New York City Center, or, later, the New York State Theater (now the David H. Koch Theater) at Lincoln Center.

Unfortunately, through a series of missteps beyond the scope of this book, the New York City Opera Company folded in 2013. It was revived in 2016, but in name only, a pale shadow of its former self, giving only a dozen or so performances a season mostly at the Rose Theater at Jazz at Lincoln Center.

City Opera's roster did not boast the international opera stars that the Met had, but did have lots of American, and a few international, up-and-comers, many who were never to make it big. In its early days in the 1940s, many of its singers were artists you have probably never heard of, but it did have a few who would go on to bigger things, most notably Dorothy Kirsten, who would become a Met favorite for more than two decades. City Opera's greatest years, 1957 to 1979, were those when Julius Rudel (1921–2014) was its director. He was a fine conductor, as well as administrator, and he led many inspiring performances. By the 1960s, the City Opera had nurtured its own garden of home-grown stars who stayed with the company for most of their careers. The two most prominent of these were bass Norman Treigle and soprano Beverly Sills. Because the Met and City Opera were, after 1966, both located on the Lincoln Center campus, for standard-repertoire operas I would mostly attend the Met to hear their more star-filled casts, but the enterprising New York City Opera often performed new and/or lesser-seen operas. In September, 1969, they unveiled a new production of Boito's *Mefistofele* starring Norman Treigle in the title role, conducted by Julius Rudel.

Mefistofele, New York City Opera, September 21, 1969 (Written 9/27/69)

This is the first staged performance of this opera in New York since 1926 and it's a shame. For, as the American Opera Society concert performance showed me a few years ago, this is one of the most beautiful Italian operas of the period. This staged performance impressed me even more and I can almost say that "Mefistofele" is as good as anything Verdi had written up to that time. Indeed, there is more in "Mefistofele" that foreshadows "Otello" and "Falstaff" than in "Trovatore," "Rigoletto," "Forza." The music of the prologue is among the most gorgeous ever composed, and Mr. Rudel made the most of it with stereophonic effect, having some trumpeters on each side of the Fifth Ring.

Most of the vocal honors of the evening, if not all, go to Norman Treigle in the title role, at the height of his very great powers. Such bass singing is a rare occurrence, and Mr. Treigle, with a cold, was singing strongly and exquisitely, and doing a marvelous job of acting.

I should note here that *Mefistofele* is an Italian opera written by Arrigo Boito, based on the famous German play *Faust* by Johann Wolfgang von Goethe. Boito is more famous in opera circles for writing the libretti for Verdi's two final masterpieces *Otello* and *Falstaff*, which is why in my review I made the comment that compares *Mefistofele* to Verdi's earlier works. But, I doubt if that review adequately conveys the impact of Treigle's astounding performance that is locked in my memory.

Aside from his vocal prowess, Triegle's writhing was a sight to behold. Indeed, over the next few years I went back to see him do that role several times. Interestingly, exactly ten days earlier, I had seen Treigle in the same role in the other *Faust* opera, the more popular one, in French, by Charles Gounod. In that performance, he was accompanied by Beverley Sills as Marguerite. Unfortunately, Rudel was not on the podium for that performance, and it suffered for it. However, Treigle, and, to a lesser extent Sills, excelled. Of the two Faust operas, I prefer the Boito, even though it's less popular. Gounod may be melodic, but he can be syrupy. Boito's music is more serious. The best way I can say to describe it is that it has gravitas, even though that term is not usually used to describe music. The prologue, which lasts nearly twenty minutes, contains some of the most sublime music I've ever heard. If the opera falters a bit in the middle, it comes back with a wallop at its stunning end. It is a work that I immediately fell in love with the first time I saw it, and it remains so to this day.

There is YouTube audio of one of Tregle's *Mefistofele* performances from two weeks after the one I reported above. It is unfortunate to be audio-only as one misses the visual aspect of his performance.
[https://www.youtube.com/watch?v=80R4HI_Iuuk&t=106s]

If you want to hear Treigle's towering performance in better sound and with a better-known supporting cast, including Placido Domingo and Montserrat Caballe, listen to his 1973 studio recording.

[https://www.youtube.com/watch?v=si2ifEGW4Gs]

You can also listen to Treigle's Mephistopheles in Gounod's *Faust* at City Opera, with Beverly Sills and Julius Rudel conducting, at a performance given a year before the one I saw.

[https://www.youtube.com/watch?v=5gvN4yEuWxk]

Sometimes I profoundly disagree with professional critics. Here is *The New York Times* music critic Tim Page's view of *Mefistofele* from a review of a 1984 City Opera performance of the opera with Sam Ramey in the title role:

> *Mefistofele* is simply not a very good opera. Boito took his text from Goethe rather than Piave or Illica, but the finished product is, in essence, just another 19th-century Italian tonsil show, with less vitality than most. One feels the force of Boito's admirable intellect, rather than any spontaneous musical gift: his love music is sexless, most of his melodies feeble, and the attempts at musical apotheosis ring consistently false. The "Prologue in Heaven," the stirring "Sabba Classico" and two or three good arias stand out, but cannot redeem what is, for the most part, a static and labored affair. (Ramey at City Opera In Boito's *Mefistofele*, NY Times, October 23, 1984).

At the beginning of *my* review of the City Opera's *Mefistofele*, quoted above, I noted that I had previously seen *Mefistofele* once before, in a concert performance by the American Opera Society. (The American Opera Society was a New York City-based musical organization that presented concerts and semi-staged performances of operas between 1951 and 1970. *Wikipedia*). So, before I return to Treigle and the City Opera, let's go back three years for my review of that *Mefistofele* performance.

Mefistofele, American Opera Society, Carnegie Hall, January 25, 1966 (Written on 1/26/66)

There was very much of interest in this performance of Boito's "Mefistofele," which hasn't been heard at the Metropolitan Opera since 1926. The first and most important is the music. I've never been so impressed with an opera at first seeing as I was with "Mefistofele. Sure, I had heard recordings, but listening to a live performance, and with such a fabulous cast, my feeling for the opera multiplied.

There is so much beauty in this opera. There are a number of lovely tenor arias, two great bass arias, a fine soprano-tenor duet, and one of the most beautiful soprano arias ever written, *L'altra notte in fondo al mare.* Best of the evening's illustrious singers was Nicolai Ghiaurov, who gave his most in the title role. His voice never sounded so gorgeous. Also in good form was Carlo Bergonzi. His lyric voice was superbly suited to the role and he gave it his best, singing an artistically and vocally arresting performance. Well, what can one say about Renata Tebaldi? She has one of the most beautiful soprano voices that I have ever heard. Today, the beauty is still there in the middle, but as soon as she leaves it for the top, the beauty disappears. Gall and bravery she has, singing the two leading soprano roles in this opera, an assignment that would make any soprano in her prime, shudder. That Tebaldi got through it, and better than I expected, is to her credit.

That performance was probably recorded by several audience members because I obtained a tape of it not long after its performance. It has also been released more than once on LP and CD at varying sound-quality levels. In subsequent years, when listening to the recording, I found myself being less critical of Tebaldi.

[https://www.youtube.com/watch?v=xw3N_7-BeWo&t=140s]
[https://www.youtube.com/watch?v=l03rKHjCyDg&t=11s]
[https://www.youtube.com/watch?v=CHIUjSgdF-E&t=2s]

Back to the City Opera and Treigle, who had a stunning career with that company. He is reported as having said he was never tempted to go to the Metropolitan because he would simply be one of many and would not get the star treatment he got at City Opera—they mounted productions around him. Beside *Mefistofele*, Treigle starred in such diverse and rare operas as Floyd's *Susannah*, Handel's *Giulio Cesare* and Rimsky-Korsakov's *Le coq d'or.* He, of course, also sang many of the leading bass roles in the standard repertory. He was just forty-seven at his untimely death in 1975.

After Treigle's death, the New York City Opera produced *Mefistofele* in 1977 with Treigle's successor, Samuel Ramey, and again in 1984. Ramey may have been vocally superior, but even his gorgeous singing could not erase my memories of Treigle's commanding presence in the role. Indeed, Ramey probably had the most beautiful bass voice of the late twentieth century. When the Met finally revived *Mefistofele* in 1999 for the first time since 1926, it was for Ramey—who, once again, was vocally superb—but on this rare occasion, with respect to the scenery, direction and even orchestral playing, the Met's production couldn't compare with the City Opera three decades earlier.

I saw Jerome Hines (1923–2003) sing the title role in *Mefistofele* in Newark's Symphony Hall with the New Jersey State Opera in 1976 and he was vocally quite fine. At least what I could hear of it, as the poor acoustics made a mockery of Boito's brilliant score. Only legendary soprano Magda Olivero (1910–2014) came out unscathed. I saw Hines many times at the Met, and elsewhere, and was always impressed by his vocal instrument. He was an imposing presence at 6' 6", but his performances were often marred by his stiff acting. The two most recent basses I've seen do the role did not impress me at all: Eric Owens, who I admired in his Wagner forays, seemed a rather lackluster Mefistofele in a concert performance by the Collegiate Chorale at Carnegie Hall in 2013, while Christian Van Horn, in the Met's most recent revival in 2018, pales by comparison to Nicolai Ghiaurov, Norman Treigle, or Samuel Ramey.

In the mid-to-late 1960s, the City Opera gave some of its best performances. Some of their performances of the standard repertoire rivaled the Met's. This was the period when Placido Domingo and Sherrill Milnes sang there. The company's other lead tenors included Michele Molese, (who I didn't care for at all), Enrico Di Giuseppe, and Kenneth Riegel (who were much better). Other baritones included Dominic Cossa and Richard Stillwell. All except Molese were to graduate to the Met. Therefore, at City Opera one could see Domingo and Sills in *Manon*, those same two in *Don Giovanni*, with Treigle in the title role, and Sills doing all three soprano leads in Puccini's *Il Trittico* with Domingo in *Il Tabarro* and Treigle singing the title role in *Gianni Schicchi*. Unfortunately, there were only one or two performances with each of those configurations, but I was fortunate enough to get to see them.

I have mixed feelings about Beverly Sills. She was one of the trio of sopranos who became international stars in the post-Callas era, essaying many of the bel canto roles that Callas had helped to bring out of obscurity and many they helped reintroduce. The two other sopranos who excelled in this repertoire were Joan Sutherland and Montserrat Caballé. I am being somewhat American-centric here. There were other sopranos who essayed the bel canto repertoire, but they were not as well-known as these three, did not perform in the United States as much, and made fewer commercial recordings. Notable among these is Leyla Gencer (who Nicholas Limansky reports in *Pirates of the High C's: Opera Bootlegging in the 20th Century,* published by this book's publisher, YBK Publishers, in 2020, had became a queen of pirated recordings).

Sills became a household name due to her regular appearances on TV. This was partly due to her effusive personality, making her nickname, "Bubbles," very apt indeed. Over the years, I've seen her give some splendid performances, but to my eyes, on some occasions, her acting seemed to be overly exaggerated, thus detracting from the performance. I recall her Rosina in *The Barber of Seville* being such a case.

[https://www.youtube.com/watch?v=SZkKIXaIHyc&t=1464s]

But, at other times, such as her Manon in Massenet's *Manon*, Donna Elvira in *Don Giovanni*, and as the three queens in Donizetti's *Tudor* trilogy (she was the first singer to do all three queen's roles in New York at the City Opera long before the Metropolitan Opera produced them), she was terrific.

Although Sills did migrate to the Met late in her career, she never left the City Opera. Upon retiring from singing, and Julius Rudel retiring around the same time as General Director of the New York City Opera, she succeeded him as the City Opera's general director.

But, I must say that the greatest performance I ever saw Beverley Sills give, and one of my greatest concert experiences, was not at the City Opera, but at a concert performance of the original 1912 version of Richard Strauss's *Ariadne auf Naxos* in 1969 at Carnegie Hall with the Boston Symphony under Erich Leinsdorf.

Ariadne auf Naxos, **Carnegie Hall, January 18, 1969 (Written 1/25/69)**

This was one of the most exciting concerts I've ever seen. It was a Boston Symphony Orchestra concert performance of the original 1912 version of *Ariadne auf Naxos* by Richard Strauss. The main difference between this version and the one we have come to know is that this [*the original version*] does not have the prologue, and the music of Zerbinetta's aria is longer and more difficult, being a full fifteen minutes and containing high Fs, a note few sopranos can reach, and, indeed, this version is rarely given. Beverley Sills had all the notes and all the voice one needs to do the role justice, and she did it so much justice she received one of the loudest and longest ovations I've ever seen. Most impressive of all was the thrilling and beautiful Strauss music, played to perfection by the reduced, thirty-nine-person Boston Symphony under Erich Leinsdorf. The concert received a standing ovation and it was deserved.

This concert, given at Carnegie Hall, followed several in Boston. Luckily, one of the Boston performances was videotaped and telecast nation-wide on PBS and has been issued on DVD. Sills's singing of Zerbinetta's aria has been posted on YouTube.

[https://www.youtube.com/watch?v=v4l6rwPVvMo]

These will give you an idea of what I saw. However, my memory of her performance was that it was even better than what one hears and sees in this recording. I wonder whether singing in Carnegie Hall to her home town audience, the audience that made her a star at the City Opera, caused her to give just a little more than she did in Boston!

The Summer of 1969 in Washington D.C.—Ellington, Schwarzkopf, and Stilwell

I spent the summer of 1969 in Washington. I was between my second and third year in Law School, doing research at the National Archives and the Library of Congress. As was usual for me, my evenings were spent at cultural events. Compared to New York City, D. C. seemed a cultural wasteland; this was especially so in the days before the Kennedy Center was built. The big performing arts center in D.C. at that time was the infamous Constitution Hall. Infamous because the Daughters of the American Revolution who owned Constitution Hall had, in 1939, denied Marian Anderson permission to perform there, because of the color of her skin. This prompted Eleanor Roosevelt to resign her membership. Because of that, it was arranged by the federal government that Ms. Anderson would, instead, give an outdoor concert in front of the Lincoln Memorial. That concert attracted 75,000 attendees! It was an utter triumph and a rebuke to the then-racist policies of the DAR.

[https://www.youtube.com/watch?v=XF9Quk0QhSE]

An audio recording of the actual concert as broadcast on NBC radio.

[https://www.youtube.com/watch?v=xodhypFAFJw]

The Daughters of the American Revolution now states that it "proudly practices a non-discrimination policy and encourages and celebrates diversity in our organization."

In 1969, as I sought out what quality entertainment there was, Constitution Hall was home to what was then still called the

Washington National Symphony Orchestra (now simply the National Symphony Orchestra) and, just my luck, they were giving their first summer series, ever, of concerts. I got to see several orchestral concerts, most of them conducted by Franz Allers, the conductor famous for being the music director of the original Broadway production of *My Fair Lady*.

At that time, Allers was increasing his classical bookings, including at the Met, where he conducted lighter fare, such as *Die Fledermaus* and *Hansel and Gretel*. That summer, in Washington, Allers conducted the National Symphony in an all-Beethoven concert, which included the Fifth Symphony; an all-Tchaikovsky program, including his Sixth Symphony and First Piano Concerto; and a concert that included Dvorak's ninth symphony, the *New World*.

During that summer of 1969 in D. C., I saw three memorable performances, two of which were with the National Symphony Orchestra, and one was not. I will start with the first one. I listen to jazz, and enjoy it, but not in the embracing way I take in opera and stage musicals. It happened that Duke Ellington and his orchestra were presenting a free outdoor concert on July 16th. It was at the Watergate Pavilion near the Arlington bridge. It was a beautiful evening and a wonderful concert, and I wrote the following about it:

"Ellington played some of his newer repertoire and some songs he made famous. Just hearing his rendition of his trademark "Take the A Train" with Cootie Williams [*on trumpet*] was worth the evening. There was one and one-half hours of music and the seventy-year-old Mr. Ellington didn't stint the non-paying audience. All the soloists were fine, but Cootie Williams and Johnny Hodges [*on saxophone*] must take precedence."

That concert was, of course, not filmed, but a concert the band gave just ten weeks later, in Copenhagen, was.
[https://www.youtube.com/watch?v=MVh6yeCTKm4&t=3776s]

I would see Duke Ellington one more time before his death in 1975. Just over a year later, in the summer of 1970, I was sitting in my Newark apartment on a Sunday, perusing the Arts and Leisure section of the *Sunday Times*, when I noticed there was to be a free joint concert given by the New Jersey Symphony and the Duke Ellington Orchestra at Branchbrook Park skating rink in Newark that day. The building I lived in was just across the street from Branchbrook Park. I could actually see the skating rink from my seventeenth story window! I checked my watch and saw that it was just a few minutes before the concert. I literally jumped up, waited impatiently for the elevator, ran across the street, and arrived just in time to hear the first few bars of the concert.

When I got to the rink, it was understandably full, and I had to stand in the back. Coincidentally, I saw an old acquaintance from the Bronx who had come specially to Newark to see the concert. After the concert we happened to walk with a small group of people who were accompanying Ellington to his car, parked a block or two away. I have pretty much no memory of the conversation that occurred, but it certainly was exciting to stroll down the street chatting with this great jazz icon.

The review I wrote the next day gives some background and flavor to that day.

New Jersey Symphony, Duke Ellington Concert, August 23, 1970 (Written 8/24/70)

The New Jersey Symphony Orchestra and Henry Lewis. The Duke Ellington Orchestra and Duke Ellington. Wow, what a concert! I walked into the rink to the opening bars of Gershwin's "An American in Paris." Then came the Duke, sitting at the piano, and Lewis, in front of the orchestra, doing a very fine modern Ellington piece, "New World A-Comin." Mr. Lewis then gave Ellington the baton and Ellington conducted "The Golden Broom and the Green Apple." It was symbolic, for Mr. Ellington conducted without a baton, and very well too, belying the second half where he would often stand around doing nothing as his orchestra played familiar pieces. While the first half lasted a good fifty minutes, the second part went on for an hour and had the Ellington band playing many of the Duke's hits from the past with the Duke at the keyboard and such old Ellington stalwarts as Cootie Williams. There was "Satin Doll," "Harlem," and, of course, the familiar bars of "Take the A Train." Every once in a while, the New Jersey Symphony got in the act, first conducted by Ellington, then backing Ellington's piano medley conducted by music director Lewis. To say it was a fantastic concert would be saying too little, for it was more than that.

Getting back to D. C. and the summer of 1969—Although I've forgotten the details of two of three of the Allers-led concerts with the National Symphony Orchestra, one of them was memorable because of the vocal soloist—legendary operatic soprano, Elisabeth Schwarzkopf. Schwarzkopf was one of the great German singers to emerge in the postwar era who had a stellar international career starting in the mid-1940s, but not so much in America, possibly because of the uncertainty about her past in Nazi Germany. She denied being a member of the Nazi Party, but there appears to be documentation that she had joined as early as 1933.

Wikipedia states, "[Schwarzkopf] is generally considered to have been the greatest German lyric soprano of the twentieth century and one of the finest Mozart singers of all time, with an "indescribably beautiful" voice." I was at her belated Met debut on October 13, 1964. She was slightly past her vocal prime by then, but, as the aging Marschallen in *Rosenkavalier*, one of her signature roles, she was in her element and vocally excellent. In the summer of 1965, she sang in two concerts with the Met at their then-summer home in Lewisohn Stadium—one of which, an all-Strauss program, I attended. She returned to the Met on December 19, 1966 for a run of *Don Giovanni*. Its first performance was also broadcast as a Saturday Metropolitan Opera radio broadcast, so I was home, listening and taping. She performed Donna Elvira, a fiendishly difficult role for a soprano of any age, but on this occasion, it was clearly beyond her capabilities.

[https://www.youtube.com/watch?v=GkcHQrlay9E&t=8s]

I will simply note that she cancelled the rest of the run and never returned to the Met. Thus, it was surprising to me that Schwarzkopf was in the U. S. giving concerts only three years after the Met fiasco.

The concert she gave at Constitution Hall on August 14, 1969 was pretty much a joy, showing that she still had enough voice to wow the crowd. I wrote then:

> This was quite a long concert, what with the encores and extended applause for Madame Schwarzkopf, who before her first encore, Dorabella's aria [*from Mozart's* Cosi fan tutte], received a standing ovation. For the most part, Schwarzkopf's performances were exemplary. Only in the *Deh vieni, non tardar*, did one feel she was going beyond her means and that her Susanna [*the character who sings that aria in Mozart's* Le Nozze di Figaro] days were over, for in that aria she had breath control and other problems. The two Mozart songs were gorgeously sung, even if trifles. The *Cosi* aria was sung with artistry and flair, and her voice sounded beautiful. Desdemona's music ["Salce! Salce!" *and* "Ave Maria" *from Verdi's* Otello] was given real meaning in Schwarzkopf's singing. Her voice again soared for Puccini [*"Addio, senza rancor" from* La Boheme], showing she truly deserved the cheers she received.

It was a generous program on her part, and it was nice that the last time I would see Schwarzkopf she was in a vocal state worthy of her reputation, even that late in her career. Along with Schwarzkopf's generous musical offering, the concert also presented Allers conducting Mozart's *Le Nozze di Figaro* overture, the *Haffner Symphony*, and Mussorgsky's *Pictures at an Exhibition* (the Ravel orchestration).

Here's a taste of Schwarzkopf's singing.
[https://www.youtube.com/watch?v=Bm_AKMV0ME0]
[https://www.youtube.com/watch?v=g2jRkp6Ucho]
[https://www.youtube.com/watch?v=HAw4iDDWby8]

I should point out that in the time between the concert above, and the one I report on next, just over a week later, many members of my generation were attending a concert and listening to a completely different type of music—*in Woodstock, New York!*

On August 22, the Washington National Symphony did, in the words of *Monty Python*, "something completely different"—an all-Rodgers and Hammerstein concert. Strangely, it was not conducted by Allers, who had spent a good part of his career conducting Broadway musicals, but by a relatively unknown associate conductor for the National Symphony Orchestra named Lloyd Geisler. My review was somewhat lengthy, as was the concert, but I will print most of it here as it explains why this was a concert I have never forgotten.

Washington National Symphony Concert, **August 22, 1969 (Written 8/24/69)**

As if the people in authority at the Washington National Symphony knew I was in town and liked concerts, they added a free one to their first summer series. I, of course, was very happy about this, but was a little disappointed when I heard it was to be a Rodgers and Hammerstein program, as I am not a big Rodgers and Hammerstein person, and I remembered those dismal Lewisohn Stadium "Rodgers and Hammerstein nights." But, it was free and inviting, so I went, and am happy to report it was one of the best concerts of light music I've ever seen. First of all, this program contained lots of music, much of the best of Rodgers and Hammerstein, and not the usual repetitions they always did at Lewisohn. Secondly, the four vocal soloists, whose names were new to me, were quite good and did a lot of singing. Suzanne Brock has a pretty soprano with personality for musical comedy. Charlotte Dixon has a frayed mezzo-soprano that was sometimes off-pitch. Their idea of switching "My Favorite Things" and "Climb Every Mountain" was not a happy one. There is a reason why mezzos always sing the latter, and sopranos the former. John Kinnamon has a pleasant tenor voice, but without much power. He was especially effective in "The Surrey with the Fringe on Top."

There is a special reason I am leaving discussing Richard Stilwell, the baritone of the concert, for last. It was he who made the concert for me. Any concert will become an exciting event with the discovery of a new star, and this concert became exciting, for in Mr. Stilwell I heard a voice of immense potential. In his first duet with Charlotte, "I Have Dreamed," I realized his voice was very beautiful. Then came "Some Enchanted Evening," which further impressed me with the singular beauty of his voice and flawless technique. The gorgeous "Carousel," "Soliloquy" convinced me of what I had only been thinking before. Mr. Stilwell wasn't just impressive because he outclassed the other three singers on the program, he was impressive because he outclassed most other baritones I've seen!

Since I was so excited about my "discovery," I, of course, had to go backstage and find out about him. The first thing I asked him, after congratulating him on his singing, was whether he had any operatic aspirations. Having heard him sing, I wasn't too surprised when he told me most of his prior experience had been in opera. In fact, he said, when he leaves the army next month, he has a scholarship awaiting with the Met. He seemed very pleased when I told him (and honestly believe) that he was one of the best young baritones I've heard—in fact, the best since the young Sherrill Milnes. He said, "that means a lot to me." It is, of course, difficult to make predictions, not having seen Mr. Stilwell in opera, and only hearing him in a few songs in a big "miked" house. But, from what I heard, if I'm any judge of singers, Richard Stilwell is a name the opera world will soon hear of.

Well, it turns out, it was much sooner than I expected. Less than a year later, on April 7, 1970, Richard Stilwell made his New York City Opera debut in no less a role than Pelleas in Debussy's *Pelleas and Melisande*. It was a new production that City Opera had debuted a few weeks before with Andre Jobin, son of the great French tenor Rauol Jobin as Pelleas. I believe I saw the second performance with Jobin before I read that Stilwell was going to debut in the production.

Pelleas was not, and is still not, one of my favorite operas, so it attests to how much I thought of Stilwell that I trekked from Newark to see his debut, despite having seen the opera less than three weeks earlier. As I was walking into the New York State Theater, I met an acquaintance in the lobby who asked me if I knew anything about this new baritone. I told him I had seen him in D.C. and thought he was one of the best young baritones I'd seen. My acquaintance was Matthew Epstein (no relation) to whom I had been introduced by Lois Kirschenbaum several years before, at the Barbra Streisand *Happening in Central Park* concert. At the time I met him, Matthew had just graduated high school. Later, in the mid-1970s Matthew Epstein had become an artist representative at Columbia Artists Management and Stilwell was one of the artists in his portfolio.

I was to see Richard Stilwell frequently at the New York City Opera. I especially remember his Dandini in Rossini's *La Cenerentola*, and his singing of the title role in Mozart's *Don Giovanni* at City Opera. By 1972 I had seen over a dozen performances of Puccini's *La Boheme* at the Met, several with Tebaldi and Corelli, but that didn't stop me from heading across the Lincoln Center Plaza to see Stilwell's first Marcello in *La Boheme* at the City Opera. It was a typical performance of a standard repertory opera at the City Opera in those days, with a mix of City Opera stalwarts and some up-and-comers who would graduate to the Met and a bigger international career.

La Boheme, New York City Opera, September 30, 1972 (Written 10/8/72)

As Mimi was Elisabeth Carron, a veteran of over a dozen years at the City Opera and though not in the first blush of youth, her voice remains effective and though not gloriously beautiful, but pretty enough to be likeable and make a very satisfactory Mimi. Jose Carreras is a young Spanish tenor making a name for himself at the City Opera and Europe these days. In the first act he had trouble with a few notes at the beginning of *Che Gelida Manina* and the very last note of the duet *O Soave Fanciulla* (which Carron held much longer than he did). However, other than that his voice showed great promise. Richard Stilwell sang his first Marcello with the company and his rich baritone voice proved most expressive and beautiful in the role.

That was the first time I had seen Carreras. It should be noted that almost exactly a decade later, in October 1982, both now established operatic stars, Carreras and Stilwell appeared together again as Rodolfo and Marcello in the *Met's* second telecast of *La Boheme*.
[https://ok.ru/videoembed/1346877196917]
Stilwell made his Met debut as Guglielmo in Mozart's *Cosi fan tutte* in 1975, where he appeared until 1996 (with some big gaps in

between). Interestingly, Stilwell's final appearance at the Met, twenty-one years later, was as Don Alfonso in the same opera. The high point of his Met career was singing the title role in the Met premiere of Benjamin Britten's *Billy Budd* in 1978.
  [https://www.youtube.com/watch?v=M8f71AqJXs8]
  That role, and his Figaro in Rossini's *Barber of Seville* opposite famed mezzo-soprano, Frederica von Stade, are among my favorite memories of his Met performances.

Il Barbiere di Siviglia, Metropolitan Opera House, January 20, 1976 (Written 1/24/76)

A beautifully sung performance of Rossini's most enduring work, which was only held back from being memorable by parts of the staging of the over-twenty-year-old Cyril Ritchard/Eugene Berman production. True, I did find many mirthful moments in this delightful performance, but there were a number of misjudgments in Patrick Tavernia's redirection. Probably the most telling was the lack of spontaneity.

  Fortunately, the singing made for a glorious evening. Richard Stilwell in his debut Met season, was even more effective than his debut Ferrando, or the Figaro I saw him do a couple of seasons ago at the City Opera. His voice sounded richer and he sang with total beauty of tone. Again, I must say that after Milnes (and excluding Gobbi, who made only one token Met appearance this season on New Years Eve), Stilwell is the best baritone at the Met today.

  Similarly, Frederica von Stade is an ideal Rosina. Perhaps the finest young mezzo singing today, the role of Rosina fits her like a glove. Her voice is beautiful and perfect for the role. Indeed, Stilwell and von Stade's voices and looks are much more suited to these roles than the singers of the last Met performance of this opera I saw, Milnes and Horne.

I never really "hung out" with opera singers, but in those days I often went backstage to see my favorites. I remember once, I believe it was a New Year's Eve sometime in the mid-70s, with Lois Kirschenbaum and another friend, Ira Kaplan, that we ended the evening at Matthew Epstein's apartment. How that came about, I don't remember, but when you hung out with Lois, those things happened. Also present were Frederica von Stade and Richard Stilwell. What I remember most vividly was Matthew attempting to persuade Richard to learn the baritone version of Massenet's *Werther*.

  I think it was sometime after the Met had revived *Werther* for Franco Corelli, and there being a version for a baritone in the title role, that it made a likely prospect for Stilwell—after all, one of Stilwell's most notable roles was Pelleas, which is the only other role in the standard repertoire I can think of that can be sung by either a tenor or baritone. He didn't take Matthew up on it. Stilwell never sang the role of Werther in New York. He did, however, sing the actual baritone role in *Werther*, Albert, at the Met, opposite Alfredo Krauss, who sang the title role

The last time I saw Stilwell in opera was in 2007, when he returned to the City Opera to portray the old doctor in Barber's *Vanessa*. Nearly forty years after I first saw him, his voice continued to stand out to me as one of the finest baritone voices I've heard. The last time I saw him was a brief appearance at Frederica von Stade's farewell Carnegie Hall recital in 2010. Stilwell and another guest artist, bass Samuel Ramey, joined her in a song from Leonard Bernstein's *On the Town*.

Richard Stilwell had a long and successful operatic career, but he never gained the kind of renown that some others had. Indeed, the baritone who has gone on to the kind of star career I thought Stilwell would have, is Thomas Hampson. Why this is, I cannot say, as I find Stilwell's voice to be as beautiful, maybe even more so, as Hampson's. Perhaps it is Hampson's intellectual cross-genre curiosity that has him singing (and recording) everything from Mozart, Verdi, and Wagner in opera, to lieder by Schubert, Strauss, and Mahler, to Broadway show tunes, to old American songs (and not just those Copland arranged). Nevertheless, if you ask me to list my favorite *American* operatic baritones of the last sixty years, my answer would be Milnes, along with Stilwell, and Hampson.

Unfortunately, Stilwell is one of those great singers who is underrepresented on commercial recordings and videos. Arguably, his most notable studio recording was a complete *Pelleas and Melisande,* again opposite von Stade, conducted by Herbert von Karajan.

[https://www.youtube.com/watch?v=LUK6qSmu8o0]

That Stilwell and von Stade appeared together frequently may be no accident, as they were both represented by Matthew Epstein. To give you an example of his art, here is Stilwell singing an aria from a 1979 Chicago Lyric Opera telecast of Gounod's *Faust*, followed by a compilation of recordings and broadcasts by Stilwell.

[https://www.youtube.com/watch?v=a6mgePKl4Ns]
[https://www.youtube.com/watch?v=ZXHTzeCGif4&t=1463s]

Finally, here is an almost complete *Don Giovanni* with Stilwell in the title role:

[https://www.youtube.com/watch?v=Ca2srU8S2GQ]

Opera Preserved

Opera and Record Companies

Commercial recordings of complete operas were rare in the pre-LP era because an opera album was bulky, requiring many discs, thus expensive to produce and, therefore, to purchase. Yet, in the years between 1934 and 1946 (just before the dawn of the LP era), Beniamino Gigli recorded nine complete operas (including the *Verdi Requiem*).

That is not to say that this proves Gigli was the best tenor of the period (although I think he was), but it does show that he was popular enough for a major record company to go to the expense of producing complete operas in which he was the lead tenor. (It was clear that he was the draw.)

By 1934, Gigli was very much a known quantity. His Met career was behind him, having quit in 1932 after twelve seasons. Except for two brief returns to the States, in 1939 and 1955, the last two decades of Gigli's career were primarily spent in Europe.

Had Gigli continued at the Met, those recordings might never have happened. If recording complete operas was sporadic in Europe, it was practically non-existent in the U.S. Giovanni Martinelli, who sang primarily in America throughout the thirties and forties, made no complete commercial opera recordings. Aureliano Pertile, who was the same age as Martinelli, but whose career was primarily in Europe, got to record three complete operas.

From the mid 1930s through the 1940s, Gigli starred in more than a dozen movies, which may not have happened had he stayed in the U.S. Unfortunately, unlike Gobbi, none of Gigli's films were operas, although he did sing excerpts from operas. While several of his films are listed on YouTube, this link is to one with English titles, *Mama* (1941).

[https://www.youtube.com/watch?v=jpj2-G8G2Gw&t=1000s]
The title song was written for Gigli to sing in the film.
[https://www.youtube.com/watch?v=TD8Ij4BpqM0]
I remember it, not for Gigli, but as a hit with English lyrics for Connie Francis in 1959, just before I became an opera lover. Strangely, it is opera singer Gigli who sings it uptempo, while pop singer Francis goes for the heartstrings.
 [https://www.youtube.com/watch?v=vB7hyJ7VNmU]
British singer David Whitfield, who I described earlier as a one-hit wonder in America, in 1955 had a hit in the U. K. with *Mama*, though the English lyrics were different from those Connie Francis sang.
 [https://www.youtube.com/watch?v=2aVrEF4XIwU]
Back to Gigli. Here he sings the title song from the 1936 film *Ave Maria*:
 [https://www.youtube.com/watch?v=3DlhKD4v39g].
and an excerpt from *La Traviata* from that film.
 [https://www.youtube.com/watch?v=5xKvKONIhpk]
In the first full decade of the LP era, the 1950s, recording complete operas became more commonplace. There were three major record companies that recorded core repertory operas using the artists they had under contract. It was like the Hollywood studio system of the thirties and forties.

EMI/Angel produced mostly Maria Callas/Giuseppe Di Stefano/Tito Gobbi or Rolando Panarai; London/Decca gives us mostly Renata Tebaldi/Mario Del Monaco/Ettore Bastianini or Aldo Protti; and RCA Victor gives us mostly Zinka Milanov/Jussi Björling/Leonard Warren or Robert Merrill. While the soprano and tenor stars generally stayed the same, the baritones (third in the listings) were often alternated. The baritone listed first is the one most often recorded.

Of course, singers under contract to competing recording companies performed onstage together in full operas. This resulted in broadcasts of operas having singers who never, or rarely, recorded together. These can now be heard as pirated recordings on the Internet, and downloaded for one's own collection. Unfortunately, many performances having such pairings were not broadcast. For instance, Maria Callas and Jussi Björling appeared together in only two legendary performances of *Il Trovatore* at the Chicago Lyric Opera in November of 1955. Also, in Tito Gobbi's 1956 Met debut in *Tosca*, the title role was sung by Zinka Milanov! As far as I know, that was the only time those singers ever sang together. Those performances were not broadcast, nor do they appear to have been otherwise recorded, as no pirated recordings have appeared.

Just as the Hollywood studios system of mainly using stars they had under contract slowly started to break down in the late 1940s, the system of opera stars under contract to a record label singing together on opera recordings began to break down by the end of the 1950s. Only London/Decca continued this practice into the late 1960s with a series of recordings of their exclusive stars, Joan Sutherland and Luciano Pavarotti.

It was difficult in those days for an artist to break into the mainstream without a recording contract. There were many fine singers who didn't record much during the 1950s because of the domination of the contracted-to-label artists. Luckily, we have broadcasts of many of them as more and more opera companies began to broadcast performances over the radio.

Today, it's completely different—there are numerous radio broadcasts that are streamed on the Internet and there are TV broadcasts, live HD cinema presentations, and performances that are video streamed. Many of these end up on CD or DVD. Even present-day lesser-known singers who would not earlier have been recorded commercially, can be found in complete performances on the Internet and on other recorded media.

Among all the opera singers who have benefited from recording contracts, I think Luciano Pavarotti benefited most. He was signed by London/Decca when he was just starting out. He remained an exclusive London/Decca artist for the entire period of his career, even after many other artists at his level turned to freelancing.

Once under contract, the London/Decca marketing department and Herbert Breslin (Pavarotti's manager) went to work. I submit it was their efforts that had a large hand in shaping his popularity, and, without that exclusive contract (and, of course the recordings that followed, along with his regular exposure on PBS), he may never have achieved the iconic status he now holds.

Since I don't much care for his voice, Pavarotti becomes the second tenor I must designate as overrated.

Broadcasts and Tapes

By the summer of 1961, I was enough of an opera fan that commercial recordings were not enough for me. On the radio, one could hear, besides the Met broadcasts, delayed broadcasts of the Salzburg and

Bayreuth Festival performances, as well as many operas that were broadcast on RAI (Radiotelevisione Italiana, the Italian broadcasting network) and other European stations, that were later broadcast in the U. S. Thus, there was lot of material I heard on the radio that was not available commercially. In those days, the only way to record radio broadcasts was by using a reel-to-reel tape recorder. So I bought a reel-to-reel tape recorder and readied myself for the 1961–62 Met broadcast season. My first taping was the first broadcast of that season, Joan Sutherland's debut Met broadcast, that took place shortly after her Met house debut, a *Lucia de Lammamoor* with the, for me, ever-ubiquitous Richard Tucker.

[https://www.youtube.com/watch?v=JwE40LtyCaQ]

For the first few seasons, I recorded only broadcasts that interested me. By the mid-1960s, I taped every Met broadcast, provided I was home that day.

During that first recording season, I recorded a *Gioconda* with Corelli some weeks after the one in which I saw him sing with Zinka Milanov, but in this one, Eileen Farrell sang the title role. It was the only Corelli Met broadcast as Enzo.

[https://www.youtube.com/watch?v=1W2We9akvww]

As he never recorded Enzo commercially, this Met broadcast recording is now the only way we can hear his splendid Enzo in excellent, but monophonic, sound.

There are other recordings of Corelli's Enzo, but they are true bootlegs from portable tape recorders when an audience member was able to sneak it into the Opera House—and they are of later performances with Renata Tebaldi. The sound quality of those recordings are obviously inferior to a professionally engineered broadcast performance. Although Corelli starred opposite Tebaldi in the premiere of the new production of *La Gioconda*, the second performance at the new Met in 1966, it was Barry Morell who sang Enzo in the broadcast performance later that season.

The other Corelli gem I recorded that first year was the 1962 Salzburg Festival *Il Trovatore* with Leontyne Price, Giuletta Simionato, and Ettore Bastianini, all in fabulous voice, much better even than the Price/Corelli Met broadcast of the previous year. Who knew that decades later, Deutsche Grammophon would commercially release the Salzburg *Trovatore*; that SONY would release the 1961 Met broadcast of *Trovatore* and many other broadcast performances that were difficult to find?—and that they would all become available commercially, or, as in the Met's case, that they would appear on SiriusXM radio; or be made available on the then-unheard-of Internet!

It annoys me that Sony released the Met broadcasts of *Tosca*, *Il Trovatore*, and *Pagliacci* with Corelli—all operas he had recorded commercially—but not the 1962 *Gioconda* or the 1966 *La Fancuilla del We*st, neither of which had he recorded commercially, and, in both cases, for which he had been in top form. Furthermore, Eileen Farrell and Dorothy Kirsten (in *Gioconda* and *Fancuilla* respectively), both wonderful artists, are underrepresented in commercial opera recordings.

Edward J. Smith and Giovanni Martinelli

The Metropolitan Opera Saturday afternoon broadcasts began on Christmas day of 1931 and continue to the present. They are the longest-running continuous classical music program in history, having become a Saturday afternoon tradition. The broadcasts are full-length live performances from the stage of the Metropolitan Opera.

During the first two decades of their transmission, there was no attempt to preserve them by either the Met or the stations that broadcast them. Also, due to the technology available at that time, very few listeners had the ability to record them, so many of those early broadcasts are gone forever.

It is something of a miracle that so many of those early broadcasts have survived because of the few individuals who had the capability to record them, did so.Thank goodness, because, were it not for the Met broadcasts, we would not have many of the treasures that are discussed and linked-to in this book.

These days one can find a huge trove of historic opera broadcasts on the Internet, on commercial and bootleg CD's, among old Metropolitan Opera broadcasts, on SiriusXM, and in many other places. This was not so when I became an opera lover more than sixty years ago, although the Met had been doing radio broadcasting for thirty years.

Reviewing the *Met Annals* (in printed book form in those days) I drooled at the casts of some of the past broadcast performances. There were complete operas with some of my favorite singers like Ezio Pinza, Lauritz Melchior, Jussi Björling, and on, and on.

At some point early in my opera-going days, someone told me about Edward J. Smith's "list," and gave me his postal mailing address so I could get on it. Smith may have been the first person to make available for sale, privately distributed LPs of live opera performance broadcasts. Every month he would mail out a short list of new releases (a few records with brief comments about the performances). When I got on the list, he already had over a hundred recordings of vintage broadcasts on his back list, many of them prior Met broadcasts. They cost $3.00 per disc and came in a plain paper sleeve; no fancy packaging or liner notes, but what a treasure!

I immediately began to purchase as many Met broadcasts as I could, but, unfortunately, he kept the run of each title limited to around a hundred copies. So, while there were quite a number of titles on the list (which he had started in the mid-1950s) many were gone, sold out. Still, I was able to obtain many wonderful performances. One of them was a 1930s *Simon Boccanegra* with Laurence Tibbett, Ezio Pinza, Giovanni Martinelli, Elisabeth Rethberg, and Leonard Warren.

[https://www.youtube.com/watch?v=esG2dm2LayU&t=11s]

Later came an *Aida* and a *Norma*, both with Gina Cigna, Giovanni Martinelli, and Ezio Pinza

[https://www.youtube.com/watch?v=qWOvo88etHo&t=673s] Aida
[https://www.youtube.com/watch?v=VFjHv33exxI] Norma

a Siegfried with Lauritz Melchior and Kirsten Flagstad from 1937:
[https://www.youtube.com/watch?v=PPDr3RFfTD0&t=101s]

a *Don Giovanni* with Ezio Pinza, Rose Bampton, Bidu Sayão, and Alexander Kipnis, conducted by Bruno Walter
[https://www.youtube.com/watch?v=DwSkBywk4Io];

and a *Lohengrin* with Lauritz Melchior and Elisabeth Rethberg.

Thus, by listening to these recordings, did I become familiar with Met stars of the 1930s and '40s

As Smith's releases of Met Opera broadcasts dwindled, his releases of European broadcasts increased. I was able to find some truly exceptional recordings of my favorite artists, such as complete broadcasts of *l'elisir d'amore* and *L'Amico Fritz* with Beniamino Gigli
[https://www.youtube.com/watch?v=SYLCjavbph4&t=519s]
[https://www.youtube.com/watch?v=0-65iDfKkqo]

and a *La Boheme* with Renata Tebaldi, Giacomo Lauri-Volpe, and Titi Gobbi from Naples in the early fifties.
[https://www.youtube.com/watch?v=PNPaXAk5jLA]

Another of my favorite Gigli releases by Smith was extensive highlights of Puccini's *Manon Lescaut* taken from a 1950 RAI broadcast. It contains the most passionate and beautifully sung version

of the third act aria, *Guardate, pazzo son*, that I've ever heard. In the aria, Gigli's character, Des Grieux, pleads to be let onto the prison boat carrying his beloved Manon to America. He does it complete with an interpolated lengthily held high B at the end (3:10), expressing his character's joy at being allowed to join Manon on the ship. Purists may scoff, but I find it appropriate and thrilling.
[https://www.youtube.com/watch?v=PLf0BkGdYKs]
Here is the entire recording, consisting of fifty-five minutes of highlights. If the opera was performed complete and a recording exists, I've never heard it.
[https://www.youtube.com/watch?v=tIPuXmwwCrg&t=17s]

 I also began to obtain bootlegs from other sources. By the mid-sixties, a number of other distributors began to put out complete opera broadcast performances. I remember getting sets of most of Callas's broadcasts—many of these are now commercially available on EMI CD's. They were still packaged with just a paper sleeve, but later, bootlegged opera LP's were boxed with booklets.

 The sound quality of these recordings varied greatly, and sometimes Edward J. Smith cheated. I got a disc of highlights from *Tosca* sung by Gigli, recorded in Rio de Janiero in 1947. While listening to it, I found places where, all of a sudden, Gigli sounded like Tagliavini. I wrote to Smith saying, "At his best I might mistake Tagliavini for Gigli, but I have never mistaken Gigli for Tagliavini!" maintaining that portions of that disc were clearly Tagliavini. He wrote back, saying that sections of the original recording had drifted off into non-intelligiblity and he inserted Tagliavini to keep the music flowing. Of course, he should have stated that up front. I wondered why he didn't just use Gigli's commercial recording of *Tosca* as the filler. I hadn't heard that disc in decades, but I found a portion of it on YouTube.
 [https://www.youtube.com/watch?v=viGxcNLPyPc]

I wondered if I could still note the difference. It didn't take long. Listen to Tagliavini from about 9:17 to 9:37, which reverts to Gigli. Can you find the other Tagliavini insertions?

 Smith was a big fan of Giovanni Martinelli. Martinelli was one of two tenors often thought of as being a successor to Caruso at the Met. The other was Gigli. Martinelli had a long Met career, debuting in 1913 and singing his last performance there in 1945. By the 1950s, the LP era was in full swing and the ability to obtain complete opera recordings without lugging stacks of heavy 78s was making the availability of complete operas soar. Gigli had commercially recorded nine complete operas in the 78 rpm era, which were being transferred to LP. Martinelli, although he had an extensive discography of arias and songs, never recorded a complete opera commercially. As many of Smith's early releases featured Martinelli, and because Smith was not only a fan, but a close friend of the aging Martinelli, it is my surmise that one of the reasons for Smith's beginning to sell bootlegs was to disseminate complete opera performances of Martinelli. This was a boon to me because many of those discs also contained Ezio Pinza. I am a big Pinza fan.

[https://www.youtube.com/watch?v=ovw5G4KmSSo]

If Smith was trying to get more people interested in Martinelli by enhancing Martinelli's discography by releasing complete opera broadcasts, with respect to me, this backfired. The more I heard Martinelli on the bootleg discs I purchased from Smith in the 1960s, the more I disliked what I heard. I think the first time this occurred to me was in a Smith release of the February 6, 1937 Met radio broadcast of *Aida*. Listen to the first eleven minutes of the complete recording with the rich, bright, resonant sound of Pinza's Ramfis, then Martinelli comes in with a thin, wan, colorless sound, followed by *Celeste Aida* smoothly sung by Martinelli, but the timbre to me has no beauty.

[https://www.youtube.com/watch?v=qWOvo88etHo]

Compare Martinelli's vocal timbre in *Celeste Aida* to Franco Corelli.

[https://www.youtube.com/watch?v=B_Zoa1241wA]

Of course, Martinelli was in his fifties when this broadcast occurred, but I've also listened to many of Martinelli's earlier recordings, and, while some are very good indeed, I find his voice drab and colorless. There are many who, like Edward J. Smith, did love Martinelli's voice. I know, too, that this is a very subjective matter. Still, this makes Martinelli the third tenor I designate as "overrated." (The others were Tucker and Pavarotti.)

As Gigli left the Met, after twelve consecutive seasons, in 1932, just as the Met was starting to broadcast, he does not have the representation in Met broadcasts that Martinelli does. His only broadcast of a complete opera at the Met occurred in 1939 when he returned to the Met for the last time for a few performances. It was an *Aida* with the young Zinka Milanov. Unfortunately, no complete recording of that broadcast has survived. Here are surviving excerpts:

[https://www.youtube.com/watch?v=4B8nO-VvtkM]

In one of his monthly lists, Smith, in 1967, told a personal story about Martinelli. He recounted how he had accompanied Martinelli to Seattle to see a performance of *Turandot*. When the performer originally scheduled, for some reason was unable to do so, the then-eighty-plus-year-old Martinelli (who was there just to see the performance), was deputized to sing Emperor Altoum, the elderly father of the title character, who has a few quivering lines in the opera. There is a video clip of this on YouTube.
[https://www.youtube.com/watch?v=x_fZ6feuJpU]

I, too, have a personal Martinelli story, maybe not worth the re-telling, but I will, even though I will have to admit to a crime. (It was over fifty years ago, so I'm sure the statute of limitations has run out.) By 1966, I was a confirmed opera lover and had seen about a hundred performances at the old Met. So, it was a must for me to be at the opening night of the new Met at Lincoln Center. Unfortunately, I was unable to get a ticket, and my usual alternate means of getting into the house were unsuccessful. So, too, in prowling the lobby, I saw there would be no possibility of getting a last-minute-no-show ticket from a patron whose friend canceled at the last minute. Suppressing panic, I saw another means. There were lots of celebrities attending the performance and whenever a celebrity went in, camera lights came on because news organizations were filming. At such moments, I noted that the ticket takers all looked away to catch a glimpse of the celebrity.

For this story, it is important to know that the Met, unlike any other theater I knew, used special passes that were given to people as they left the hall to go into the public lobby, usually at intermission, so that they would be able to return later. I noted that, as usual, there were stacks of these passes on the ticket taker's stands. Being desperate, I saw my chance. Senator Jacob Javits was coming in. I got on the line behind him. Sure enough, as he got to the ticket taker, the camera lights flashed on and, as he passed through, I picked up a pass with my right hand, immediately switching it to my left to then hand it to the ticket taker who simply took it and let me through. That was the one, and only, time I have ever used that method to get into the Met. It was because I was desperate to get into the historic opening night of the new Met, and because I knew this probably wouldn't work going forward without the distractions provided by the cameras and celebrities.

I was now in the house and needed to find the standing room

section where I figured I could probably go unnoticed. It was the new Met and I had never been there before. It was opening night. I saw the stairs and darted to them. On the staircase between the Parterre and Grand Tier I was barreling up them so fast that I very nearly collided with a elderly man coming down the stairs. Luckily, I saw him just in time to swerve out of the way so that we only brushed against each other. He must have thought I was a madman.

The moment I glanced at him I knew who it was. His mane of white hair looked quite the same as the dark hair in his photographs from decades before. It could only be, and was, Giovanni Martinelli! He was taller than me, and much wider than me, but he was eighty and I was twenty. I was running fast, and had I encountered him head on, the headlines would have read "Gigli Fan Topples Met Star, Martinelli." Luckily for me, that didn't happen. I found the Family Circle standing room area (it is now at the back of the Family Circle, not the sides, where it had been in the old Met) and I did get to see the world premiere performance of Samuel Barber's *Anthony and Cleopatra* without further incident.

It was momentous for all who attended this historic performance, but for me—my adventure getting in to see it was even more memorable than the performance.

Lauritz Melchior, Others, and Pirated Recordings

Some say that Lauritz Melchior (1890–1973) was the greatest Heldentenor who ever lived. I disagree! I believe Lauritz Melchior was the *only* true Heldentenor who ever lived. All others were imposters.

I know that I am doing great injustice to the many tenors who studied and spent much of their careers performing Wagner— for example, Leo Slezak in the pre-Melchior era and Wolfgang Windgassen in the post-Melchior era. However, the fact is (as much as fact can exist in the opinionated and subjective world of judging opera singers) that, while one may argue the relative merits of sopranos such as Frida Leider, Kirsten Flagstad, Helen Traubel, Marjorie Lawrence, Astrid Varnay, and Birgit Nilsson, most would agree they were all great Wagnerian sopranos. When it comes to tenors though, I can't think of any other tenor who specialized in Wagner, who compares to Melchior. Simply, he was in a class of his own.

Why was he greater than all the others? He had everything Wagner would ask for of a tenor meant to sing the roles he created. This was especially true for the later, heavier roles such as *Tristan, Tannhäuser,* and *Siegfried*. Melchior had the power, stamina, and, most of all, vocal beauty. For me it *all* comes down to vocal beauty. The others who are described as Heldentenors lack one or another of the elements needed to be a true Heldentenor—usually vocal beauty. Melchior had it all.

We are happy today if a tenor can just get through a *Tristan* or *Siegfried*. If so, we won't quibble if his voice is something less than beautiful. Melchior sailed through those roles with astonishing ease, carrying a warm, rich, vibrant, and almost jaunty sound—together with a ringing top. There you have my unscholarly and weak attempt to describe Melchior's voice. I found a more erudite description than mine in the introduction to *Lauritz Melchior: A Discography*, originally published in Copenhagen in 1965. In that introduction, the compiler, Hans Hansen, states: "The rich baritone warmth, the truly masculine ring of all registers, the impact and brilliance of his top, his ability to color phrases meaningfully, those thrilling perfectly sustained legatos—these are Melchior virtues."

Can it be said, even in a stretch, that Wolfgang Windgassen, Set Svanholm, Hans Hopf, Siegfried Jerusalem, Jess Thomas, or any other tenor who has sung those Wagner roles since then, is in the same class as Melchior?

Actually, we need imposter-Heldentenors. Without them, opera houses would be unable to produce a *Ring Cycle* or a *Tristan*, and the world would be a poorer place. So they work at it, and they study the scores, and they often give admirable performances. It is because of these so-called Heldentenors that we can go to the opera house to see Wagner performed live. That they are not in Melchior's class should not diminish what they do. Given that this is so, and to seek to make up for my trashing of them, I give them my heartfelt thanks.

There is one more category to consider. I do not think one can be considered a Heldentenor if one does not have most of the heavier Wagner roles in one's repertoire. This lets out Sándor Kónya, Jon Vickers, James King, Ben Heppner, and many others who have sung Lohengrin, von Stolzing in *Die Meistersinger*, and, say, one more of the heavier roles, but not more than just those.

To be fair, I should mention that Melchior does have a few detractors, mainly for being a little sloppy musically and having grown lazy late in his career—as well as, like Corelli, holding high notes excessively. Remember my maxim, "if you have it, flaunt it".

As Melchior sang before my time, my judgment is based on recordings. His recordings of various arias and segments of Wagner operas are never less than thrilling. Melchior recorded Siegfried's Forging Song, several times over more than two decades. Listen to this early 1924 recording, in which his voice fairly bounces, putting to shame every other performance of this aria, live or recorded, that I've ever heard. Because of the time limitations of 78 rpm discs, it's in two parts.

[https://www.youtube.com/watch?v=5s8U88Lp7BQ]
[https://www.youtube.com/watch?v=ZXxWEA27CXw]

Unfortunately, there were very few complete commercial opera recordings produced in Melchior's day, and the few that were made were mostly Italian and French operas which are much shorter than the later Wagner works (making them better adapted to the briefer playing time of early 78 rpm records). Also, Melchior spent the last two decades of his career in America where hardly any complete opera recordings were made during this period (the 1930s and 1940s). We do have the wonderful 1935 Bruno Walter-led Act I of Die Walküre, with Lotte Lehmann and the Vienna Philharmonic

[https://www.youtube.com/watch?v=TdejK01vpVA]

and some extensive excerpts from Siegfried, but nothing near to a complete commercially recorded opera.

[https://www.youtube.com/watch?v=DV8sEecjAV8&t=37s]

Luckily, we have treasure-trove of Melchior performances because of the Metropolitan Opera broadcasts. The decades of the thirties and forties were the first for the Met broadcasts, and, although many performances from the 1930s, especially the early thirties, didn't survive, many from the late thirties did, including a fair number of Melchior's. More survived from the forties. These have better sound, so we can more accurately judge Melchior in complete opera performances.

Because of Melchior and the pre-Nilsson sopranos, the Met was doing a lot of Wagner in those days. For example, between 1935, the year Kirsten Flagstad made her Met debut, and 1941, her last year at the Met before the War, there were nine, yes, *nine*, broadcasts of *Tristan und Isolde*, all with Melchior and Flagstad. (Evidently, in those days, the Met didn't mind broadcasting the same opera more than once in a season.)

I don't know how many recordings survived, but I have three in my collection—the first in 1935, the last, in 1941, and one from in between. (There were also two Covent Garden *Tristan*s recorded in the late 1930s with Flagstad and Melchior, conducted by Thomas Beecham and Fritz Reiner that are more complete, as they do not suffer the Bodanzky cuts. (Artur Bodanzky was an Austrian-born conductor who came to the Met in 1915 as the head of the Met's German wing conducting most Wagner performances until his death in 1939. (*He was notorious for cutting scores.*) Due to the war, Flagstad did not appear at the Met between 1941 and 1951, therefore, in Melchior's last decade at the Met (1941–1950), when he appeared in another seven Met *Tristan* broadcasts, they were all with Helen Traubel. I have one or two of these. They seem strangely harder to come by than the 1930s *Tristan*s.

Here are six complete performances of *Tristan and Isolde* with Melchior and Flagstad currently available on YouTube:

[https://www.youtube.com/watch?v=0-5vJYNTdq0&t=14s] Met (1935) Bodanzky conducting

[https://www.youtube.com/watch?v=LqJjVb4u9ho&t=1s] London (1936) Fritz Reiner conducting

[https://www.youtube.com/watch?v=nxx-NBaFzoU] ; Met (1937) Bodanzky conducting

[https://www.youtube.com/watch?v=4YWcLaTz4lw&t=5s] London (1937) Thomas Beecham conducting

[https://www.youtube.com/watch?v=iEY6E-m41Qc] Met (1940) Erich Leinsdorf conducting

[https://www.youtube.com/watch?v=TZ3yxQezbWY&t=1852s] Met (1941) Leinsdorf conducting

Unfortunately, none of the 1940s Met *Tristan*s with Melchior and Traubel are on YouTube (I did mention they are harder to come by), but there is a 1943 broadcast from the Teatro Colon, Buenos Aires.

[https://www.youtube.com/watch?v=8BYJXoQ1KTQ&t=7s] Fritz Busch conducting

To give you a better idea of Lauritz Melchior's absolute dominance at the Met as Tristan, from the first Met broadcast season in 1932 through 1949, there were a total of twenty-one broadcasts of *Tristan und Isolde*. Melchior was Tristan in all but one of those broadcasts!

Between 1932 and 1948, Melchior appeared in twelve of the thirteen Met *Tannhäuser* broadcasts. Between 1936 and 1941 they were all with Kirsten Flagstad. After that, they were divided between Helen Traubel and Astrid Varnay.

[https://www.youtube.com/watch?v=c5sNTERGzkg&t=22s] Met (1936) Flagstad, Bodanzky conducting

[https://www.youtube.com/watch?v=NI1cfr80sds&t=250s] Met (1941) Flagstad, Leinsdorf conducting

[https://www.youtube.com/watch?v=H3wyiZqvFlw&t=126s] Met (1944) Varnay, Breisach conducting

There are also many *Lohengrin*s with such diverse sopranos as Lotte Lehmann, Kirsten Flagstad, Elisabeth Rethberg, Astrid Varnay, and Helen Traubel. In Melchior's last Met broadcast appearance, which was a *Lohengrin* in January of 1950, Traubel sang Elsa, while Varnay, who had sung Elsa in four previous *Lohengrin* broadcasts with Melchior, undertook the mezzo role of Ortrud.

[https://www.youtube.com/watch?v=mb1akz5pIWg] Met (1935) With Lehmann, conducted by Bodanzky.

[https://www.youtube.com/watch?v=9xEQWhS7Te0&t=80s] Met (1950) Melchior's last Met broadcast with Traubel and Varnay, Fritz Stiedry conducting.

Among three of the seven roles that Melchior sang at the Met during his twenty-four seasons there, *Siegfried* and *Parsifal* were broadcast only a few times. Most of those broadcasts were in the early thirties and, therefore, have not survived intact. *Parsifal* was broadcast only three times during the thirties and forties, and only the last one, (with Flagstad, in 1938) survives.

[https://www.youtube.com/watch?v=kKnGGheAprM&t=7277s] Of Melchior's four *Gotterdammerung* Siegfried broadcasts, only the third, in 1936, with Marjorie Lawrence, is to be found.

[https://www.youtube.com/watch?v=avb_RjgZ0no&t=1623s] The last was a 1939 broadcast with Flagstad, that I'd love to hear, but it may not have survived as I have not found any recording of it. There is only one complete *Siegfried*, with Flagstad, in 1937, in somewhat better sound than the *Parsifal* and *Götterdämmerung* broadcasts, both of which are quite primitive in sound and suffer from breaks of several secondwas every seven or eight minutes due to the person who was recording it having to change the recording disc. None of these three operas were broadcast with Melchior during the forties when they might have been captured in better sound. Still, to have Melchior in a complete performance of *Siegfried* (or as complete as conductor Artur Bodanzky would allow) is marvelous.

[https://www.youtube.com/watch?v=ugZ-VJ-TStY&t=4966s] Having provided links to many of Melchior's performances with

Flagstad, Traubel, and Varnay during the last fifteen years of his Met career, we should not overlook the first decade-and-a-half of Melchior's career as a Heldentenor.

Melchior made his operatic debut in 1913 as a baritone. After an extensive period of retraining, he re-emerged in 1918 as a tenor. Throughout the 1920s, until the mid-1930s, just before Flagstad made her Met debut, Melchior frequently sang with the great Wagnerian soprano of that earlier era, Frieda Leider. To give you an idea of that partnership, here are surviving segments (totaling over an hour) of a very early, March, 1933, Metropolitan Opera broadcast of *Tristan und Isolde*.

[https://www.youtube.com/watch?v=UB7iuH2bjnA]

As opera broadcasts are so few from those early years, and the primitive sound of early Met broadcasts not the best way to judge their partnership, here are Leider and Melchior in a 1929 studio recording of the love duet from *Tristan*.

[https://www.youtube.com/watch?v=_XSYCFnPST0]

Another example is this studio recording of the final fifteen or so minutes of act I of *Die Walküre* from five years earlier.

[https://www.youtube.com/watch?v=Zsbo_5zRFn8]

I have saved writing at length about Melchior's *Die Walküre* for last, because I have a story that goes with it.

One of Edward J. Smith's successors in the opera pirating business was William Seward. Although the quantity of his releases were smaller than Smith's, the quality was much higher; they had excellent sound and included a handsome box in which they were packaged. I bought a few of his releases, including the Björling/Sayao 1947 Met *Romeo and Juliette*, which were sold out when I first got onto Smith's mailing list (perhaps luckily, because I learned later that Smith's release was incorrectly pitched). Decades later the performance was issued commercially on SONY records.

[https://www.youtube.com/watch?v=LIalLiKcIDk]

At any rate, at some time in the mid-sixties, I was with a friend who had made Seward's acquaintance, and we visited in Seward's apartment. I was impressed by his record collection, but even more impressed when he showed us, and played a bit of, a complete *Die Walküre*, that he had on original 78 rpm transcription discs. These needed a special record player as they were played from the center going toward the rim, the opposite of commercial discs. The sound was excellent, and what I heard of the performance was terrific, so I asked if there was a way that I could get a copy. He had made a tape, which he lent to me so that I would be able to make a copy.

That *Walküre* was the December 6, 1941 Met broadcast with Lauritz Melchior, Helen Traubel, Alexander Kipnis, Kirsten Thorborg, Frederick Schorr, and, making her Met debut as a last minute replacement, the twenty-four-year-old Astrid Varnay as Sieglinde. Hearing the complete performance was a revelation. Rarely was the conductor, Erich Leinsdorf, in better form, here conducting a taut, intense performance. I expect he was driven by the magnificent singing he was hearing on the stage, because the entire cast was just about perfect. Traubel, who I had heard lacked the trills to do "Ho jo to ho" justice, here just blazed through the aria, trills and all, in what remains one of the best versions I've ever heard; she continued singing Brunhilde on that level for the entire rest of the opera. After Ezio Pinza, Alexander Kipnis had one of the most beautiful bass voices of that era, and it was wonderful to hear a voice of that caliber sing Hunding. And the twenty-four-year-old Varnay, a novice who had never appeared on any opera stage before, was absolutely thrilling—a young, pure-voiced Sieglinde singing beautifully, unfazed that she was singing opposite the fifty-one-year-old veteran "Heldentenor of Heldentenors." You would think that Melchior, because he was partnered with a young unknown, might hold back a little. Far from it, he, too, blazed forth, his voice sounding as beautiful as ever, and thereby, perhaps, igniting Varnay to greater heights. The last half hour of Act I never sounded better. This immediately became my "desert island" *Walküre* recording, the one by which I judge all others.

[https://www.youtube.com/watch?v=j3OAHSWs5-4&t=3s]

Compare the last fifteen minutes of act I [at 43:00] to his recording with Freda Leider from nearly twenty years earlier. His voice rings out fuller and warmer in 1941, the timbre actually more beautiful, and, in the white heat of performance, the visceral excitement makes his earlier recording sound rather tame.

Also in 1941, there is a more musically exemplary performance of the final section of Act I of *Walkure*, although it is less exciting than the December 6, 1941 Met Broadcast. It is an NBC Symphony performance conducted by Toscanini. This time Helen Traubel partners with Melchior as Sieglinde.

[https://www.youtube.com/watch?v=RruHdPssz8U]

Looking back, we know that Varnay would go on to a spectacular career, and not just by default because Flagstad could not return

to the Met due to the war, which the U. S. entered the next day (the "day of infamy"), or because Marjorie Lawrence was felled by polio. As pointed out, in the forties, Traubel and Varnay were the go-to Wagnerian sopranos at the Metropolitan who were most often partnered with Melchior. Although Flagstad's name may be more familiar to the general public, especially in association with Melchior, I am most partial to Traubel's mighty and beautiful soprano and Varnay's powerfully dramatic soaring voice. According to what I've read, Melchior got along much better with these later partners, than with the colder Flagstad; especially Traubel, who had the type of sense of humor that enjoyed his practical jokes. (Melchior loved to play practical jokes.) Her sense of humor is illustrated by Traubel's appearances with Jerry Lewis on his short-lived television show in the early 1960s. (Traubel appears on episodes five, seven and nine which can be found free (with commercials) on Tubi TV, a TV streaming service or:
https://www.youtube.com/watch?v=EdxRalCGe0s.

Early in my opera record-buying, in the sixties, I picked up a copy of Traubel's RCA Camden LP. Surprising to me, my favorite track was not a Wagner aria, but "Salce, salce" from the fourth act of Verdi's *Otello*. Her voice was big, powerful, and absolutely gorgeous; one of the best recordings of that aria I have ever heard. It is said that Melchior wanted to sing Otello at the Met, but the general manager, Edward Johnson (a former Metropolitan Opera tenor himself), not wanting to offend Giovanni Martinelli, (who owned the role of Otello at the Met during that period) wouldn't let him. I can only imagine what a Melchior/Traubel *Otello* would have sounded like!

Traubel's recording of *Salce, salce* is followed by excerpts from Melchior's *Otello*, with, finally for contrast, Martinelli in two of the *Otello* arias. I personally find Martinelli's voice thin and anemic compared to Melchior's rich and robust timbre.

[https://www.youtube.com/watch?v=du6f8evOk28] Traubel
[https://www.youtube.com/watch?v=CKdetuNRz9k] Melchior
[https://www.youtube.com/watch?v=xitMkGsP4-0] Martinelli
[https://www.youtube.com/watch?v=swgYWlMt-9M] Martinelli

The Melchior clip notes state that Melchior sang *Otello* thirty-one times in venues other than the Met. Unfortunately, there is no complete broadcast of *Otello* with Melchior. Martinelli's dominance in the role at the Met is illustrated by the fact that, between 1938 and 1941, Martinelli appeared in all four broadcasts of *Otello*, all of which can be found, complete, on YouTube.

[https://www.youtube.com/watch?v=cjRqFxOw2f4&t=13s] 2/12/38
[https://www.youtube.com/watch?v=9_in7tPhEsk] 12/3/38
[https://www.youtube.com/watch?v=c5TPWBZT-EE] 2/24/40
[https://www.youtube.com/watch?v=uQU7ow32Px8&t=10s] 1/18/41

If Martinelli dominated *Otello* at the Met, this was nothing compared to Melchior's absolute domination of the Wagnerian repertoire at the Met during the 1930s and 1940s. It also shows how much more frequently Wagner was performed at the Met when they had artists of this high caliber to perform them. As an example, the 1941 *Walküre* was just one of many Melchior *Walküre* Met broadcasts.

To give you an idea of how frequently the Met broadcast Wagner operas in those days, there was a broadcast of *Walküre* with Melchior, Flagstad as Brunhilde and Marjorie Lawrence as Sieglinde on February 17, 1940.

[https://www.youtube.com/watch?v=EwuyKZbm_H4&t=181s]

Barely six weeks later, on March 30, 1940, while on tour in Boston, the Met again broadcast *Walküre*, once more with Melchior, but this performance had Marjorie Lawrence as Brunhilde and Lotte Lehmann as Sieglinde. Note Melchior flaunting his ability to hold high notes, in this record-setting *Wälse!* (the first *Wälse!* held for seventeen seconds; the second for thirteen seconds)—one of the few places in Wagner where a tenor gets a chance to do just that. First, a short clip of his *Wälse!* then the full performance.

[https://www.youtube.com/watch?v=OfNm_KPs5Ak]
[https://www.youtube.com/watch?v=FHhxX77xsDI&t=71s]

Superb as the two 1940 performances are, I think my "desert island" 1941 broadcast is vocally and dramatically superior, even if Melchior's *Wälse!* in that performance is *very slightly* shorter. (Yes, I timed them.)

Before I leave my discussion of Melchior, I should mention his movie career. It would have been terrific if we had films of Melchior in his great Wagner roles, but no studio in the thirties and forties was going to film a four-hour Wagner opera.

Thus, MGM, in the forties, gave us Melchior in supporting roles in several musical trifles, such as *Thrill of a Romance* (1945)

[https://www.youtube.com/watch?v=qbfnB5s44EQ],

Two Sisters from Boston (1946)

[https://www.youtube.com/watch?v=nHFOUC6Y9QE&t=22s]
[https://www.youtube.com/watch?v=e0qnB9Ksyc4]

and *Luxury Liner* [1948).

[https://www.youtube.com/watch?v=Ke5urMBhycw&t=4s]
[https://www.youtube.com/watch?v=-CecPO4J-yw]
[https://www.youtube.com/watch?v=-VbwiQEaq80]

We can also see Melchior in kinescopes of some of his television appearances.

[https://www.youtube.com/watch?v=Uz6FLFhw_pg]

The last song on that compilation was Jerome Kern's *The Song is You*. Now listen to it in unaccented English as sung by Mario Lanza.

[https://www.youtube.com/watch?v=-VbwiQEaq80]

In the days before the Met could be found on SiriusXM, the Internet, or pirated LPs and CDs, the only way to obtain vintage broadcast performances, besides purchasing bootlegs, was to exchange tapes. I was doing a lot of that at the time. One of the people I traded tapes with, when he learned that I had the 1941 *Walküre*, implored me to lend it to him. I finally broke down and did so, even though I may have promised Seward I would not let anyone borrow it. That person was Ed Rosen. Not too long after that, Rosen began to release opera broadcasts on LP and one of his first releases was that *Walküre*. Having lent it to him in good faith, I had no idea he would capitalize on it commercially. I felt terrible that I had betrayed Seward, even though I never saw Seward again after having earlier returned his original tape.

Rosen continued to sell pirated opera recordings into the CD and digital era, until his death in 2016. I stopped trading with him after the *Walküre* incident, and, by the 1970s I had completely stopped trading entirely. I continued, for my own collection, recording live opera broadcasts on the radio. It wasn't until the Internet era that I would be able to augment my collection of historic performances from sites that offered free downloads or, more recently, from YouTube.

I am of two minds about piracy. I feel that those who bootleg commercial recordings should be dealt with, although this is problem of greater severity in popular music. However, most pirated opera recordings are taken from broadcasts or from in-house tapings that are not available commercially. These include performances, such as the historic 1941 *Walküre* broadcast, that deserve to be heard by the opera-loving public. If those performances that may be under copyright are not disseminated by its copyright owner, then I don't begrudge anyone else who gives the public access to it. That someone may make a profit in doing this is a more troubling issue. It appears to me that the early pirates, like Edward J. Smith and William Seward, seemed to be doing it for the right reasons. It's hard to believe that the Met was not aware of what they were doing, even though they were attempting to be discreet about it. Ed Rosen was much more overt and in-your-face about it.

My experience with Ed Rosen was not unique. There is a whole book on opera pirating I referred to previously that is humorously titled *Pirates of the High Cs: Opera Bootlegging in the 20th Century* by Nicholas Limansky (YBK Publishers, New York, 2020).

In a review of *High Cs* on the Opera Nostalgia blog [https://www.operanostalgia.be/html/Limansky-pirates.html], Jan Neckers relates a story analogous to mine: "From 1968 on I went on a yearly pilgrimage to Verona. In 1974 I was at a performance of *Tosca* (Domingo, Santunione, Mastromei) when a very American and very Jewish lady made her entrance on the *prima gradinata*. She had a portable cassette recorder with her and started to play it.... I started talking with the lady and she told me she came from Israel where she attended a Tucker concert. She had recorded it for her friend Ed. Not Ed Rosen, I asked? She was surprised I knew his name and I told her I regularly bought reels from him. In earnest she said she didn't believe it. Ed was only a fanatical collector and never sold things. In those paper-happy days and by sheer coincidence I had a copy of my latest payment as proof and she uttered the kind of expletives that were censured on the famous Nixon tapes."

As I pointed out, recording companies have recently come around to making many historic performances available. Thus, EMI has released most, if not all of the Callas live performances that I had purchased in the sixties as pirates, and the Met made a deal with SONY to release many Metropolitan radio broadcasts, while the Met, itself, has a SiriusXM channel where they play old broadcasts as well as live performances. Unfortunately, no complete Melchior opera broadcast has been released by mainstream recording companies and the pirate issues have varying sound quality. Considering that Melchior never made a complete studio opera recording during his career, we have the Metropolitan Opera broadcasts and the pirates who released those performances to thank for the many full-length opera performances we are now able to hear of this unparalleled Heldentenor.

Opera lovers with collections of rare performances are now posting many performances on the Internet, especially on You Tube, where one can access them for free. The people who post these recordings are not profiting from doing so, but do it because they love the art and want to share them with other opera lovers. It is the modern equivalent of my tape-trading days when opera-lovers traded taped recordings with no thought of making a business out of it. There are still pirates who use the Internet to sell their product, but as the numbers of performances available on the Internet for free (still, they are, technically, pirated recordings) grows, will it mark the end of opera piracy as a business?

Classical Music Stations in New York in the 1960s and Now

In the 1960s, when I first became interested in opera and classical music, there were several radio stations in New York that regularly programmed classical music. It was the early days of FM radio being commercialized with its greater audio quality while, at the same time, the old AM radio networks (CBS and NBC) were in their twilight days as they were concentrating on TV.

There were two full-time classical FM stations then in New York, WQXR (then owned by *The New York Times*) and WNCN. A few others played classical music often; WNYC (then owned by the City of New York), two college-owned stations WKCR (Columbia University) and WFUV (Fordham University), and listener-supported WBAI, which, on Washington's Birthday (now known as President's Day), would broadcast the past year's Bayreuth Festival's *Ring* cycle in its entirety for eighteen or so hours.

ABC had AM and FM radio stations in New York that played popular music. During the day, ABC's FM station mirrored (simulcast) what was on their AM station, but in the evening, the FM station would split off and became all-classical. (The interviews with Feruccio Tagliavini and Tito Gobbi referred to on pages 20 and 36 were broadcast on WABC–FM). During most of the 1960s, the Riverside Church in Manhattan had a radio station with the very appropriate call letters WRVR, which sometimes programmed classical music. Sad to say this all of these are gone now, save for WQXR.

Now owned by New York Public Radio, WQXR is no longer owned by the Times, and currently is the only full-time classical music station in New York City. WNCN is long defunct and WNYC (now owned by the same organization that owns WQXR) leaves all classical programming to its sister station. The college-owned stations and

WBAI seem barely to have any classical programming. WABC–FM simulcasts its all-talk programming, and WRVR was sold long ago.

It is a crime that the largest city in the U. S., its greatest center for the arts, has only one radio station that plays classical music, and that station plays mostly short works from commercial recordings and has programming called "drive time" that plays only upbeat short classical pieces. Their website schedule doesn't even tell you what recording they are going to play until the day they play it! You're not going to find a complete Beethoven, Mahler, or other symphony on their regular daily programming. They do carry the Saturday afternoon Metropolitan Opera broadcasts, New York Philharmonic broadcasts, and, occasionally, a live concert from Carnegie Hall, so you do get a complete opera or symphony on those rare occasions. Although many major American orchestras create syndicated broadcasts, WQXR doesn't carry them, and they carry very little from Europe. Their programming of live broadcasts (when I say live I also include delayed concerts or operas) pales in comparison to, say, Chicago's WFMT.

The sad state of affairs in New York City classical radio would be devastating if it were not for modern technology. We now have the Internet to provide a plethora of choices one could only dream of in the 1960s. Just about every classical radio station in the world streams their programming over the Internet. Although the sound quality of these streams vary, some being superior in bandwidth to FM radio (see https://www.hiresaudio.online/cd-quality-internet-radio/ and other searchable sites to find sites that broadcast lossless [maximum resolution] streams), on any given day you can find numerous broadcasts of live concert and opera performances.

In the U.S., Saturday afternoon became the traditional time to hear opera on the radio because of the Met broadcasts, but in Europe, it appears to be Saturday night. Saturday night in Europe, being Saturday afternoon in the U. S., on some Saturday afternoons there could be a half dozen or more live opera broadcasts to choose from being streamed and available to listen to over the Internet. Sometimes the choices are tough. But wait, sometimes you don't have to choose. Many European stations keep their programs available as on-demand for a week or more. And, you don't even have to check a given station's schedule. There are several Internet websites that do that for you. The two best are Operacast [http://www.operacast.com/] for opera and vocal music and World Concert Hall for concerts and operas. [https://www.worldconcerthall.com/]

There is now also SiriusXM radio, a paid-for service that can only be received on special radio receivers or the Internet, which, for over a decade has had a Metropolitan Opera channel that, besides carrying the Saturday afternoon Met broadcast, also broadcasts from one to three live weekday performances throughout the season—including the Met's first performance of the season of each opera (which the Met also streams for free on the Internet). When SiriusXM's Met channel is not broadcasting live performances, they play old Met Saturday afternoon broadcasts throughout the day. The Met has a "Met Opera on Demand" *subscription* website with a huge archive of Met broadcasts and telecasts.

[https://www.metopera.org/season/on-demand/]

One can find many old (and new) concerts and operas on the Internet on YouTube and on many other sites. So, while I decry the paltry amount of classical music on local radio in the New York City area, I am absolutely thrilled that we have these other avenues to make up for and replace it.

Conductors

Arturo Toscanini and My Toscanini Legacy

Arturo Toscanini (1867–1957) was arguably the most famous conductor of the twentieth century. His career spanned sixty-five years, from 1887 to 1955. Conducting for less than a decade, by 1896 he was already recognized as Italy's foremost conductor. In that year, he conducted the world premiere of his friend Puccini's *La Boheme*. Fifty years later he conducted an anniversary concert performance of that opera with the NBC Symphony Orchestra, which was broadcast on the radio, and later released on disc.

[https://www.youtube.com/watch?v=G923Sk1cyTQ]

Even more amazingly, Toscanini, who made his conducting debut in 1887, at age nineteen, with Verdi's *Aida*, in 1949, more than sixty years later, conducted a concert performance of it with the NBC Symphony Orchestra, which not only was broadcast and released on records, but was also telecast and is now available on DVD and YouTube. Be forewarned, the recorded version on YouTube is of very poor quality.

[https://www.youtube.com/watch?v=Ozyezf9dUyA&list=RDOzyezf9dUyA&start_radio=1]

Over the years Toscanini was the principal conductor at the Metropolitan Opera and La Scala, music director of the New York Philharmonic, and, finally, for seventeen years, music director of a radio orchestra created especially for him—the NBC Symphony Orchestra. As a radio orchestra, all of his concerts were broadcast, and a few were even telecast. Possibly, it was his exposure on the radio, and the numerous recordings he made, that accounted for his fame beyond the world of classical music—especially in America. His fame was such that, when he died, his obituary and photograph appeared on the front page of *The New York Times*.

Many consider Toscanini to have been the greatest conductor of his time. Obviously, I never saw Toscanini in live performance, so any assessment I could make is limited to the many recordings he made, along with various broadcasts and telecasts. Also, the sound quality of many of these recordings is far below today's standard, making it more difficult to evaluate the tonal clarity of a full orchestra compared to an operatic voice. Still, you can gather from many of these recordings that Toscanini was certainly one of the greats.

In the early 1960s, a local New York radio station (WRVR-FM) engaged in a project, in association with the estate of Arturo Toscanini, of restoring and broadcasting all of Toscanini's NBC Symphony Orchestra concerts in chronological order. I thought this to be an invaluable service and listened to it regularly. Unfortunately, it ended after having broadcast only the first two seasons of the orchestra's seventeen-year existence. This caused me to do something I rarely did then. I wrote a letter to the station about how appreciative I was of what they had done, and how disappointed I was that they were not continuing.

What resulted from that letter was unexpected. No, they didn't continue the broadcasts, for which I believe they had lost their funding. Shortly after I wrote, I received a letter from Don Gillis, who had been a producer of those Toscanini broadcasts. He informed me that NBC radio was going to do a radio series on Toscanini called *Toscanini: The Man Behind the Legend*, which he was producing. He invited me to be interviewed on that show. Also, some time before the interview took place, I was invited to visit with Walter Toscanini (Arturo's son) at the Toscanini home in Riverdale, where his son still lived.

The visit to Toscanini's home was thrilling, although the trip there was not. Though I lived in the Bronx, and Riverdale is in the Bronx, Riverdale is in the northwest and I lived in the northeast. All subways in the Bronx go from north to south (toward Manhattan and Brooklyn or Queens). Getting from the east to the west by public transportation in the Bronx was, and continues to be, a nightmare. I had to take a subway into Manhattan, change to a train on another line that goes back up the other side of the Bronx, and then take a bus to Toscanini's home! That is the kind of pain one sometimes must exchange for living in a city with the riches of arts that New York provides. Seeing where Toscanini lived and worked, and the various memorabilia that Walter Toscanini (playing a tour guide) showed me, made it all worthwhile.

During my visit, I mentioned to Walter that I was considering taking a few music courses. I was quite surprised by his response. He said if I was not planning to become a professional musician, I shouldn't, but to just continue to enjoy music as a layman. While I didn't understand why he said that, in later years I think I have come to a fuller realization of what he meant. For example, if I were more educated in music, could I enjoy Corelli as much, knowing how he often deviated from the written score? Instead of sitting back to enjoy the performance, would I be wincing at artistic lapses? I might have become more knowing of the music, but at what cost to my enjoyment of the performances? Would I be able to write this book, the gut impressions of one audience member among many who have only a lay appreciation for music? It was a strange statement to be heard from the son of a conductor renowned for his strict adherence to the score.

Luckily, I didn't have to make the nightmare trip home. I was going to the opera that evening (*Aida* with Corelli) and, as Walter had some business in Manhattan, he drove me to 57th Street in Manhattan. He asked me who was conducting the performance I was to see. When I told him Kurt Adler, he commented, "He's heavy-handed."

Soon thereafter, I went to the NBC studios and was interviewed by Ben Grauer, who had been the announcer for the NBC Symphony Orchestra broadcasts in their final years. At the time, I wondered why they would choose to interview me, when all the other interviewees were friends, composers, and musicians who knew Toscanini. I realized during the interview that they wanted the perspective of someone from the younger generation. I, of course, taped the interview at home when it was broadcast. That tape is somewhere in my basement, but I no longer need to store it.

While writing this, I googled "Toscanini: The man behind the legend" to ascertain the year in which it was broadcast. It took me fewer than five minutes to find all of the episodes, digitized and archived at the "UNT University of North Texas." Digital Library –I put my name in the search box and quickly found the October 2, 1963 episode that included my interview. It was excruciating to hear my seventeen-year-old-self again. I found it even more embarrassing, perhaps, than some of my early, clearly youthful, written reviews. I sounded *very* young. I wonder why!

[https://digital.library.unt.edu/explore/collections/TNMBL/browse/?q=Leslie+Epstein&t=fulltext&sort=]

Toscanini's Rivals

During the course of his sixty-five-year-long career, Arturo Toscanini had a rival during each phase of his career. In the last phase of Toscanini's career, that was Wilhelm Furtwängler. I don't know whether they ever actually interacted. Toscanini was mostly active in America, while Furtwängler conducted very little in the U.S. Still, critics and fans seem to like to compare and contrast their recordings and style—and many prefer Furtwängler.

[https://www.youtube.com/watch?v=Hp_OZEPwDQU]
[https://www.youtube.com/watch?v=bimhicdrPUs]

In his mid-career, Toscanini shared the directorship of the New York Philharmonic with Willem Mengelberg. There seems to have been a real personal rivalry, which Toscanini ultimately won, and Mengelberg was ousted so that Toscanini became the sole music director of the NY Philharmonic. I am particularly fond of many of Mengelberg's recordings, mostly with the Concertgebouw Orchestra. Humperdinck's *Hansel and Gretel Overture* is heard, first with Mengelberg conducting the New York Philharmonic in 1930, then Toscanini and the NBC Symphony in 1952:

[https://www.youtube.com/watch?v=nvsPf33x2oo]
[https://www.youtube.com/watch?v=eg_J_4Hpawc]

For the first two decades of Toscanini's career, he made no recordings, as the acoustic process was not able to properly capture large orchestras. This was also true for another conductor who was already considered the greatest conductor of his time when Toscanini was emerging. As they both conducted at the Met early in the twentieth century, they may have interacted. Unfortunately, this first great rival died in 1911, two years into his tenure as music director of the New York Philharmonic. So, with no recordings from either conductor during this period, we cannot make any comparisons between them.

Most conductors of the pre-recording era are barely remembered (with some exceptions, like Hans von Bülow, remembered as a friend and champion of Richard Wagner, and perhaps even more for the fact that his wife, Cosima, Franz Liszt's daughter, left von Bülow for Wagner). Going unremembered might have become the fate of Toscanini's first great rival, had he not also been a composer. While alive, his fame as a conductor eclipsed his compositions which were not highly thought of, nor frequently performed, during his lifetime.

However, decades after his death, Gustav Mahler's time did come (as he had predicted it would in a 1909 letter to Bruno Walter in which he also proclaimed himself to be better than Beethoven). He is now one of the more frequently performed and recorded composers, despite the massive length and complexity of many of his nine symphonies. Indeed, his second symphony is my all-time favorite symphony.

Despite Toscanini's conducting career lasting nearly forty-five years beyond Mahler's death, Toscanini never conducted Mahler's music.

The Golden Age of Conductors

While I revere Arturo Toscanini as a great conductor, he was one among those who were part of an era of great conductors. That era had many more great conductors than just the rivals I mentioned earlier. As the first half of the twentieth century was the dawn of recorded sound that didn't exist in the 1800s, we would now have ways of judging a conductor's performance.

In the United States, besides Italian-born Toscanini, who led the New York Philharmonic and NBC Symphony Orchestra, respectively, there was Russian-born Serge Koussevitsky (1874–1951), the music director of the Boston Symphony for a quarter-century (1924–1948) [https://www.youtube.com/watch?v=pfwuXg6GmPU], and British-born Leopold Stokowski (1882–1977) who was, also for a quarter of a century, the music director of the Philadelphia Orchestra. (More about him in the next chapter).

[https://www.youtube.com/watch?v=FHrQPmEd5q8]

England also gave us Sir Thomas Beecham (1979–1961) (whose knighthood was not for his contribution to music, but one inherited from his grandfather who had founded the company that manufactured Beecham's Pills that were taken to "cure bilious and nervous disorders"). Because of his family wealth, he founded two orchestras that still perform in London, the London Philharmonic and Royal Philharmonic Orchestras.

[https://www.youtube.com/watch?v=QGpDkaOYjAA]
[https://www.youtube.com/watch?v=vA83lt-Kg0M]

France gave us Pierre Monteux (1875–1964), who was music director of the Boston Symphony in the early 1920s and the San Francisco Symphony in the 1940s.

[https://www.youtube.com/watch?v=W_Rc3EChFy0]

Austria gave us Bruno Walter (1876–1962), who, while never

officially named the music director of the New York Philharmonic, was closely associated with it during the 1940s.

[https://www.youtube.com/watch?v=A8nS3JO-BzQ]

[https://www.youtube.com/watch?v=5mAcSi4jKxw]

In the Netherlands, Willem Mengelberg (1871–1951) led the Concertgebouw Orchestra for over forty years and, as noted, was music director of the New York Philharmonic in the 1920s.

[https://www.youtube.com/watch?v=STWCSjkHHGw]

In Switzerland, Ernest Ansermet (1883–1969) founded, and then led l'Orchestre de la Suisse Romande for fifty years.

[https://www.youtube.com/watch?v=jFducftqsbg]

These eight were arguably the greatest of the international conductors of that fabulous generation.

There were many other well-known conductors during this era. In England were Sir Adrian Boult (1889–1983)

[https://www.youtube.com/watch?v=DwJqhXbS2xE]

and Sir Malcolm Sargent (1895–1967)

[https://www.youtube.com/watch?v=67YOE2PAoMw] (both of who *did* earn their titles for their contribution to music). Unlike their great contemporary, Sir Thomas Beecham, who had a robust international career, both Boult and Sargent's careers outside Great Britain were much more limited.

Another, slightly younger, British conductor, John Barbirolli (1899–1970), at the age of thirty-six, succeeded Arturo Toscanini as music director of the New York Philharmonic. Perhaps anyone following, arguably, the most famous conductor in the world would have a hard time of it, it was especially tough for this young and little-known conductor who faced a hostile press and, soon, Toscanini's own NBC Symphony. Barbirolli became music director of the Philharmonic in the fall of 1936.

Just a year later, the NBC Symphony was formed to lure Toscanini back to New York, and this new orchestra, with it's world-famous conductor, performed right down the street, and sometimes actually *in* Carnegie Hall. (Most NBC Symphony Orchestra concerts were broadcast from Studio 8H, currently the home of *Saturday Night Live*, in the NBC studios in Rockefeller Center, just a few blocks south of the Philharmonic's then home, Carnegie Hall. On occasion a special NBC Symphony concert was broadcast *from* Carnegie Hall.)

Barbirolli's tenure in New York lasted until 1943, but his time in New York was not a happy one and did nothing for his reputation.

Returning to England in 1943, he became music director of Manchester's Hallé Orchestra, which, under his leadership for the next quarter century, became acknowledged as one of the great orchestras of the world. As the years progressed, his reputation and international career flourished, and he, too, earned a knighthood. He even did a stint as music director of the Houston Symphony from 1960 to 1966 (succeeding Leopold Stokowski).

[https://www.youtube.com/watch?v=kBYtbcPqeN0]

In Czechoslovakia, Vacliv Talich (1883–1961) was the chief conductor of the Czech Philharmonic for more than two decades, and was especially noted for his performances of Czech works, as these links to performances of Dvorak's "Slavonic Dances" shows: Op. 46

[https://www.youtube.com/watch?v=OZb2GEUmDPQ&t=644s]

and Op. 72.

[https://www.youtube.com/watch?v=dXFR_amAZIM&t=414s]

The Hungarian, Fritz Reiner (1888–1963)

[https://www.youtube.com/watch?v=vhMcZlzdCbU],

and Greek-born Dimitri Mitropoulos (1896–1960)

[https://www.youtube.com/watch?v=Kl-dSoNHx8Y], both had substantial careers in the United States. There were two fine Italian conductors who stuck mainly to the operatic repertoire: Tullio Serafin (1878–1968) and Victor de Sabata (1892–1967). I've already heaped much praise on Austrian Karl Böhm (1894–1981). And there was also German-born Wilhelm Furtwängler (1886–1954). I've no doubt missed a few, but that period was certainly an era that was deserving of being what I call "the golden age of conductors." It is not that subsequent eras have not given us many great conductors, but never so many at the same time.

Many of the conductors discussed here are featured in an excellent, almost-three-hour, documentary about great conductors of the past.

[https://www.youtube.com/watch?v=gn6yf4jd4mg]

Leopold Stokowski

Most of the conductors in the golden age of conductors were before my time. I only got to see two of them live. I saw Ernest Ansermet conduct twice. Especially memorable was a concert with the New York Philharmonic on July 12, 1966, which included a complete performance of Stravinsky's *Persephone*. The other was Leopold Stokowski, who died in 1977 at age ninety-five. I was able to see him numerous times. He conducted a great deal in New York in his later years, especially with the American Symphony Orchestra, which he founded and bankrolled. I also saw him conduct a concert with the New York Philharmonic and another with the Philadelphia Orchestra, not to mention my first Met *Turandot*. Indeed, he was the conductor of the first orchestral concert I attended on November 11, 1963.

If Toscanini was the most famous conductor in the world, Leopold Stokowski was probably a close second, at least in America. After all, Toscanini didn't get to shake hands with Mickey Mouse. That *honor* fell to Stokowski in Walt Disney's famed 1940 film, *Fantasia*, for which Stokowski and the Philadelphia Orchestra provided the musical soundtrack.

[https://www.youtube.com/watch?v=wxNZg1WyeVI]

Stokowski also appeared as himself in three other Hollywood movies. In 1937, he had a featured role in the Deanna Durbin film *One Hundred Men and a Girl*. Here's a clip.

[https://www.youtube.com/watch?v=wSo88XUMZZ8]

He also appeared in *The Big Broadcast of 1937* and, with lots of other classical music performers, in *Carnegie Hall* in 1946. These forays into pop culture raised eyebrows among some who may have questioned his integrity as a classical conductor. Added to this were Stokowski's many foibles, as the next two paragraphs reveal.

Although born in London, he often claimed to have been born in Poland, to the extent that he once walked off a radio interview when the interviewer stated he was born in London. His rather strange speaking-voice accent was hard to place. It wasn't recognizably British, Polish, or American. Perhaps it was something he might have just "made up." See if you can place the accent in this interview of Stokowski by Morton Gould.

[https://www.youtube.com/watch?v=_xUNc7a0zeE]

Stokowski's personal life was sometimes fodder for the tabloids. In 1938 he had a romance with Greta Garbo during which some gossip columnists predicted marriage. That didn't happen, but in 1945 he married heiress Gloria Vanderbilt. She was twenty-one and he was three days past his 63rd birthday! They had two children, divorcing ten years later.

Stokowski was sometimes criticized for his lush orchestrations of some of Bach's popular organ works. I personally love them as I am not especially fond of the sound of the organ. Listen to the original organ version of Bach's Toccata & Fugue in D Minor, BWV 565, followed by Stokowski's orchestration.

[https://www.youtube.com/watch?v=Nnuq9PXbywA]
[https://www.youtube.com/watch?v=rB9Lt30y9NM]

Stokowski was a solid musician and a great conductor, but oh so different from Toscanini, whose fidelity to the score was legendary. Stokowski was known to occasionally play fast and loose with the score. He was very concerned with how a piece sounded. If he thought it would make the sound in the hall better, he would change the seating of the orchestra to better accommodate the particular musical selection or the acoustics of that concert hall. For the last half century of his nearly seventy-year career he was among very few major conductors who conducted without a baton. While conducting, his hands were very expressive. At times it seemed as if he was molding the music out of his very hands.

Unlike Toscanini, who only sparingly performed contemporary works, Stokowski very often programmed and championed new works and contemporary composers. Stokowski also liked to work with and teach new generations of musicians. This was one of the reasons for the creation of the American Symphony Orchestra. It was to be made up of experienced, retired musicians from well-known professional orchestras who sat as the principals and first chair musicians, while the bulk of the orchestra was made up of young musicians recently out of conservatories. These recent graduates were hand-picked by Stokowski, and would be mentored by him and the first chairs.

One of the more memorable American Symphony Orchestra concerts I attended was on April 26, 1965. Stokowski (with the help of two assistants, David Katz and Jose Serebrier) conducted the world premiere of Charles Ives forty-year-old Fourth Symphony, which, although composed in the 1920s, had never been performed. There is a video of this performance on YouTube, which includes an enlightening explanation of who Ives was and how he presented the music.

[https://www.youtube.com/watch?v=-xXv55ARtsM&t=4s]

On that program (but not part of the video) were the Beethoven Fifth, Sibelius's *The Swan of Tuonela*, and Wagner's *The Flying Dutchman* overture. I was not prepared for Ives to be heard among all these more familiar classic works, but such a concert was typical of Stokowski's programming: tried and true popular works together with something new or relatively obscure.

On November 7, 1967, at Lincoln Center, I saw Stokowski conduct the Philadelphia Orchestra for the only time. Here is what I wrote at the time:

Philadelphia Orchestra Concert, **November 7, 1967, Philharmonic Hall, Lincoln Center, (Written 11/12/67)**

It was at the beginning of the 1912–1913 season that the thirty-year-old, newly appointed music director of the Philadelphia Orchestra, conducted his first concert with that group at the Philadelphia Academy of Music. It began an association that lasted twenty-five years and made musical history, with superb performances and that lush sound that came to be associated with the Philadelphia Orchestra and Leopold Stokowski. Mr. Stokowski retired as music director in 1936, but remained an active conductor leading most of the great orchestras of the world, becoming, for a while, music director of the Houston Symphony and founding orchestras, such as the present day American Symphony Orchestra. Though Stokowski did not conduct the Philadelphia Orchestra from 1940 to 1960, he finally returned for guest appearances in 1960 and has been returning for guest appearances with the orchestra that will forever be associated with his name ever since. And, on this occasion, I finally got my chance to see one of my idolized combinations together, and it certainly was an unforgettable event.

It is doubtful that there is even one member of the orchestra who remembers that occasion fifty-five years ago when the young Leopold Stokowski first stood on the podium facing the Philadelphia Orchestra. It is even doubtful as to whether there are many people in the orchestra who played under Stokowski during his last season as music director in 1935–36. Yet Eugene Ormandy (Stokowski's successor as music director of the Philadelphia Orchestra) has been able to maintain that unique Philadelphia/Stokowski sound, so that, on those rare occasions when Philadelphia's great musical patriarch of the past does return, it can sound like he never left.

Mahler is a composer I would not ordinarily associate with Stokowski and I didn't know what to expect from a Stokowski Mahler Second. I almost forgot that Stokowski, being a champion of new music, and being around when Mahler was active, was also a Mahler proponent, to the extent of premiering in America, with this ensemble, the gigantic Eighth Symphony ("Symphony of a Thousand"). Well, if these facts weren't enough to convince me of Stokowski's prowess with a Mahler score, the performance certainly was. It was rousing and beautifully played, with the kind of intensity and meaning too often lacking. The performance shook the walls and souls.

The program also included fifteen minutes of Bach's "Magnificat," which was played with full orchestra and therefore sounded a little more than Bach would have wanted. The concert was truly a great one, and I hope this combination could appear more often together, yet this program, being the only one they are doing together this season, it seems quite unlikely, and more likely this will be my only exposure to what the "golden age of orchestral playing and conducting" was like.

Two days later that concert was given in Philadelphia and taped for broadcast.
[https://www.youtube.com/watch?v=yVNDEZJPIns]

It should be noted that that concert was the last time Stokowski conducted the Philadelphia Orchestra in New York. This brought his career full circle in New York, so to speak, as it was in 1916 that he first brought the Philadelphia Orchestra to New York to premiere Mahler's Eighth Symphony (at the Old Metropolitan Opera House). The Eighth was nicknamed the *Symphony of a Thousand* because that's almost the number of people it needed on stage to perform that massive work. That concert made front page news and put Stokowski and the Philadelphia Orchestra on the map, probably also resulting in their recording contract. So, it was fitting that he should close out his New York appearances with that orchestra with another great Mahler symphony.

Over the next decade I would get to see the Mahler Second many times, including two more times conducted by Stokowski, but now with the American Symphony Orchestra. I also saw it during this period with William Steinberg conducting the Boston Symphony and Leonard Bernstein conducting the New York Philharmonic. With each performance, my love of the work grew until I finally realized it is my favorite symphony. It's not just the outer beauty of the music, but there is an inner depth in this piece that speaks to me as few other pieces do.

Although I continued to attend American Symphony Orchestra concerts conducted by Stokowski, I never again saw him conduct the Philadelphia Orchestra. In September, 1972, on the sixtieth anniversary of his debut with the Philadelphia Orchestra, he was scheduled to conduct them at the Academy of Music in Philadelphia in a duplicate of his 1912 debut program. (He had done so in 1962 for the fiftieth anniversary of his debut there.) I bought a ticket. Alas, the ninety-year-old maestro did not return to America that season and, although he continued conducting in Europe until his death five years later at the age of ninety-five, he never returned to his adopted home. I sent the ticket back for a refund, but in retrospect, considering the ticket cost of $2.50, I probably should have kept it as a memento.

Leonard Bernstein

Perhaps I'm wrong about there being a golden age of conductors. Perhaps *every* era has its golden age.

There have been many conductors in the last sixty years who I've come to admire: Herbert von Karajan, Seiji Ozawa, Michael Tilson Thomas, and, most notable for me, both Daniel Barenboim and James Levine. Leonard Bernstein was ubiquitous in the sixties when I became a classical music lover. As he was music director of the New York Philharmonic at that time, I got to see him conduct a lot of concerts, including my first-ever Philharmonic concert in 1965. It was an all-Bernstein program that included the world premiere of his *Chichester Psalms*. I was not all-in as a fan of Bernstein, the conductor. I considered him a much better composer than conductor, especially his more popular works (several of his Broadway musicals are among my favorites). I thought of him as overrated as a conductor, although I agree, he was a musical genius.

Among the many performances in which I saw Bernstein conduct the New York Philharmonic during his tenure as its music director, the most memorable for me (as an opera lover) were the three Wagner programs he conducted in his last three seasons. He conducted one each season, all three with the wonderful Eileen Farrell among the soloists. Farrell left the Met prematurely in the mid-sixties, never having sung a Wagner opera there, but most agree that she is the only soprano of that era who could have given Birgit Nilsson a run for her money in Wagner operas. (Astrid Varnay, the great Met Wagnerian soprano of the 1940s and 1950s was, by the mid-1960s, past her vocal prime even though she was the same age as Nilsson!)

Wagner: Die Walkure, Act I, Leonard Bernstein, New York Philharmonic, Philharmonic Hall, May 25, 1968 (Written 6/31/68)

This was the last regular subscription concert of the Philharmonic's 1967–68 season, and it featured Act I of "Die Walkure," a work this orchestra performed the U. S. premiere of in 1876. This may be the biggest year for Act I of Walkure in the U. S., as besides this performance, both the Boston Symphony under Leinsdorf and the Pittsburgh Symphony under William Steinberg opened their 1967–68 season with Act I of *Walkure,* and the Met presented the entire opera in a new production directed and conducted by Herbert von Karajan. I, of course, saw the Met's production, and though I didn't get to Boston or Pittsburgh, I did listen to their broadcasts, so I am able to make comparisons. I must say Bernstein and the New Yorkers come out favorably.

There was a certain brightness and musical lyricism to this performance, yet Bernstein did not neglect the dramatic urgency of the score. Both Mr. Bernstein and the orchestra were in top form. Eileen Farrell, though she has virtually deserted staged opera, is still one of the finest dramatic sopranos in the world and showed off her mettle here. Though a little unfocused at times, her voice soared, and she made a commanding Sieglinde, somewhat undercut by the fact she was the only one of the three singers on stage who had the score in front of her. James King as Sigmund was at his best, clear-voiced, singing with vigor and to great dramatic effect. Michael Langdon was satisfactory, but not outstanding as Hunding." [*Both King and Langdon were veterans of many stage performances of Walküre, but this may have been Farrell's only Sieglinde, thus her need for the score.*]
https://www.youtube.com/watch?v=hJv1b58QJAY]

In February of 1969, Bernstein and the New York Philharmonic, along with Farrell, tenor Jess Thomas, and mezzo-soprano Joanna Simon (Carly Simon's sister) performed highlights from Wagner's *Tristan und Isolde* at Philharmonic Hall.
[https://www.youtube.com/watch?v=qldRIJsmZlc]
Finally, in January, 1970, Bernstein, the Philharmonic, Farrell, and Thomas got together again for a program of highlights from Wagner's *Gotterdammerung.*
[https://www.youtube.com/watch?v=-cim3B08TwY]
[https://www.youtube.com/watch?v=HTtaKNG1YyE0]
[https://www.youtube.com/watch?v=QYG8hkDuCHI]

One of Bernstein's great contributions as a conductor was his early and continued championing of the music of Gustav Mahler. Bernstein was in the forefront of those who brought Mahler to the attention of the broader public; that public who were soon to embrace Mahler. Although he left the music directorship of the Philharmonic in 1969, Bernstein continued to appear with the orchestra in the early seventies.

There was a time, from approximately the late-seventies to the mid-eighties, when Bernstein did not conduct the Philharmonic, centering his conducting in Europe. His first commercially recorded Mahler cycle (the complete symphonies) in the fifties and sixties was mostly (except for the Eighth) with the New York Philharmonic. His second, in the seventies and eighties, was with various European orchestras. A video cycle from that period was mostly (except for the Second) with the Vienna Philharmonic. Following are links to each symphony in this video cycle.

[https://www.youtube.com/watch?v=ISBfOpztUZM] First Symphony

[https://www.youtube.com/watch?v=9MNXqXXfMoM] Second Symphony with the London Symphony Orchestra

[https://www.youtube.com/watch?v=HXVueK5sjlQ] Third Symphony

[https://www.youtube.com/watch?v=UMQiATUXg00] Fourth Symphony

[https://www.youtube.com/watch?v=9KSESLJ0LWA] Fifth symphony

[https://www.youtube.com/watch?v=goXH3NUhUFk] Sixth Symphony

[https://www.youtube.com/watch?v=_v7BmR3pPAk] Seventh Symphony

[https://www.youtube.com/watch?v=NSYEOLwVfU8] Eighth Symphony

[https://www.youtube.com/watch?v=IoNEeKJ2x44] Ninth Symphony

[https://www.youtube.com/watch?v=vHyV8noUXC0] Tenth Symphony—adagio movement, the only movement completed by Mahler before his death.

Americans are very familiar with Bernstein's appearances on TV as host of the New York Philharmonic's Young Peoples Concerts, his Harvard lecture series, and others, making the sound of his voice immediately recognizable. So, it comes as a jolt to hear this rehearsal clip of the Mahler First with the Vienna Philharmonic, in which that voice speaks in perfect German. Also, at the end of this clip, speaking English, Bernstein talks about his affinity to Mahler.

[https://www.youtube.com/watch?v=TxjQSqr70Po&t=4s]

In the mid-eighties, when Bernstein returned to guest-conduct the New York Philharmonic, I found him to be a totally different conductor—now a great one. I saw a number of his concerts then, including an all-Copland program, a program of American symphonies including the Copland Third, a concert with his newly composed *Songfest* (he sported a white beard then, which he, thankfully, soon abandoned), and performances of the Mahler Third and Seventh symphonies.

It was two other concerts, however, that stand out as being among the greatest concerts I ever saw. In 1987, I saw Bernstein conduct a Mahler Second again, but it was two years later, in 1989, when he, once more, led the Mahler Second, that I was overwhelmed. It was to be his last performance of that work and it moved me more than any other I have seen before, or since. It was as though the accumulated knowledge of more than three decades of Bernstein's championing, studying, and conducting Mahler had coalesced in this one performance. It was as if Bernstein knew it would be the last time he would conduct this work, so dear to his heart, that he poured his soul into the performance.

In 1988, I went to a concert at which Bernstein conducted the finest version of the Tchaikovsky Fifth I'd ever seen. Tchaikovsky was one of the greatest romantic composers, whose gorgeous melodies abound in his Fifth symphony, my favorite of his symphonies, but nothing prepared me for what Bernstein did with it. It runs approximately fifty minutes, depending on the conductor. I once saw Valery Gergiev do it in forty-five minutes, flat. Bernstein's performance of the Fifth at this concert lasted a full hour! The performance had an intensity and depth I had never heard in this symphony before. Like the Mahler Second of the next year, this performance moved me, such that, even three decades later, it stays in my mind as one of my great musical experiences.

Having here summed up my feelings about Bernstein's 1989 performance of the Mahler Second, I debated whether to include my review of that concert. On rereading it, I found it to be one of my better-written reviews. I feel I have improved as a writer, given there were twenty-five years since the sophomoric efforts of the Tebaldi/Callas "Tosca" reviews on pages 30–32.

New York Philharmonic, Mahler 2nd,
April 4, 1989 (Written 4/15/89)

Simply the finest performance of my favorite symphony I've ever seen. I've seen Bernstein conduct the Mahler Second twice before, in the early seventies, as his thousandth concert with the Philharmonic and just two years ago, but never like this, where everything was just right, well-nigh perfect. Bernstein's utter control made this performance just about definitive. It was Bernstein's grasp of the depth of the Mahlerian feeling that is intrinsic in this sublime score. As a champion of Mahler for forty years, Bernstein is steeped in the music, and the performance seemed to ooze from his soul. Bernstein has long ago won the war. Mahler has long been recognized as one of the musical giants of the romantic era.

Over the years, Bernstein's vision of the Mahler Second has matured. I calculated this performance came in at just about ninety-seven minutes, longer than any performance I've ever seen. It should be said the Philharmonic, which doesn't always sound like the greatest orchestra in the world, sounded like it here. For a rare second or two, a French horn was oh so slightly off, but, for the rest, the orchestra blazed forth with Mahlerian perfection and the seventy-year-old Bernstein leaped above the podium during the greatest of the climaxes.

Benita Valente and Wendy White were the superb soloists and the New York Choral Artists were the fine chorus, but it was Bernstein's show, and rightly so. This Mahler Second was Mahler seen through the eyes of one of his greatest interpreters, and that interpretation gave us an unsullied, beautiful, and visionary performance. Now that Mehta is leaving the Philharmonic, one almost wishes for the return of Bernstein to his "home" orchestra, or at least an expanded role for him; for he is now the conductor he sought to be in the past. Judging from this performance, and Bernstein's recent Tchaikovsky Fifth with the Philharmonic, Bernstein has achieved a new level in his conducting.

My wish for an expanded role for Bernstein at the Philharmonic *almost* came true. A few months later it was announced that, during the Philharmonic's search for a new music director, a triumvirate of conductors would share the bulk of the concerts. One of the three was Bernstein. Sadly, in late summer 1990, Bernstein announced a temporary withdrawal from conducting for health reasons. Within two months, he had died.

James Levine

Having previously acknowledged the elephant in the room, I will now speak of James Levine. I've seen Levine conduct more performances than any other conductor. He is among my favorite conductors of the past fifty years. Levine made his Met debut on June 8, 1971, conducting *Tosca*. The cast was Grace Bumbry, Franco Corelli, and Peter Glossop. Despite Corelli's presence, I missed that performance. I did, however, see Levine's second Met performance, with the same opera and cast. About that June 12, 1971 performance, I wrote:

"Another debut in last week's *Tosca* was conductor James Levine, and he did a superb job, making the orchestra sound more colorful than it normally does in this opera."

Two months later I was visiting friends in Los Angeles. It was there I got to see James Levine for the second time in a rather unusual circumstance. I will let my almost contemporaneous account speak for itself (I was writing about the morning of August 12, 1971 on August 24, when I was back home,):

"Visiting L.A., I was a bit annoyed that I was just going to miss the big musical event of the L.A. season on August 14 when at the Hollywood Bowl there was to be a performance of "La Traviata" with the golden age cast of [Beverly] Sills, [Placido] Domingo and [Sherrill] Milnes. So, the day before I was to leave, I went to the Bowl in the morning, hoping I might at least see a rehearsal of it (knowing they have free public rehearsals in the morning, though I felt it more likely they would rehearse that evening's concert.) Quite to my surprise, the conductor, James Levine, came out and began an orchestral run-through of Act III of "Traviata," after which I assumed he would do the same for the other two acts, but to my further surprise, out came Mssrs. Sills, Domingo, and Milnes, and with the orchestra and conductor and other soloists, but minus the Los Angeles Master Chorale under Roger Wagner who are to appear at the concert, they rehearsed the third Act again, and then went to the first scene of Act II. Thus, at least, I got half my wish. The three soloists were in excellent voice. Also, though I believe in [labor] unions, I was appalled by the fact that at 12:00 noon [the rehearsal had begun at 9:30 a.m.], in the middle of Milnes' "Di Provenza," the orchestra stopped and the rehearsal was over. With less than three minutes to go to the end of the scene, I thought that a crime. What would the tyrants of yore, such as Toscanini, say to such goings on? Certainly there can be some minor (three minutes) flexibility for the sake of art."

Although I never got to see the full performance, I did get to hear it over fifty years later when it was posted on YouTube.
[https://www.youtube.com/watch?v=pHdQkQ6oY8Y]

During the next forty-seven years, Levine would prove that one doesn't have to be a musical tyrant to make great music. But, little did I know then, how great a conductor he was to become, nor how ignoble would be his fall from grace. In the years that followed I would see numerous Levine performances at the Met, and it soon became apparent that the orchestral playing of the Met orchestra under his baton was superlative; and the orchestra that he fashioned was among the best in the world. Many of his performances, especially of Verdi and Wagner, were beyond compare. I saw him conduct two full *Ring* cycles and they were among the greatest of my musical experiences. This, from my review of the first *Ring* cycle I saw, given the week beginning April 30, 1990:

"Richard Wagner's *Der Ring des Nibelungen* remains a deeply moving musical experience, especially when seen in close proximity and when conducted by a master. These were the strengths of this third and last "Ring" cycle at the Met this season, only the fourth season in the last thirty years the Met has given us complete "Ring" cycles, and my first visit to one. The real star of the show was it's guiding musical light, the Met's music director, James Levine, who is one of the finest conductors of our era, and he guided the "Ring" with control, and produced magnificent sounds from his Metropolitan Opera Orchestra, which under him sounds the equal of a great symphony orchestra. Of course, musically, the "Ring" requires an orchestra the equivalent of a symphonic ensemble and Levine and the Met were able to give it. It is doubtful if any of the Met "Rings" of yore had this moving, beautiful, and deeply felt orchestral underpinning, Furthermore, Met "Rings" previously, at least in my memory, were given over a space of several weeks to accommodate house subscribers, so that the intense experience of viewing the work within a short period of time was denied patrons. But, starting last season, and again this, two "Ring" cycles have been given each within a week and it certainly makes for a more compelling musical and dramatic experience."

One-and-a-half Met *Ring* cycles conducted by Levine were telecast. The first complete cycle was during the late 1980s. In the second, in the early 2010s, he conducted only *Das Rheingold* and *Die Walkure*, after which he had to take a sabbatical from the Met for health reasons and the cycle was completed by Fabio Luisi. Here is a taste of Levine's monumental Wagner conducting in this clip of *Ride of the Valkyries* from the second cycle.

[https://www.youtube.com/watch?v=xeRwBiu4wfQ]

Now to my final review of a Levine performance. As the years went by, my writing of these reviews often became more delayed, so I didn't get to write about Levine's November 27, 2017 performance of the *Verdi Requiem* at the Met, until December 13. By that time, a lot had happened:

"What a difference a week makes. It is extremely likely this was the next-to-last performance conducted by James Levine at the Met (and, perhaps, anywhere). This also may be the saddest and most difficult-to-write discussion of a performance I've ever written. The next performance Levine conducted was the last of this season's scheduled "Requiem's" on Saturday (Dec. 2), the first matinee broadcast of the season. The next day the news broke that he had been accused of molesting a fifteen-year-old boy in the late 1980s. In this post-Harvey Weinstein era, he was immediately suspended by the Met, pending an investigation. The Met may claim they are "shocked"—"shocked" to hear of this allegation—but the likely fact is they have known of some of this for decades. I heard rumor of an arrest in Cincinnati, I believe, decades ago that the Met was able to hush up. Several articles over the past years, about Levine, touched on these rumors, all denied by Mr. Levine. When I heard of his arrest I thought it was for soliciting and didn't think much about it. Since it was hushed up, I never knew the details. I figured he learned his lesson and would not risk it again.

"About the performance. It was a solid, beautiful performance, again more due to the conducting than to any contribution of the soloists, who, for the most part, were strong. This may not have been Levine at the peak of his powers, but it was still a spine-tingling performance that showed his utter mastery of the idiom. But that mastery will not likely be heard again because of the credible allegations of his conduct over the past decades."

Musicals and Musical Theater Performers

My First Broadway Musical

That I became an opera lover didn't stop me from becoming a fan of Broadway musicals. While pop music was going in the direction of rock music, the stage musicals of the 1960s were still producing the type of songs I grew up with, so it was natural that I should start going to see Broadway musicals (and, because I had/have other interests beyond music, the Broadway drama stage as well).

My first onstage musical was a school trip in what was then called junior high school, now called middle school. The teacher gave the class a choice between two musicals: *My Fair Lady* or *Fiorello!*. While I knew *My Fair Lady* was the better musical, I had heard the cast album of *Fiorello!* several times and was quite taken with it. As *My Fair Lady* was in its third cast by that time, and *Fiorello!* still starred Tom Bosley, who originated the title role, I voted for *Fiorello!*. I was greatly outvoted by my classmates, some of whom probably never heard of *Fiorello!*, so *My Fair Lady* became the first Broadway musical I saw, then starring Michael Allinson and Pamela Charles in January of 1961.

Fiorello! has a great show business back story. It was originally planned as a vehicle for Lou Costello, fresh from his break with Bud Abbott, but early in the rehearsals, Costello died, and his understudy, the then-unknown Tom Bosley got the role. Bosley performed in every performance of its two-year run. He went on to greater fame on TV in *Happy Days*, later starring as Father Dowling in a series of TV mysteries, returning occasionally to Broadway. Unfortunately, there is no video of Tom Bosley in *Fiorello!*. Although he played the title character, he had only two songs in the show, probably because Lou Costello was not a singer—nor was Bosley, really. From the original cast album, these are Bosley's two numbers.

[https://www.youtube.com/watch?v=vHw_fdjc5v4]
[https://www.youtube.com/watch?v=tvN1sfwgSgk]

It wasn't until 1964 that I began to regularly go to Broadway shows, because, in the earlier sixties, I went mostly to see opera at The Met. Therefore, I never did get to see the Broadway production of *Fiorello!*, although I have seen it in an Equity Theater production, two City Center Encores! revivals, and one Off-Broadway revival. I continue to be surprised that *Fiorello!* has not had a Broadway revival or a screen version, while lots of lesser musicals have. Perhaps because it's so New York-centric?

Howard DaSilva of the original 1959 production singing *Little Tin Box*.

[https://www.youtube.com/watch?v=XrJMnONes2w&t=75s]

This is the only video I know of with an original cast member reprising their performance.

Kate Baldwin singing *When Did I Fall in Love?* from the 2013 City Center Encores! production of *Fiorello!*

[https://www.youtube.com/watch?v=gzRgZSQGWfo]

I have seen *My Fair Lady* numerous times since my middle school days in 1961. There was the City Center revival in the late '60s, the twentieth anniversary Broadway revival in 1976 (with Ian Richardson), a West End (London) revival in 1980, the twenty-fifth anniversary Broadway revival in 1981 (with Rex Harrison returning to the role he originated), and a National Tour production recently with Christopher Cazenove. Of course, I've watched the movie version several times.

A Listing of Great Musicals

Let's discuss my criteria for determining a great musical. That I am an opera lover affects my perspective. In opera, being entirely sung, it is the music that is the dominant element. The libretto can be second rate, but if the music is great, the opera can still succeed. Is the reverse true?

I think of Lorenzo Da Ponte (1749–1838). He wrote more than two dozen libretti, but only three are operas that have stood the test of time. Those three happen to be wonderful librettos, but the reason the operas are performed is not because of its libretto. These were the only libretti he wrote in which the music was composed by a genius named Wolfgang Amadeus Mozart—*The Marriage of Figaro, Don*

Giovanni, and *Cosi fan tutte.* It is possible that some of his other libretti are as strong as these three, but, paired with music of lesser quality, they are mostly forgotten.

Musicals are not entirely sung (with a few exceptions such as *Sweeney Todd),* so many critics will give almost as much weight to the book as to the music. I don't. For me, a strong book is a plus, but it's the music that counts. I cannot consider a great musical one that has a strong story but only the occasional great song. It is why I cannot consider two of the longest running musicals of the 1960s great musicals. However popular *Hello Dolly* and *Fiddler on the Roof* were, each of these musicals has only two, or maybe three, great or near-great numbers. Much of the rest of the score is uninspired filler.

There are a few prolific composers for theater who have written many great songs, but have no shows that appear on my list of great musicals. This is because their great tunes are spread across the inventory of all of their shows, with no production having more than one or two gems. Most notable among such composers is Kurt Weill.

In his second Broadway show, *Knickerbocker Holiday* (1938), Weill, a refugee from Germany, gave us the bittersweet, classic *September Song,* but little else to match it in that score
[https://www.youtube.com/watch?v=E3mAT-4FdP4],
Lady in the Dark (1941) gave us *The Saga of Jenny*
[https://www.youtube.com/watch?v=8jl3_aOHn6k],
and *One Touch of Venus* (1943) gave us *Speak Low,* performed in the clip by Kurt Weill, himself.
[https://www.youtube.com/watch?v=VgQJvNhuiAE]
In his last Broadway show *Lost in the Stars,* the title song is hauntingly beautiful.
[https://www.youtube.com/watch?v=5dCcGorrT0Q]
Again, little else in those scores matches those songs.

In his German years, in *The Threepenny Opera* (1928), we have *Mack the Knife* and *Pirate Jenny*
[https://www.youtube.com/watch?v=oZecKsm0Mfw].
In *The Rise and Fall of the City of Mahagonny* (1930) there is *Moon over Alabama* [https://www.youtube.com/watch?v=Yi-hEFKs9gk], but few of the other songs in those works come near this level.

Here is a list of productions that meet my criteria of having every, or almost every song, be a gem. They are chronologically listed with their composers from 1927 to 1970.

1) *Showboat* (1927) - Jerome Kern
2) *Anything Goes* (1934) - Cole Porter
3) *Oklahoma* (1943) - Richard Rodgers
4) *On the Town* (1944) - Leonard Bernstein
5) *Annie Get Your Gun* (1946) - Irving Berlin
6) *Carousel* (1947) - Richard Rodgers
7) *Kiss Me Kate* (1948) - Cole Porter
8) *South Pacific* (1949) - Richard Rodgers
9) *Guys and Dolls* (1950) - Frank Loesser
10) *The King and I* (1951) - Richard Rodgers
11) *The Pajama Game* (1954) - Richard Adler and Jerry Ross
12) *My Fair Lady* (1956) - Frederick Loewe
13) *West Side Story* (1957) - Leonard Bernstein
14) *Gypsy* (1959) - Jule Styne
15) *How To Succeed In Business Without Really Trying* (1961) - Frank Loesser
16) *Company* (1970) - Stephen Sondheim

I defy someone to find more than a song or two in any of the above musicals that is *not* a gem.

Don't expect to find Gershwin's *Porgy and Bess*. It's not on this list. Although it premiered on Broadway, I consider it an opera—perhaps America's greatest opera!

There is an honorable mention list. Each has an array of wonderful songs, but, in sum, these don't quite reach the same criteria as above—but are *very* close.

1) *Call Me Madame* (1950) - Irving Berlin
2) *Wonderful Town* (1953) - Leonard Bernstein
3) *The Most Happy Fella* (1956) - Frank Loesser
4) *Candide* (1956) - Leonard Bernstein
5) *Fiorello!* (1959) - Jerry Bock
6) *Camelot* (1960) - Frederick Loewe
7) *Milk and Honey* (1961) - Jerry Herman
8) *She Loves Me* (1963) - Jerry Bock

Sondheim and the Post-1970 Musicals

Since 1970, there have been very few musicals that meet my criteria for great musicals, and all that do, with one exception, were written by Stephen Sondheim. In the decade of *Company* (1970), Sondheim wrote

Follies (1971), *A Little Night Music* (1973), *Pacific Overtures* (1976), and *Sweeney Todd* (1979). All but *Pacific Overtures* would make it to the list.

In the 1980s, Sondheim gave us *Merrily We Roll Along* (his only flop in the decade), *Sunday in the Park with George* and *Into the Woods*. *Into the Woods* is definitely on the list, while *Merrily* and *Sunday* would probably get only honorable mention. While first thinking that *Sunday* was among Sondheim's best ever, two revivals, one by the Roundabout Theater in 2008 (an imported British production that won several Olivier Awards there) and an Encores! presentation in 2016, which starred Jake Gyllenhaal and Annaleigh Ashford (who brought it to Broadway the next year), showed me that without Mandy Patinkin and Bernadette Peters who starred in the original production, it just wasn't as good as I remembered it.

Unfortunately, in his last three decades, Sondheim's powers seem to have declined, and two viewings of *Assassins* (1990) (at Roundabout and Encores!) could not convince me of its worth—but I would give *Passion* (1994) an honorable mention. Following these, there were a revised *The Frogs* and several versions of *Bounce/Road Show*, none of them top-quality Sondheim.

The only *non*-Sondheim show since the 1970s that would make the list is *The Producers* (2001). Who knew Mel Brooks could write so many wonderful songs? I think it was apropos that Brooks, on accepting the Tony for *The Producers*, thanked Sondheim for *not* writing a musical that year!

Musicals from the pens of Kander and Ebb, Stephen Schwartz, Cy Coleman, Marvin Hamlisch, and others, as noteworthy as they are, just don't make the cut, however many fine qualities they have. Like Weill, their great songs are not concentrated in a single show

The fabulously successful Andrew Lloyd Weber doesn't make the list because he's British, and although I hadn't made it previously clear, I am discussing American musicals, and secondly, like Weill and the others, none of his works have more than two or three great songs.

Were I to include non-American musicals, *Les Miserables* would definitely be on that list. It has a brilliant musical score with one great song following the next.

Company

I saw the original production of Sondheim's *Company* about as many times as Joanne was married (three or four times—Joanne is the

Set design by Boris Aronson for the original production of *Company*.

character in the show who was played by Elaine Stritch). I loved it the first time I saw it, and I continue to do so. There has been no actor in any of the many subsequent performances of *Company* that I've seen, that comes near the perfect performances of the actors who created these roles. I saw it in Los Angeles in the summer of 1973 with a few original cast members still playing in it, and I've seen every Broadway revival (except the one in 2021). I've seen many off-Broadway and non-professional productions, as well as the New York Philharmonic's semi-staged production in 2011. There was also the twenty-third anniversary reunion concerts at Lincoln Center's Vivian Beaumont Theater. I saw that one *twice*!

Company wasn't a show I at first had a great desire to see. This was due to a review I remembered from years earlier when *A Funny Thing Happened on the Way to the Forum* opened in 1964. *Funny Thing* was Sondheim's first Broadway show for which he wrote the music. The critic I heard on the radio opined that Sondheim was a terrific lyricist, but a second-rate composer. Nearly a decade later I still remembered that statement. What got me interested in the show was Larry Kert

joining the cast soon after it opened in 1970. I loved him in the original cast recording of *West Side Story*, especially after hearing the tepid singing of a dubbed-in Tony in the film version.
[https://www.youtube.com/watch?v=0oVM1LXOids]

Still, I wasn't rushing to the box office for tickets to see *Company*. But, on October 20, 1970, I was on my way to see *Don Pasquale* at the Met. One of my main reasons for going to that performance was to see the young soprano, Reri Grist, as Norina. She had recently made her Met debut and I was hearing good things about her. Unfortunately, when I got to Lincoln Center, I found that Grist had cancelled. In those days, Broadway curtain time was 8:30; while the Met's was 8:00. So, having just enough time, I walked quickly downtown to see if I could get a ticket to a Broadway show. The first one I came to was *Company* at the Alvin Theater (since renamed the Neil Simon Theater) on 52nd Street. They had a balcony ticket still available. Thus it was that I got to see the musical that would become my all-time favorite. This is what I wrote about that performance:

Company, **October 20, 1970, (Written 10/25/70)**

I've been waiting for this a long time. Personally, I think it's the best musical since Frank Loesser's "How to Succeed in Business Without Really Trying" back in the early sixties. None of the big Broadway musical hits since then, including "Fiddler on the Roof," "Hello Dolly," "Cabaret," and others, come up to the class of these two, or the greats of the fifties such as "West Side Story and "My Fair Lady." Incidentally, speaking of "West Side Story," the lyrics and the music of this one were written by Bernstein's lyricist for "West Side Story," namely Stephen Sondheim. Although he is not new to Broadway as a composer either ("A Funny Thing Happened on the Way to the Forum," etc.) he finally came into his own with this brilliant musical, which, while it seems to derive much from Bernstein's influence, is totally fresh and appealing. I am speaking of the music now—which is beautiful. I just can't recall a song I didn't like, and I can recall many that shall always from now on move me.

However, this show had more than a fresh and beautiful score. It had a literate and absorbing book by George Furth. Some may not realize it, but "Company," in its own way, may be as revolutionary as "Oklahoma" was supposed to be thirty years ago. For, if I'm not mistaken, this is the first musical to deal with a psychological emotional problem. At least it's the first *successful* musical to do so.

The story was absorbing, even though I'm not certain I fully understood it. It was provokingly like a Fellini or Bergman film. [*Little did I know then that Sondheim would soon do a musical adaptation of a Bergman film,* A Little Night Music, *adapted from Bergman's 1955 film,* Smiles of a Summer Night—*not one of his later serious dramas, but one of his earlier romantic comedies.*] I'm pretty sure what it sought to document was the emotional change in the character of a man and his inhibition about becoming deeply involved—and about marriage. I'm far from certain what the ending meant, but it seemed to be saying that Robert was finally changing, and changing for the better.

As for the cast, it was about as good as you can get. In the lead was Larry Kert, best remembered as the original Tony in "West Side Story," and he was excellent. He may have been a little stiff, but somehow he was very believable. His singing voice is very warm and appealing, and he seems to have an innate feeling for proper phrasing. He certainly must be far superior to Dean Jones, the original Robert, who left the show after a few weeks.

Elaine Stritch is perfect as Joanne, combining her fine comical personality and her rough voice to great advantage. Steve Elmore showed a fine baritone in the beautiful "Getting Married Today," while Beth Howland showed an amazing deadpan singing and Teri Ralston showed off a beautiful voice. Barbara Barrie added her fine personality to the evening. Pamela Myers was superb as the oddball blonde, especially in her show-stopping number "Another Hundred People." I could go on and on with praises, but I'll just add that everyone in the cast was great and almost every song in the show was great. What more can one ask for."

Some works grow on you. You only come to love them after multiple hearings. This was the case for me with Mahler's Second, my favorite symphony. Obviously, that was not the case with *Company*. I clearly immediately loved it that first time I saw it. By some coincidence, New York's local channel five happened to show the D. A. Pennebaker documentary, *Original Cast Album: Company,* about the making of the original cast recording, within a week of my first attending *Company*. The documentary, which was also broadcast on PBS decades later, is currently available on DVD from the Criterion Collection, as well as Criterion's subscriber streaming service and HBO Max. It can also be viewed on YouTube
[https://www.youtube.com/watch?v=tWsG2dEoUsA&t=326s]

Unfortunately, there is no video recording of the original production of *Company*. This is especially egregious because the scenic design by Boris Aronson was quite ingenious. Usually, scenic design is not something I'm concerned with, and I didn't mention in my review, but Aronson's design, looking something like an Erector-set version of cubes and rectangles, (each one used as a different apartment that the lead character, Bobby, visits) was revolutionary and, like the cast, was never surpassed in other productions I saw later.

In 1993, there were concerts given in California and New York with the original cast, celebrating *Company*'s twenty-third anniversary. Those concerts contained all the songs, but cut most of the dialogue and, of course, did not have the Aronson set. The first, hosted by Angela Lansbury, was given in Long Beach in January and a second set of three concerts was given at Lincoln Center's Vivian Beaumont Theater in April, hosted by Patti LuPone. Bootleg videos of both concerts exist, but I think the New York video, which is on You Tube, is the better one.

Performers often say that their performance can be affected by the audience. I think that was the case with the reunion concerts. At the two New York reunion concerts I attended, most people in the audience were long-time *Company* lovers like me. Many of them had, no doubt, seen the original Broadway production several times. Audience reaction to the songs was *so* overwhelming that I suspect it fed the cast's desire to give it their all. They did three performances over one weekend; two performances on Saturday, April 11, and a single performance the next day. I attended both Saturday performances. Amazingly, most of the cast was as good as they had been twenty-three years earlier.

It was a love fest. I wrote this about the concert:

"The electricity for both performances I saw could have lit up the City, and when George Furth, Harold Prince, and Stephen Sondheim came out to take their bows, the theater was filled with excitement, love, and warmth."

Elaine Stritch was as magnificent in 1993 as she was in 1970. Pamela Myers who "owns" *Another Hundred People* may have outdone herself in the 1993 concert—it seemed even better than twenty-three years earlier! Beth Howland's rendition of *(Not) Getting Married Today* was, perhaps, a tad less coherent than originally, but still awe-inspiring. Here are the two concerts. The first is the January concert from California, cut down to thirty-six minutes, the second is the complete April New York concert, coming in at eighty minutes.

[https://www.youtube.com/watch?v=H4IflVde1Is&t=1944s]
[https://www.youtube.com/watch?v=8QRQzVvgT-A&t=110s]

The 1993 reunion concert was my first opportunity to see Dean Jones do the role of Bobby. I was more impressed than I expected. I always felt that Larry Kert was probably better in the role because he had a better singing voice than Jones. (Kert was a musical theater regular who had created the role of Tony in West Side Story, while Jones was a visitor from the world of Disney movies.) Dean Jones left *Company* only one month after it opened. It was reported that he was going through a painful divorce and performing an emotionally charged show about marriage and relationships eight times a week exacerbated the pain.

Some say Jones acted the role better, although I found Kert compelling, especially in the scene toward the end with Stritch (as the *married* Joanne)—when she asks him, "When are we going to make it?" and, a bit later, maintains, "I'll take care of you," to which Bobby queries, "But who will I take care of?" Joanne understands the epiphany he is having, even if *he* doesn't do so quite yet. They then sit motionless, in complete silence, staring at each other. The audience will soon realize, that, in those moments of silence, he is finally having the epiphany that results in his emotional breakthrough as he sings one of Sondheim's most masterful and poignant songs, *Being Alive*. I just can't imagine that scene being done better. In all of the subsequent productions that I saw, I did not see two actors duplicate that silent, motionless scene. Of course, much of the credit probably goes to the Broadway director, Harold Prince.

It should be noted that Kert was nominated for a Tony that year, not Jones, and, as far as I know, that was the only time a replacement cast member in an original production was nominated. Strangely, Kert lost to Hal Linden (later of TV's *Barney Miller* fame) for his role in *The Rothschilds*. (I saw *The Rothschilds*, and I barely remember it, having no memory of Hal Linden's performance in it. Sometimes the "Tonys" get it wrong.) *Company* was nominated for a record thirteen Tonys, and won six, including Best Musical and Best Score.

Larry Kert singing the last half of Being Alive from *Company*: [https://www.youtube.com/watch?v=z6WmcSi9aZ4]

Company opened in London in 1972 with most of the original Broadway cast and Larry Kert. There is a London cast recording of *Company*, but it's a hybrid! Kert recorded Bobby's songs in London, before the production opened there, and his songs were integrated into the original cast recording, making it the "London" cast recording.

It is well known that Oscar Hammerstein was Sondheim's mentor and surrogate father. Sondheim often said that if Hammerstein had been a butcher, he would have become a butcher. Yet Sondheim's lyrics are a world apart from Hammerstein's. Indeed, Sondheim's lyrics are much closer to those of Cole Porter, perhaps also Noel Coward, and even Richard Rodger's first great collaborator, Lorenz Hart. Hammerstein wrote pseudo-religious anthems: *You'll Never Walk Alone, Climb Every Mountain*, polemics like *You've Got to be Carefully Taught*; and, of course, lots of emotional love songs. Subtlety, sophistication, and wit-and-fun wordplay were not the hallmarks of Hammerstein's lyrics as they became with Sondheim after *West Side Story*.

When watching *Company* the first time, I realized I was watching something new and, perhaps, revolutionary. The first glimmerings of this came to me early on, in the first act song, *Sorry–Grateful*. In response to Bobby's query about being married, a friend sings:

> You're always sorry,
> You're always grateful,
> You're always wondering
> What might have been--
> Then she walks in.

Of course, like the rest of those in the audience who hadn't seen the show or heard that song before, I was expecting a soaring melodic musical climax accompanied by lyrics that are an ode in praise of the wife of the character singing the song. That's what Hammerstein would have done. Not Sondheim! In a moment of genius, he tones the music down and the song continues with:

> And still you're sorry,
> And still you're grateful,
> And still you wonder
> And still you doubt--
> And she goes out."

No, this is not a song about idealized love, this is a song about real life and real-life relationships.
[https://www.youtube.com/watch?v=HVoFRwniZMI]
There are plenty of love songs that have been written about a mythically perfect person who the singer has not yet met—and the ideal life they will have together, but, Bobby, in his great song of emotional discovery near the end of *Company*, *Being Alive*, has come to a more realistic understanding of the commitment he (and in a broader sense anyone) must make in a marriage and the need it fulfills:

Someone to hold you too close,
Someone to hurt you too deep,
Someone to sit in your chair,
To ruin your sleep."

With all the great songs that came before, this final song of emotional discovery sealed *Company*'s fate of becoming my favorite musical of all time.

Being Alive sung by Dean Jones in the original cast recording [in the first clip], then by Larry Kert in the London cast recording [in the second]:

[https://www.youtube.com/watch?v=WmVwshV5ecw]
[https://www.youtube.com/watch?v=e9Ci_bVz8L4]

Of course, after seeing *Company*, I had to see the original Broadway production of every musical Sondheim wrote thereafter, including the short-lived *Merrily We Roll Along*.

Encores! and the City Center

Many musicals I saw were performances at Encores! Those readers who do not live in the New York metropolitan area are probably not familiar with Encores! It is a company that gives concert performances of previously performed Broadway musicals mostly not given again since their initial Broadway run. Encores! began in 1994 with *Fiorello!*. Often, especially in Encores! early days, the cast would perform with score in hand. They do three musicals a year; one each in February, March, and May. Each musical gets a one-week run, starting on Wednesday and including four performances on weekends. What makes them better than most other companies that do Broadway revivals, is that they employ a full orchestra and often get bona fide Broadway stars to perform. Their prices are lower than for most Broadway shows, and they do their performances at the New York City Center, a relatively large (over 2000 seats) venue that was the original home of the New York City Opera and the New York City Ballet.

The New York City Center is located on West 55th Street, two blocks south of Carnegie Hall. It was originally built in 1923 as a home for the Shriners (a fraternity having its foundations in Freemasonry) and called Mecca Temple. Twenty years later, the Shriners were unable to pay its real estate taxes and the building became the property of New York City. Fiorello La Guardia, mayor at the time, had the foresight to turn it into a budget-conscious performing arts theater (and probably why Encores! debut show was *Fiorello!*). Besides being the home for the New York City Ballet and Opera companies, in its early days, it presented stage plays and musicals. [https://en.wikipedia.org/wiki/New_York_City_Center]

By 1994, when Encores! was launched, both the City Opera and Ballet companies had already moved to Lincoln Center, the City Center had become mainly a showcase for smaller ballet companies, albeit prestigious ones, like Alvin Ailey, as well as various touring groups including theater companies from other countries. [https://en.wikipedia.org/wiki/Encores!]

In recent years, Encores! sometimes has added a two-week run of a fully staged musical in the summer, and begun what they call "Off-Center," reviving Off-Broadway musicals, usually three each summer. Even their regular concert performances have become fuller productions, often with sets, and very rarely now do you see cast members with just score in hand. Indeed, I remember a performance of *Irma le Douce* a few seasons ago with a very elaborate and beautiful set. Even with all these added performances, the Encores! series takes up only a total of under two months of the City Center's yearly calendar, but somehow they seem to have become the City Center's flagship attraction, and rightly so I think. I have seen about 80% of all of Encores! productions.

Encores! wasn't the first group to revive Broadway musicals at the City Center. In the mid-1950s, the City Center Light Opera Company began reviving Broadway musicals at City Center. It was still going strong a decade later when I began attending musicals and I saw several of their productions. They were completely staged with a full orchestra. They usually did four productions a season, each during one month in the spring, each show having a week-long run. The company was run by Jean Dalrymple and they could afford to do full-scale productions for as little as a week-long run because Ms. Dalrymple purchased the sets of closing Broadway musicals! (While I read that at the time, I also wondered what the cost of *storing* those sets was?) The City Center Light Opera Company folded after their 1968 season, but I got to see quite a few of their productions in their last half dozen years of existence. For a listing of their productions, see https://ovrtur.com/biography/10134312. The listing in IBDB is incomplete and inaccurate.

Among the more memorable performances I saw there was *Porgy and Bess* in its operatic version, with little dialogue, starring William Warfield as Porgy and conducted by the City Opera's General Director, Julius Rudel, *Wonderful Town* with Elaine Stritch as Ruth Sherwood, *Guys and Dolls* with Hugh O'Brian as Sky Masterson and Vivian Blaine recreating her Miss Adelaide. There was also *My Fair Lady* with Inga Swensen and Fritz Weaver, who not long after that, starred together on Broadway in *Baker Street*, a Sherlock Holmes musical!

Broadway Bootlegs

I have previously written about pirated opera recordings and my view of them. There are many Broadway theater performances that can be found on YouTube. Both pirating and copying to YouTube are technically illegal but, in actuality, a treasure.

In large part, what I write here is a response to a comment I read on a YouTube bootleg video of the Encores! production of Sondheim's *Anyone Can Whistle* starring Sutton Foster and Raul Esparza. The person commenting said he would get immense satisfaction if the person who had sat in a darkened theater and recorded the show for two-and-a-half hours was arrested. I see it differently. There is no movie or TV version of *Anyone Can Whistle*, nor is there likely to be. Other than seeing an actual live performance, the pirate is the only way you will see the important show that immediately preceded *Company* in the development of one of Broadway's greatest composers.

Sutton Foster is a magnificent musical theater performer, but watching movies and TV you will learn little of this facet of her art. No producer has made a movie version of *Thoroughly Modern Millie* or *Violet* with Foster. For those who only know her from the TV shows *Younger* and *Bunheads*, or the movie *Gravy*, we can see the full glory of her performances in *Millie* and *Violet* because someone sat in a darkened theater and recorded them. This applies to numerous other theater performers whose film appearances don't do justice to their stage achievements, such as Patti LuPone and Bernadette Peters.

If the owner of the copyright material isn't exploiting it, it is probably because he or she doesn't believe there is any profit in doing so. Should we be deprived of wonderful performances because of the whim of those producers? Are Foster, LuPone, and Peters lamenting the fact that people can see these performances on YouTube for free and they are not being paid a royalty—or are they happy that these performances exist for present-day viewing and posterity? I can't answer for them, but I hope it is the latter.

It is because of the whim of short-sighted producers that posterity has Audrey Hepburn's Eliza Doolittle, not Julie Andrews; and Rosalind Russell's Mama Rose, not Ethel Merman's. Had the technology to record shows from the audience existed in the 1950s and *My Fair Lady* been secretly recorded with its original cast, do you suppose Julie Andrews might be overjoyed, even if she's not collecting royalties? I get no satisfaction from someone being convicted for preserving theatrical history. (I would, however, get intense satisfaction from the conviction of persons who foment insurrection.)

I should highlight that I am talking specifically about people who post on YouTube to disseminate to a wider audience for free. If someone is *selling* those recordings for more than cost, that is another matter, as they are profiting from someone else's labors. Still, the fact that the performance exists for posterity is wonderful. It may also be true that the person who posted the bootleg on YouTube is not the person who actually recorded the performance, but someone who just acquired it. Of course, the person who recorded it, not being the actual owner of the property, has no standing to demand it be taken down.

Disclaimer: I have never recorded a live performance. I just enjoy the fruits of others' labors.

Ethel Merman, Patti LuPone, Sutton Foster, and More

Ethel Merman and Patti LuPone are two of my all-time favorite female musical theater performers. Then there is Sutton Foster who is one among several current female performers whom I greatly admire. She is to be the representative in this group because she fits in with LuPone and Merman, having played a role in common. All three played Reno Sweeney to great acclaim in Cole Porter's *Anything Goes* on Broadway.

Ethel Merman

Ethel Merman was a true original, a force of nature, and one of the greatest musical theater stars ever to grace the stage. Ethel Merman defines the term, "Broadway belter." Indeed, the term was coined in recognition of her Broadway performance debut in Gershwin's, *Girl Crazy* in 1930 in which she shook the rafters with *I Got Rhythm.*

[https://www.youtube.com/watch?v=0pWug6_RoQA]

Yes, I know there are people who can't abide her; who think she simply screams a lot. This is the part where I should tell you what I think makes her great, but I can't. Is it that unique, *powerful* singing voice and phrasing? Partly, but she was also a larger-than-life brash personality who transcended the art form she was a part of. This may not paint a complete picture, but it's all I can come up with. Hopefully the links will help you make your own determination.

I had the privilege of seeing "the Merm" on stage five times. In 1966, she starred in a limited-run revival of one of her greatest roles, Annie Oakley, in Irving Berlin's masterpiece, *Annie Get Your Gun*. At the age of fifty-seven, she was much too old to play the teenaged character, Annie, but once she stepped on stage, no one cared. She had that voice of steel and outsized personality to carry off and dominate the show, making her age irrelevant. I loved it so much I went to see it three times!

[https://www.youtube.com/watch?v=rhOTMf84gFo]

Hello Dolly! premiered in January, 1964 with Carol Channing in the lead as Dolly Gallagher Levi. It ran for nearly seven years. The show's composer-lyricist, Jerry Herman, said that he wrote the show with Ethel Merman in mind for the lead, but she turned it down, leaving it open for Carol Channing to get the role of her career. Somewhere along the road, Merman must have had a change of heart, because in 1970 she became the final Dolly in the original Broadway production. Jerry Herman wrote two new songs for Merman to sing, or perhaps they were two songs he had cut when Channing, whose vocal capabilities were completely different from Merman's, came aboard. That was the only time Merman was a cast replacement in a Broadway show and it was her last appearance on Broadway. I saw it in March, 1970.

I saw Merman one more time, on May 10, 1982, in a concert with the American Symphony Orchestra at Carnegie Hall. By that time, while she still was loud and brash, her singing voice had developed a wobble. Still, she was marvelous! It was to be her last live concert.

Ginger Rogers and Ethel Merman became stars in 1930 when they co-starred in Gershwin's, *Girl Crazy*. In both cases, their last Broadway appearance, decades later, was as the main character, Dolly Gallagher

Levi, in *Hello Dolly!* Rogers played the role from 1964 through 1967; Merman played the role in 1970. While Ginger Rogers abandoned Broadway to become a major movie star after *Girl Crazy* (she only did one short stint in a Broadway show between *Girl Crazy* and *Hello Dolly!*) Merman had a spotty Hollywood career, but as we all know, one of the all-time great Broadway careers. Merman created the leading roles in about a dozen shows in the '30s, '40s, and '50s. Among them were *Panama Hattie, Du Barry Was a Lady,* Sally Adams in *Call Me Madam* and, finally, one of her greatest triumphs, Mama Rose in *Gypsy*.

Sondheim and Merman

Stephen Sondheim was one of my favorite Broadway composers, and Ethel Merman was one of my favorite Broadway performers. So, whose side do I take when they are in conflict?

The story goes that the young Stephen Sondheim (then age twenty-seven), who had quickly gained fame in his initial Broadway outing as the lyricist for *West Side Story* in 1957, was eager to write the music, as well as the lyrics, for a Broadway musical. He was initially attached to *Gypsy* to write both the music and lyrics, but Merman would only agree to do the show if the music was written by a more experienced composer. So, Sondheim reluctantly agreed to relinquish the composing chores, and Jule Styne came aboard.

Given the success of Sondheim's subsequent career, one might think that Merman should have given the newcomer a chance. Ultimately, it proved to be the right decision. Jule Styne wrote what is clearly *his* masterpiece. It is, far and away, better than *High Button Shoes, Gentleman Prefer Blondes, Bells are Ringing, Funny Girl,* and others that Styne wrote. Some critics even call *Gypsy* the greatest American musical.

As much as I am a fan of Sondheim, I will agree that there is no way, in 1959, so early in Sondheim's career, that he would have equaled, let alone surpassed, the music that Styne composed for *Gypsy*. Sondheim's *Saturday Night* and *A Funny Thing Happened on the Way to the Forum*, are the musicals that Sondheim composed the music for before and after *Gypsy* appeared. Whatever musical merits they have, they do not come near the musical peak achieved by Styne in *Gypsy*. It wasn't until 1970 and the appearance of *Company* that Sondheim matured into the composer who could surpass Styne. So, Ethel was right.

Merman's Screen Career

It is unfortunate that Ethel Merman didn't get to recreate most of her wonderful stage roles for the movie screen. So how does one, today, see for themselves the art of Ethel Merman? Her film career began with a number of shorts made in the early nineteen-thirties.

[https://www.youtube.com/watch?v=dSqKOtR0vSo]
[https://www.youtube.com/watch?v=LkF3Qp44NdE]
[https://www.youtube.com/watch?v=kb8qG7LDyok]
[https://www.youtube.com/watch?v=B2iTBCl5Ce4]
[https://www.youtube.com/watch?v=EPkgU3cc7Ck&t=84s]
[https://www.youtube.com/watch?v=EPHNxgffM2c&t=18s]

She graduated to feature films later, in the mid-thirties, when she co-starred in two Eddie Cantor films and two with Bing Crosby. Here's a clip from one of the Cantor films, *Strike me Pink* from 1936.

[https://www.youtube.com/watch?v=MtI8sa1VoWU]

The second film she did with Crosby should have been the best film showcase for her at that time. It was Cole Porter's *Anything Goes* in 1936, but Paramount truncated the score, rewrote the book, and turned the main character, Reno Sweeney, into a supporting player for their big star, Bing Crosby. Among the songs cut was *Blow, Gabriel. Blow.*

[https://www.youtube.com/watch?v=8PfMR1jpkw4]

They even cut the title song down to a fifteen second snippet just before the opening credits. Instead they inserted second-rate songs by composers other than Cole Porter. Here's Ethel and Bing singing *You're the Top*, followed by a link to the full movie

[https://www.youtube.com/watch?v=LCfqIXiLxSE]
[https://www.youtube.com/watch?v=hrB8oX5lP_U]

You may notice in the credits the movie is titled *Tops is the Limit*. That is because, when Paramount sold the film's television rights, their 1956 film version of *Anything Goes* was then running in theaters. Bing Crosby returned to star in that later version, but Ethel was nowhere in sight. Except for the songs, the 1956 film version also strayed from the original book.

Merman's last film during the '30s was *Alexander's Ragtime Band* (1938), again a supporting role, but it had an assortment of Irving Berlin classics, making it, perhaps, her best film exposure during that period.

[https://www.youtube.com/watch?v=c-TBIuY9jUY] (Ignore the fourteen-second "introduction.")

A brief appearance in *Stage Door Canteen*, in 1943, was her only screen appearance in the 1940s.

[https://www.youtube.com/watch?v=UUizqStPMww&list=PL3ARSnVuWufxXEWd011DSR889bEM7oARd]

She returned to the screen strongly in 1953, recreating one of her great stage roles as Sally Adams in Irving Berlin's, *Call Me Madam*. It was the high point of her screen career. She is in top form in a movie that was a faithful adaptation of the stage show, enhanced by support from the ever-charming Donald O'Connor, as well as Vera Ellen, and George Saunders. If you want to know what the fuss about Merman was, this is the film to see. The first two links below are of the duet *You're Just in Love,* the show-stopping duet and one of Berlin's greatest songs. The first clip is Merman with her original co-star from the 1950 Broadway production, Russell Nype. The second is from the film version with Donald O'Connor. After seeing those, I know you will want to see the entire movie; the third link.

[https://www.youtube.com/watch?v=BJ0YAOyxEXU]
[https://www.youtube.com/watch?v=2LAijDQ2cIE]
[https://www.youtube.com/watch?v=aw06yeOhbQQ]

I'd like to digress here to write about Russell Nype, as *You're Just in Love* would not have been written were it not for him. He had a wonderful rapport with Ethel, as you can see in the clip. During the *Call Me Madam* out-of-town tryouts, Merman was so impressed with young Nype that she told Berlin, "I want a number with the kid." (For a more detailed account, see:

[https://www.irvingberlin.com/youre-just-in-love]).

Twenty years later he co-starred with Ethel in *Hello Dolly!* I wouldn't be surprised if she specifically asked for him.

The clip of Merman and Nype singing *You're Just in Love* is the only recording I know of the two of them, together singing that duet. The original production of *Call Me Madam* was financed by RCA Victor, who held the rights for the original cast recording. Unfortunately, Merman was under contract to Decca records (now MCA) and Decca refused to lend her out. Victor went ahead with an "original cast recording", substituting Dinah Shore for Merman, while Decca put out its own *Call Me Madam* recording with Merman. Thus, on vinyl, Merman is heard singing *You're Just in Love* with Dick Haymes!

[https://www.youtube.com/watch?v=nJ9Wn37BXBU]

Ethel's standby in *Call Me Madam* was a much younger lesser-known actress, Elaine Stritch. Stritch never had to go on for Merman, but when Merman left the show during the national tour, Stritch took over the role. Nype was equally at ease singing with her. If you can take listening to *You're Just in Love* twice more (I always can), here are two video clips of Nype and Stritch, clearly made about fifty years apart. It's rather touching.

[https://www.youtube.com/watch?v=4kmOjZfcR0U]
[https://www.youtube.com/watch?v=oL1QhCQuhhA]

Nype won two Tony Awards. His first was for *Call Me Madam* in 1951, the second, eight years later, was for the musical *Goldilocks,* which happened to star Elaine Stritch.

The year after the movie version of *Call Me Madam* in 1954, Merman starred in another big-budget movie musical, *There's No Business Like Show Business*, the title coming from the Irving Berlin show-business anthem first performed by Ethel in *Annie Get Your Gun*. With more Berlin standards, and co-stars that included Dan Dailey, Donald O'Connor (again), Marilyn Monroe, and Johnny Ray, this is another must-see for Ethel fans—and would-be Ethel fans.

[https://www.youtube.com/watch?v=Lhn9rIx3y_s] (Full movie)

Between those two movies, television enabled Merman to partially redress some film grievances.

In 1954, TV's *Colgate Comedy Hour* presented an abridged performance of Cole Porter's *Anything Goes* in which Merman recreated her stage role of Reno Sweeney. Unfortunately, it had to be cut to fit the one-hour time slot (including commercials). If it strayed a bit from the original book, it, however, retained most of Porter's great score and put Reno Sweeney back as the central character. It also was extravagantly cast, co-starring Frank Sinatra and Bert Lahr. It also had a few added songs, but they were all by Cole Porter. Most notably was the duet *Friendship,* which was taken from the 1939 Porter musical *Du Barry Was a Lady,* which had starred Merman and Lahr, who reprised *Friendship* on this telecast. Since that telecast most stage revivals of *Anything Goes* have included *Friendship*. First is a clip of *Friendship,* followed by the complete telecast minus the commercials.

[https://www.youtube.com/watch?v=Q_t82ir4REQ]
[https://www.youtube.com/watch?v=YeX2tNEFRQI]

As usual, Merman was not chosen to repeat her stage role in the 1943 movie version of *Du Barry Was a Lady*. The part went to Lucille Ball. That film also marked the screen debut of Zero Mostel. Here's the film version of *Friendship* with Ball and Red Skelton, followed by the trailer for the movie.

[https://www.youtube.com/watch?v=Qm1AZOmNxbw]
[https://www.youtube.com/watch?v=c8ZnIzAQ_YI]

Another bit of trivia here, one of Merman's replacements in the original production of *Du Barry Was a Lady* was Gypsy Rose Lee! Here's Ethel Merman and Gypsy Rose Lee in a 1967 segment of Gypsy Rose Lee's talk show, talking, among other things, about the musical *Gypsy,* wherein Merman had played Gypsy Rose Lee's mother.

[https://www.youtube.com/watch?v=yqCgnX0s0M8]

Also in 1954, according to IMDB, there was a telecast of *Panama Hattie* with Ethel Merman and Art Carney. Unfortunately, I was able only to find a few minutes of song highlights of it on YouTube.

[https://www.youtube.com/watch?v=kUb1U44v3JE&t=85s]

Hopefully, it exists somewhere in complete form and someday will be made available. Perhaps someone reading this has a copy and will post it on YouTube.

One would hope that, over a decade later, in the videotape age of the 1970s, I would have found a copy of the 1967 telecast of an abridged version of the 1966 *Annie Get Your Gun* revival, but that has not happened. It was abridged to seventy-five minutes (for a ninety-minute time slot), but, even so, all the musical numbers were there (including the terrific *Old Fashioned Wedding* counterpoint duet written especially for that production.)

[https://www.youtube.com/watch?v=H4qWAESB17E].

I, of course, saw the TV show when it aired. It was a treasure and an antidote to Betty Hutton's tacky movie portrayal in 1950. That the telecast appears to have been erased or otherwise destroyed is a crime. Perhaps this, too, exists somewhere in whole form.

A telecast of *Annie Get Your Gun* from a decade earlier, with Mary Martin and John Raitt, still exists and can be found on YouTube.

[https://www.youtube.com/watch?v=qHhjqjylP60]. (Full telecast)

Merman's friend and rival, Mary Martin, is fine in the title role, ten times better than Hutton, but nowhere near Merman's definitive portrayal. I am also struck by John Raitt's Frank Butler, and how much he appears to be enjoying himself. Incidentally, the terrific Frank Butler in the 1966 production was Bruce Yarnell, who had a magnificent baritone voice. He was a rising young operatic baritone when his life was cut short a few years later in a plane crash in 1973.

Merman recorded *Annie Get Your Gun* three times: the original cast recording in 1946, the 1966 revival cast recording and, again in 1973 with The London Festival Orchestra and Chorus. She was great in the two earlier recordings, but, by 1973 you can hear a slight diminution of her vocalizing with the beginnings of the earlier-mentioned "wobble."

While it is understandable that Merman did not play Annie Oakley in the movie version, as she was over forty when the film version was made, what might be forgiven onstage and on the small screen would have been glaring on the big screen. Judy Garland, who was originally slated to do the movie, would have been perfect. Betty Hutton wasn't in their league. What we have left of Judy's performance are two numbers filmed by Judy before she was fired. In *Doin' What Comes Naturally* the second song on the clip, she's terrific. However, in *I'm an Indian Too*, the first song shown here, she clearly seems off, probably headed to the nervous breakdown that caused her being fired from the film. Incidentally, *I'm an Indian Too* has been cut from recent revivals as being insensitive to Native Americans. The first clip, with Garland, is followed by the way it *should* sound as done by Merman (from the 1966 revival cast recording when she was fifty-seven), and the final clip is Betty Hutton. As far as I'm concerned, the less said about Hutton's version, the better. However, I seem to be in the minority based on the comments accompanying the clip on YouTube.

[https://www.youtube.com/watch?v=ucmdcigpeos]
[https://www.youtube.com/watch?v=yI-0DMTmx9M]
[https://www.youtube.com/watch?v=T7pLm2VPntQ]

What is not understandable is why Ethel Merman did not get to repeat her Mama Rose on screen. That Julie Andrews didn't get to recreate Eliza on screen, and Merman didn't get to recreate Mama Rose, are two of the greatest failings of the transfer of stage musicals to the big screen.

The movie version of *Gypsy* was made in 1962. Merman was passed over for Rosalind Russell. Russell enjoyed success on Broadway in the Bernstein/Comden/Green presentation, *Wonderful Town*, a musical version of *My Sister Eileen*, the non-musical movie version of which Russell had starred in a decade earlier, but she wasn't really a singer. One must assume that her songs in *Wonderful Town* were geared to the limitations of her voice, as Bernstein knew who he was writing for when he wrote the songs. In *Gypsy*, Russell was asked to sing songs written for the magnificent voice of Ethel Merman—Russell's renditions are a pale substitute. One might purchase the original cast album to luxuriate in Merman's vocalizing; but one seemingly wouldn't get the movie soundtrack album to hear Russell sing the songs.

The following links provide an interesting contrast. First is Rosalind Russell in *Rose's Turn* from the *Gypsy* movie. The second is that same fragment, but, this time, some enterprising "YouTuber" spent hours synchronizing Ethel Merman's voice to Russell's clip. *What a difference a voice makes.!*

[https://www.youtube.com/watch?v=VhYzZXA2gL0]
[https://www.youtube.com/watch?v=Totzt9duNNE]

While I did not see the original production of *Gypsy*, I saw all four of its Broadway revivals—starring, in chronological order: Angela Lansbury (1974), Tyne Daly (1989), Bernadette Peters (2003), and Patti LuPone (2007 at Encores!—where I saw it, and in 2008 on Broadway). In another role she has in common with Merman, LuPone also did Annie Oakley, but only one benefit performance in New York (1998). Lansbury, Daly, and LuPone each won a Tony for their portrayal of Mama Rose in *Gypsy*; Merman and Peters did not.

Here's LuPone's intense version of *Rose's Turn* to lead us into the next segment.

[https://www.youtube.com/watch?v=OTdPWmHstjE]

Patti LuPone

I love classic and dramatic plays and often attended the small repertory companies that populated Off-Broadway and Off-Off-Broadway in the 1960s and '70s, which I write about in some detail in the next section. So, I certainly was not going to miss the inaugural New York engagement of the newly formed City Center Acting Company in 1972. The company was made up of the first graduating class of the Juilliard School's new Drama Division, created when the school moved to their new quarters at Lincoln Center. The Drama Division and the repertory company that grew out it, the Acting Company, were headed by John Houseman. I had seen a wonderful production of Sheridan's, *The School for Scandal* with the APA/ Phoenix Theater (more details about this company in the next section) in 1966, but that didn't stop me from going to the Good Shepherd-Faith Church on West 66th Street, where the Acting Company was performing its production of *The School for Scandal*, and was I glad I did. Among other things, it introduced me to a young actress who was to become one of my favorites, and, ultimately, a sort of successor to Ethel Merman. This is what I wrote of Patti LuPone, the day after the September 29, 1972 performance of *The School for Scandal*, and the first time I saw her:

"Patti LuPone was an absolute doll as Lady Teazle. Miss LuPone, with the cutest nose and lips, made you love her from the beginning, so you can understand Sir Peter's feelings for her."

I was clearly smitten!
[https://www.youtube.com/watch?v=WBdF2_-Zt24]
[https://www.youtube.com/watch?v=eELrTLyGCeE]

While I found a number of actors to admire who were then performing in various classics throughout the city, few of the actresses impressed me. Therefore, Patti LuPone was like a breath of fresh air as one of the few actresses I'd seen who could do justice to some of the female roles in classic plays. I should state that, among the other actors in that first performance of the City Center Acting Company I saw who later became well known, were David Ogden Stiers and Kevin Kline. (Kline was romantically involved with LuPone at the time). Mr. Kline, who subsequently became one of my favorite actors, didn't impress me very much then. Primarily because of Miss LuPone, I made up my mind to try to see everything the Acting Company did when they were in New York. I went back three times to see the remainder of their productions that season. LuPone was in only one of the others, Gorky's, *The Lower Depths*. As they were a touring company, their appearances in New York were limited and, when in New York, they performed in various venues.

The next season, in 1973, with the Acting Company now at Broadway's Billy Rose Theater, I saw LuPone in Chekhov's, *The Three Sisters*, as well as a more contemporary play that I didn't care for, because, for the most part, I couldn't understand it, and what little I did, I found implausible. It was a play originally written in 1962 by James Saunders, titled *Next Time I'll Sing for You*. The three performances given at the Billy Rose Theater are that play's only Broadway credit. That said, I loved Patti in it. This is what I wrote a few days after the January 2, 1974 performance I saw:

"Here, Miss LuPone plays the unpredictable Lizzie absolutely delightfully and was the hit of the show. She was especially campy, and she is an actress with a flair and personality that should make her go far."

Despite its title, *Next Time I'll Sing for You* is not a musical. Patti did perform in a musical that season, *The Beggar's Opera*. I didn't see it. I can't imagine why not! Ultimately, I got to see LuPone in a wide variety of dramatic roles with the Acting Company and she certainly fulfilled the acting promise she showed the first time I saw her. Until I saw her in *The Robber Bridegroom* the following year, I had no idea that she sang. And *could* she sing! Everything I'd seen her in earlier were dramatic performances.

In *The Robber Bridegroom*, which I saw on October 10, 1975 in the since demolished Harkness Theater near Lincoln Center, Patti did something that could not have been done a few years earlier. She sang her big number, aptly titled *Nothin' Up*, with *nothing on*! The fearless Miss LuPone, standing straight up on top of a bed and facing an audience of hundreds, with her co-star (Kevin Kline, of course) still on stage (I'm not sure—I wasn't looking at him), she sang the entire three-minute or so song stark naked. Obviously, it made a great impression on me, but it seemed all in a day's work for LuPone. She doesn't even mention it in her memoir. Here's a clip, sorry, it's just the audio:

[https://www.youtube.com/watch?v=WMSXafjv_9g]

If Ethel Merman had done that in her early career, she would have been arrested—as her contemporary, Mae West, who was arrested for a lot less, would have advised her.

Merman did, however, have the perfect song, had she wanted to be that daring. It goes like this:

> In olden days, a glimpse of stocking
> Was looked on as something shocking.
> But now, God knows,
> Anything goes.

Cole Porter was clearly seeing forward from 1934.

Almost exactly twenty years later, on October 19, 1995, I saw Patti do her solo show, *Patti LuPone on Broadway*. In the second half of what actually was a concert, she did a retrospective of big numbers from shows she had been in earlier. The idea was to take something from each earlier show, like wear a stole she *stole* from another show to sing that show's big number, thus wearing what she wore in the show from which the song came. She did not sing *Nothing Up*, but I recall thinking that if she asked for audience requests at the end of the performance it would have been humorous had I asked her to sing *Nothin' Up* in the same costume she had worn in *The Robber*

Bridegroom. Since the Acting Company's *Robber Bridegroom* that Patti had appeared in played only a very limited run (for about two weeks) in New York—and it was before she was well-known—I expect there would have been only a couple of people in that audience who would have gotten the joke.

Shortly after the Acting Company's, *The Robber Bridegroom,* Houseman produced a Broadway production of that musical that ran for four months. Patti LuPone wrote in her memoir in 2010 (*Patti LuPone: A Memoir*) that she had been livid that she was asked to audition for that production, when, despite doing only fourteen performances in New York, she was nominated for a Tony as featured actress for her performance in that show. She refused to audition. She relates that Kevin Kline did audition, but didn't get the part. Barry Bostwick did!

As well as *The Robber Bridegroom*, I also saw Patti that season in Marlowe's, *Edward II,* in the trouser role of the title character's son, and in Saroyan's, *The Time of Your Life* as Kitty. Thus, despite her positive impression singing in *The Robber Bridegroom*, I still thought of LuPone as a dramatic actress and expected her career to be more along the lines of Ethel Barrymore than Ethel Merman. Her breakthrough role in *Evita* changed all that.

Starting with *Evita*, LuPone took her voice and oversized personality off to become a Broadway musical theater icon.

[https://www.youtube.com/watch?v=7aqst6B8h5A]

But, unfortunately, by the 1970s, when Patti became a star, fewer Broadway musicals were being written for that type of personality, so Patti created very few roles. In the thirty-year period between 1930 and 1960, Merman created twelve roles in Broadway musicals written for her. In the forty-plus years since *Evita*, LuPone has created only two roles: a supporting role in *Women on the Verge of a Nervous Breakdown*, and a co-starring role with Christine Ebersole in *War Paint*. There actually should be three, because, in 1976, after leaving the Acting Company (and before *Evita*), she created the title role in what was to be a Broadway-bound musical, *The Baker's Wife*. It never made it to Broadway, but she got a lovely song out of it, *Meadowlark*.

[https://www.youtube.com/watch?v=sWVGyzqXZ3w]

It should be remembered that Patti did not create the role of Eva Peron in *Evita*, it was premiered in London by Elaine Paige. The reverse of that happened years later with another Andrew Lloyd Webber musical LuPone starred in, *Sunset Boulevard*.

[https://www.youtube.com/watch?v=jejUMxyUOIE]

LuPone was signed to create the role in London and then bring it to Broadway. She did create the role in London, but before the Broadway production, Webber mounted a production in Los Angeles with Glenn Close in the lead. Evidently, he was so taken with Close's performance, he hired her to star in the forthcoming Broadway production. Patti was not amused. Actually, she was devastated. She sued Andrew Lloyd Webber who settled out of court for something in the area of a million dollars. According to her memoir, she used the money to fix up her Connecticut home and build a swimming pool.

First a news clip about the LuPone/Close *Sunset Boulevard* controversy, then Patti singing *Just One Look* from *Sunset Boulevard*, followed by the complete show with Patti from the Sydmonton Festival Workshop performance of September 5, 1992. In light of things to come, the final shot of Patti and Lloyd Webber hugging is rather bittersweet. The last link is to the full West End version in 1993 with Patti and the elaborate sets. Unfortunately it's in washed-out black and white.

[https://www.youtube.com/watch?v=pZzbGfVQ974&t=12s]
[https://www.youtube.com/watch?v=jejUMxyUOIE]
[https://www.youtube.com/watch?v=257pxUReamU]
[https://www.youtube.com/watch?v=-BP3rWfSUt0]

If you want to make your own decision about who was better, go to page 101 where you can find a link to a performance with Close.

Interestingly, after the *Sunset Boulevard* fiasco, LuPone did several Sondheim shows:
Sweeney Todd
[https://www.youtube.com/watch?v=mYpVwhvQgWg],
Passion
[https://www.youtube.com/watch?v=sAeKgJl5fiE],
Anyone Can Whistle (unfortunately, not in New York)
[https://www.youtube.com/watch?v=2YZUriv64Wc],
and *Company*.
[https://www.youtube.com/watch?v=Scq_qR5v1GY]

Patti's Broadway musical career is most notable for revivals: *Oliver* (1984), *Anything Goes* (1987), *Sweeney Todd* (2005), *Gypsy* (2008), and, most recently, *Company* (2022), for which she won her third Tony. She has also appeared in several straight plays and two Broadway concert runs, the aforementioned *Patti LuPone on Broadway* (1995) [https://www.youtube.com/watch?v=aIVtm0_3BZ4] and *An Evening with Patti LuPone and Mandy Patinkin* (2011).

[https://www.youtube.com/watch?v=xenYa9cmsn4]
[https://www.youtube.com/watch?v=HDbOLuG0MGI]

I can't help it. Here's that pesky Irving Berlin duet again, as sung by Patti and Mandy in their show.

[https://www.youtube.com/watch?v=UEyC3nECpz8I]

I saw her in most, but not all of her Broadway performances, missing only *Oliver* (1984)

[https://www.youtube.com/watch?v=-FAxxSqE0sQ]

and *Women on the Verge of a Nervous Breakdown* (2010).

[https://www.youtube.com/watch?v=-0gilcLKe30]

I had seen *Gypsy* in its initial Encores! run in 2007, and I intended to see it again on Broadway just at the end of that run, but it closed suddenly, two weeks before its announced closing date.

She did a fine *Pal Joey* with Encores! in 1995, opposite Peter Gallagher.

[https://www.youtube.com/watch?v=2YJmLCVaZig]

She appeared in Bernstein's *Candide* in 2004 with the New York Philharmonic alongside Kristen Chenoweth.

I did see both her New York Philharmonic and Broadway performances of *Sweeney Todd* (in 2000 and 2005 respectively). I missed her Lincoln Center performance in Sondheim's *Passion* (a very limited run of only two or three performances in 2005), but, luckily, it was telecast on the *Live From Lincoln Center* series.

[https://www.youtube.com/watch?v=Nfubo4hf2NM&t=3219s]

I didn't get to see her in *Company* on Broadway, but I did see her do it with the New York Philharmonic in 2011.

[https://www.youtube.com/watch?v=6M8pxgF2NbU&t=10s]

There's a video of LuPone in a 1983 Acting Company performance of Blitztein's *The Cradle Will Rock*,

[https://www.youtube.com/watch?v=KqzeTwrWA8M]

which I saw on stage, but missed her second appearance, decades later, with her son. Patti LuPone is the actress I have seen onstage more often than any other.

Like Merman, LuPone has had a spotty big screen career. None of her stage successes were filmed and, in most of the movies in which she appeared, she had supporting roles—none were musicals. It is on the TV screen that one can find greater representations of LuPone's art. The earliest of these is a taping of the Acting Company's, *The Time of your Life* in 1976, but it is a relatively small role.

[https://www.youtube.com/watch?v=w-2os5TkvhI]

On the TV screen, besides the already-mentioned *Passion* and *Cradle Will Rock*, there were tapings of Mamet's, *The Water Engine*, as well as musicals such as *Sweeney Todd*, Weill's, *The Rise and Fall of the City of Mahagonny*, and the New York Philharmonic's *Candide* and *Company*. You can find a bootleg of her Mama Rose in *Gypsy* on YouTube.
[https://www.youtube.com/watch?v=gFTnBdH99Zg]
A 2022 *Company* bootleg was on YouTube for a short time.

For four years, LuPone starred in a TV series, *Life Goes On* (1989–1993), a family drama, wherein she plays the mother of a boy with Down Syndrome and since then has had a host of guest spots on various TV series, such as *Frasier, Law and Order, Touched by an Angel, Will and Grace, Ugly Betty, 30 Rock, Girls,* and *Mom*. I thoroughly recommend the tapings of her stage performances cited above, and if you can find it, her turn as Lady Bird Johnson in the 1987 TV movie, *LBJ: The Early Years*.
[https://www.youtube.com/watch?v=tZrh3Bbp5g4]

Sutton Foster

Writing about Sutton Foster in the same comparative section as Merman and LuPone may seem a bit of a stretch as she is not quite (or perhaps not *yet*) the iconic Broadway performer as they, but she is *one* of the best among a more recent group of female musical theater performers I will write about who have gained fame in the last decade or two. Sutton Foster has one of those great show business stories that is almost worth making a movie about, somewhat similar to Tom Bosley's story that I related earlier. When *Thoroughly Modern Millie* came to Broadway in 2002, it had been in tryouts in San Diego with Erin Dilly. Young, unknown, Sutton Foster was in the ensemble. When Dilly quit because of "artistic differences," the show's creators chose Sutton to replace her and bring it to Broadway. The rest, as they say, is history. The show was a hit, as was Sutton, who won a Tony for her performance. She was never in an ensemble again.

Thoroughly Modern Millie, **Marquis Theater, August 21, 2003, (Written 8/31/03)**

"Thoroughly Modern Millie" is a further musicalization of the delightful 1967 musical film that starred Julie Andrews. The film had a wonderful title tune composed by Jimmy Van Heusen (lyrics by Sammy Cahn) and a host of period (1920s) songs. The Broadway version retained the title song and had two or three period songs (most notably Victor Herbert's, *I'm Falling in Love with Someone*, done as a comic number!), but the bulk of the songs are original, composed by Jeannine Tesori, with lyrics by Dick Scanlon. Those songs were fun and serviceable, but not really memorable. What makes the show so enjoyable is the fun plot and, especially, some terrific performances.

Sutton Foster was a treasure in the title role. Ms. Foster has a face and manner that grow on you as the show progresses and she gave an endearing and memorable performance, singing and mugging with the best of them."

Here is a clip from the Tony awards show, followed by the two acts of the full Broadway production.

[https://www.youtube.com/watch?v=0wwzXdwM1C0&list=RDQM6D9sX-QYAM4&start_radio=1]

[https://www.youtube.com/watch?v=v212UUWicbU&t=1672s]

[https://www.youtube.com/watch?v=Jk1rJrb2EaQ&t=200s]

Unfortunately, unlike LuPone, I did not make it my business to see everything she was in, thus missing her next four performances on Broadway. I saw *The Drowsy Chaperone* (2006) and *Young Frankenstein* (2007) after Sutton left the cast of those shows, but never saw *Little Women* (2005) or *Shrek* (2008), both of which had much shorter runs. I did see her in the 2010 Encores! presentation of Sondheim's *Anyone Can Whistle*, wherein she did a lovely version of the title song and was abetted by fine performances from Raul Esparza and Donna Murphy. Following is a rehearsal clip and the full show.

[https://www.youtube.com/watch?v=PkOxoyOPPHQ]

[https://www.youtube.com/watch?v=fG485DFjj5k&t=4440s]

This is part of what I wrote about Sutton Foster's *Reno Sweeney* in the January 18, 2012 performance of *Anything Goes* that I saw at the Stephen Sondheim Theater:

> In the last Broadway revival of "Anything Goes" some two decades ago, Patti LuPone was a terrific Reno Sweeney, but (saying this is almost sacrilege for me, as Patti is one of my all-time favorites), if anything, Foster was even better and with a less mannered singing voice than LuPone (and she's probably a better dancer). It was an all-around star-making performance if Sutton Foster wasn't already a star."

Like LuPone, Foster won a second Tony for her Reno in *Anything Goes*.

Following is LuPone at the 1988, and Foster at the 2011 Tony awards singing *Anything Goes*.

[https://www.youtube.com/watch?v=UpjaqswBVIA]
[https://www.youtube.com/watch?v=j3b5XRd15KM]

There's also a bootleg copy of Sutton's Broadway Reno on YouTube.

[https://www.youtube.com/watch?v=k0GPg1GkCvA&t=75s]

She reprised the role in London a decade later, where it was recorded professionally, and telecast on PBS

The London performance is beautifully shot while the Broadway one rudimentarily shot by an audience member, but I think, performance-wise, the Broadway production was superior.

I've since seen Sutton in two Encores! Off-Center projects, *Violet*, which also had a brief Broadway run (in 2014),

[https://www.youtube.com/watch?v=SGT6Nih8yiY]

and *The Wild Party* (2015).

[https://www.youtube.com/watch?v=tevBzvcIN9E]

She won raves opposite Hugh Jackman in *The Music Man* (2022), which I missed, but there's a bootleg I can watch. On television, she starred in two series, the short-lived *Bunheads* (2012–2013) and the much more successful *Younger* (2015–2021). She clearly is well on her way to iconic status.

Following is a video compilation of Sutton in most of the shows discussed above.

[https://www.youtube.com/watch?v=s4vGIRQNlBA]

More

By calling this section "More," I don't mean to suggest that the performers that follow are less talented than any already discussed. There have just been so many terrific female musical theater performers in the last quarter of a century (or so) that I'm doing a little compressing.

I'll start with Audra McDonald.

I first saw McDonald in what was her first-Tony-winning role in *Carousel* in 1994, as well as in several other shows over the years. Short of commenting on each show, here is a 2014 review:

Lady Day At Emerson's Bar & Grill, Circle in the Square Theater, August 20, 2014 (Written 8/24/14)

When I walked into the Circle in the Square for the first time in a long time (decades?), I immediately loved the set with the thrust stage being a bar and actual members of the audience sitting at tables having drinks (those must be the $250.00 premium seats) while a jazz combo played. Audra McDonald came in as Billie Holiday and, within a few minutes, I knew this was going to be bravura performance worthy of winning her record-breaking sixth Tony Award. Her walk, her posture, her speech and yes, her singing, was pure Holiday—the Audra Mc Donald we know was completely submerged in her character. But long before the end of the show, I realized this was more than a bravura performance, it was also a brave performance! We are seeing Holiday at near the end of her life as she intersperses songs with stories and reminiscences of her life as she gets drunker and drunker—and at times she can barely walk—needing help from those audience members sitting at the "bar." This just wasn't deserving of McDonald's sixth Tony, it was deserving of all six of them, being simply one of the finest dramatic performances I've ever seen.

We all know that Audra McDonald is a terrific singer, but she managed to make her classically trained voice sound like the self-taught jazz vocalist, Billie Holiday, though clearly in better shape than Holiday's voice was at the end of her career (McDonald is nearly the same age as Holiday was when Holiday died, but McDonald is at the height of her vocal and dramatic powers now). Still, good as her renditions of Holiday's songs were, it was her dramatic performance that I will remember longer and may explain why she won Best Actress in a play, not a musical. (She has won the Tony in all four female acting categories.) A memorable deconstruction of a jazz and American icon.

McDonald's performance was recorded and shown on HBO. Although it doesn't quite have the same impact as seeing it live, you can still get the essence of her magnificent performance. You won't find the complete show on YouTube, but to give you an idea of how perfect McDonald's inhabiting of Billie Holiday was, here's a clip from an appearance on *The View*. However, before that, make a comparison to Billie Holiday herself.

[https://www.youtube.com/watch?v=9m7WAQE1SOs]
[https://www.youtube.com/watch?v=-TXfxI18J9k]

For contrast, this is McDonald in her first Tony-winning role, in her own voice, singing *When I Marry Mr. Snow* from *Carousel*.

[https://www.youtube.com/watch?v=-4Wok-iG2jo]

Kelli O'Hara is another treasure. I saw her in the short-lived Frank Wildhorn, *Dracula, the Musical* (2004), but missed her in her breakthrough role in *The Light in the Piazza* (2005), which I saw after she left the cast. The PBS *Live from Lincoln Center* telecast was also after she left the cast. I did see her in *Nice Work if you Can*

Get It (2012) [https://www.youtube.com/watch?v=nkZYf3O7lgw], *Brigadoon* at City Center Encores (2017)
[https://www.youtube.com/watch?v=5ftJuerpl-4&t=775s]
and in *Kiss Me Kate* (2019).
[https://www.youtube.com/watch?v=0B6-U_-6K7Y']
[https://www.youtube.com/watch?v=K9ESKVuZlTE]
[https://www.youtube.com/watch?v=e48U6Uh53Ug]

Like Audra, she is classically trained and owns a magnificent soprano. She is, to my knowledge, the only Broadway diva who has appeared in opera at the Met while maintaining a Broadway career. (Grace Moore, a famous Met soprano of the thirties and forties, abandoned Broadway, where she began her career, once she began to sing at the Met.) O'Hara's first role at the Met in Lehar's, *The Merry Widow* (2015) [https://www.youtube.com/watch?v=rVaTj8jCSFM] was probably closer to musical comedy than to opera, but she also did Mozart's *Cosi fan tutti* (2018), which is definitely not a musical comedy, although it is musical and a comedy.

[https://www.youtube.com/watch?v=E7kYU5YPgZg]

For her third outing at the Met, she did a contemporary opera, Kevin Puts's, *The Hours* (2022).

[https://www.youtube.com/watch?v=N9djqHsy6g0]

This shows Kelli O'Hara's versatility, as these are works in very different styles. Kelli's vocal versatility is at the center of this next clip which also gives us another chance to see the wonderful Audra McDonald.

[https://www.youtube.com/watch?v=Q2PBOAbdIcU]

Laura Benanti, whom I initially saw with LuPone in *Gypsy* at Encores! [https://www.youtube.com/watch?v=BmdRgvGeoFE] also did a beautiful job a few years later, in an Encores! revival of Loesser's, *The Most Happy Fella* (2014). It was her turn in the revival of *She Loves Me* (2016), however, that made me a fan. She was an utter delight in that Roundabout production, which, happily, was live-streamed and was later broadcast on PBS. I attended the performance that was live streamed.

[https://www.youtube.com/watch?v=RjRhvf-w8TE]

While I could go on with "more," as there are many other wonderful female musical theater performers with superb singing voices, I will pause with a nod to the always-delightful Kristen Chenoweth and her *Wicked* co-star, Idina Menzel. Then, too, there is a newer batch of female performers who have arrived in the last decade.

Among them are Laura Osnes, Katrina Link, and Jessie Mueller, but I'm going highlight one who wowed me the first time I saw her. Unfortunately, this was after she had already appeared in several Broadway and Off-Broadway shows. I had not heard of Lindsay Mendez when I went to see Moross and LaTouche's *The Golden Apple*" at Encores! on April 10, 2017. I thought the cast was talented and did their best to bring the show to life. I wrote:

"Ultimately, though, the only memorable performance came from Lindsey Mendez, a real find, who portrayed Helen delightfully and absolutely nailed *Lazy Afternoon*, making it sound as good as even Tony Bennett's recording. As good as everyone else was, she was worth the whole price of admission."

[https://www.youtube.com/watch?v=iMggiJYGkfA]
[https://www.youtube.com/watch?v=jJyTrMjTYLw]
[https://www.youtube.com/watch?v=SpEjaDW3feI]

You can bet I did not miss what ended up being her Tony-winning performance the next year in *Carousel*.

Judy Garland

That Judy Garland is regarded as one of the greatest popular singers and performers is unquestionable. From the moment she came into the lives of moviegoers as a teen-ager in *The Wizard of Oz*, she captured the hearts of America and the world. As Dorothy, singing *Somewhere Over the Rainbow*, which became her signature song and one of the most-recorded songs ever, she revealed a shimmering, gorgeous voice. Although a natural for musical theater, she only appeared in movie musicals (M.G.M). After her M.G.M. days, starting in 1951, she also performed stage concerts.

Her most famous concert performance was at Carnegie Hall on Sunday April 23, 1961. According to Wikipedia, that concert has been called "the greatest night in show business history." The double album derived from the concert was an enormous best seller, charting for seventy-three weeks on Billboard, including thirteen weeks at number one. It won four Grammy Awards: Album of the Year, Best Female Vocal Performance, Best Engineered Album, and Best Album Cover. The album has never been out of print. She also performed at Broadway's famed Palace Theater in 1951, 1957, 1959 and the last of them in the summer of 1967, two years before her death. It was at that time that I got my only chance to see this iconic artist onstage.

You may note that most of the reviews I've chosen to reproduce in this book are laudatory. If I didn't care for a performer or his or her performance, I may mention that here, but I will generally choose not to dwell on it. In the case of Judy Garland, a now legendary and ultimately tragic figure, about whom a great deal has already been written (perhaps by some who never saw her perform live), that I feel it is important to report on what I may be able to add that is not previously of record. I don't know whether there exists a detailed description of one of her later concerts as this one that follows. While I will not dwell on it, to my ears the performance was a disaster. This was not so, apparently, to the majority of the audience! The following is my review.

Judy Garland at Home at the Palace,
August 3, 1967 (Written 7/5/67)

Judy Garland had some of the greatest successes of her, by-now, legendary career, when she previously came to the Palace in the 1950s. Now, eleven years since her last appearance at the Palace, although she has appeared in New York at Carnegie Hall and the Old Metropolitan Opera House, she is back, perhaps trying to recapture the success of yore.

The program presented by Sid Luft, a former husband of Miss Garland, and the father of the two children of Miss Garland who appeared with her on stage, begins with the juggling act of Francis Brunn—which I suppose is fine, and probably enjoyable if you like juggling acts, which I don't. It continues with veteran vaudevillian John Bubbles, soft-shoeing a little, singing a little (minus a voice), and telling corny jokes. The first half ended with comedian Jackie Vernon, who had some funny material, some of which was lost on me due to poor acoustics.

The program really began after the intermission, when Judy Garland, to the cheers of the audience, walked down the orchestra aisle, onto the stage. Then she opened her mouth to produce the voice that a couple of dozen M.G.M. movies over the past thirty years have proved to be one of the most beautiful voices of any female popular singer. But, as most of us know by now, and for those in the audience who hadn't yet found out, that gorgeous voice—that has thrilled movie-goers for so many years—is a total wreck. She sang. And, every once in a while, maybe every three or four songs, for the duration of one note, that Garland sheen would return as she would slide into a note. But, her mostly slow singing was close to a whisper with no vocal quality, and she would tend to crack on her low notes. By any standard, it would rank as less-than-amateur singing. No one who once had what Miss Garland had, should be allowed to appear in public, as a singer, with as little remaining as she now has. It's not that she should not be allowed, but that she should have better sense.

Certainly, she is aware of her present state, for what made it even more ludicrous, is that she herself admits her failing vocal powers. When she cracked during *The Trolley Song* she stopped singing for a couple of lines and, afterward, told the audience that, being familiar with her all these years, they should understand and forgive those things. Indeed, one member of the audience, amidst a vocal lapse, shouted to her, "We'll cheer you whatever you sing, even "Popeye, the Sailor Man," at which point Miss Garland whispered a few words of that song. She tried to sing a new slow song and it died in her mouth. She stopped in its middle, made a face, and joked that at least she was following the music, then went out to get a drink while the orchestra covered her absence. But the audience was there not to cheer Judy Garland's singing, but to cheer Judy Garland, as both the audience and Judy knew. When she came back with a glass (of water?) she said, "Well, at least I'm living up to my image"—which, in fact, was what this show was, and should have been titled, "The Image of Judy Garland.

During the course of her program, which lasted nearly one-and-one-half hours (much of which was audience applause), Judy presented two of her children, Lorna Luft, who sang pleasantly, but only very rarely displayed the vocal splendor of her mother when her age, and twelve-year-old Joey Luft, whose drumming made noises not dissimilar from many another twelve-year-old drummer. They all came out in a cute "Me and My Shadow" number led by John Bubbles, demonstrating how bad a state Miss Garland's voice was, that Mr. Bubble's singing sounded fresher than hers.

The question is, what happened to that gorgeous voice that captivated America? Was it the marriages, drinks, and drugs that contributed mightily to the downfall? But, this result in a loss of vocal splendor, is too painful to dwell on. *You Made Me Love You* was a shambles the way she sings it now. She always had a tendency to slur over words and to not enunciate properly, even in her greatest years, but this was slurred, breathless, and without one iota of charm or beauty. The best thing she did was "Ole' Man River," because she didn't crack once and I have no old Judy Garland recording of it to compare it to. The final encore, of course, was "Over the Rainbow," which was screeched out and had a very bad, and big, crack in the middle, with none of the beauteous sheen of the little girl called Dorothy in *The Wizard of Oz* who introduced it to the world twenty-nine years ago.

For those who love Judy Garland the entertainer, whatever state her voice is in, this concert was for them. For those, like me, who love the voice of Judy Garland, the best thing to do is to watch those old M.G.M. musicals and forget you ever saw this.

The problem is, it's been over fifty years and I have unfortunately never forgotten it! I still remember how shocked I was that most of the audience was eating it up, applauding and cheering at every opportunity. I wondered whether I was the only one who thought that what I saw was rather sad. Actually, I soon realized that what I had witnessed was not a performance, it was a love fest between Judy and her fans.

Several years later I picked up a copy of the ABC Paramount LP of that Palace performance. While the voice on it pales in comparison to the Judy of her Decca (now MCA) years, what I heard on it were credible performances of the songs, with no cracks in the voice and few of the problems I recounted above. One would like to think maybe she was just having a very bad day when I saw her. The performance I saw was early in a four-week engagement. Of course, the real explanation is that they probably taped and merged several performances using engineering mastery to make her voice sound better than it did at the live performance. After writing this, I Googled for information about that album and found this statement on Discogs. com sites: "Sadly, the master tapes from the three nights of recording are lost. Only the master tapes of the final album are known to exist."
[https://www.discogs.com/release/2521320-Judy-Garland-At-Home-At-The-Palace])

I suspect the master tapes were not lost, but justifiably destroyed—on purpose. Here's the final recording:

[https://www.youtube.com/watch?v=tekrJEd2Zds]

I hesitated to add this next link, but it is a performance very similar to the one I saw with John Bubbles and Lorna and Joey Luft, in Hartford, this one made a little over two months after the performance I saw. You shouldn't listen to it if you feel it will taint your memories.

[https://www.youtube.com/watch?v=x4dy8vcWC7c]

There's actually a performance from that 1967 Palace engagement on YouTube, but it's less representative of what I saw as it was the final night when she was joined by the twenty-one year old pre-*Cabaret* (by five years) Liza, singing, among other things—*Cabaret*! [at 4:44]

[https://www.youtube.com/watch?v=HxTerOTii7c]

This is where I originally ended this Judy Garland section, but very near to publication, someone posted a concert on YouTube claiming to be Judy's last, from Copenhagen, nearly two years after the one I reported on. Again, while not near Judy in her vocal prime, it is actually quite fine with much of her timbre in place, just some screaming in vocal climaxes she used to sail through and some quivering in places. It's only thirty-six minutes and it was a radio broadcast, so I don't know whether it was the full concert or there was any electronic fiddling (although it claims to be newly remastered in 2023), but if she had sounded this good when I saw her, I would have written a very different review.

[https://www.youtube.com/watch?v=Sv7a1A5AGcA]

Barbra Streisand

Barbra Streisand is sometimes thought of as a "kind of" successor to Judy Garland (perhaps even more so than Judy's own daughter, Liza Minelli). Unlike Garland, Streisand started out on the musical stage, appearing in two Broadway musicals before her rise to movie stardom. Like Garland, she has a glorious singing voice that isn't just beautiful, but so unique it can't be compared with anyone else. Thus, I have never heard anyone say that one is better than the other. They both are incomparable artists. There is a wonderful segment during Garland's 1963–64 TV series in which she and her guest, the young Barbra Streisand, sing together, and were joined at the end by a *surprise* appearance—Ethel Merman!

Barbra and Judy:
[https://www.youtube.com/watch?v=UxFvQEanqbQ]
joined by Ethel.
[https://www.youtube.com/watch?v=kPKO-s3uATg]

I did not see Barbra in the two shows she did on Broadway. The only time I saw her live was during a free Central Park concert, *A Happening in Central Park*. I got there early and met up with Lois Kirschenbaum, who had gotten there even earlier and had a nice spot very near the front.

A Happening in Central Park, June 17, 1967
(Written on 6/24/67)

I'll never forget the first time I heard the original cast recording of *I Can Get It for You Wholesale* soon after it first came out, and the song *Miss Marmelstein,* sung by the unknown Barbra Streisand. [https://www.youtube.com/watch?v=_i3W3n1fty4] It was the highlight of the record and a most wonderful performance by someone I knew, at once, was destined to become a big star. Certainly, her overnight success as Miss Marmelstein, and her unbelievably fast rise showed that my opinion was shared by many others. Thus, after success in nightclubs, performance as Broadway's *Funny Girl*, a multi-million dollar television contract, and with no motion picture yet to her name, she's already been signed to star in two.

A free Central Park concert would generally be beneath stars of her caliber, but being paid by Rheingold Brewery, who sponsored the event, and being taped for television (meaning about $1,000,000 for her), she probably made more than she would have in front of a paying audience. Certainly, that it was free didn't dent her program. Though it started forty minutes after its scheduled starting time of 9:00 P.M., due to television complications, she treated the audience to over thirty selections. Despite the outdoor surroundings and not too great acoustics, much of it came out very well. Her voice is very unique and can be extremely beautiful, especially in the upper register. On occasion, she sometimes sounded a bit hoarse, but, when she did sing out, it was with stunning effect. She sang some of her hits, such as "People" and "Second Hand Rose" and they were deservedly cheered.

Incidentally, Miss Streisand was there before the concert, from about five to seven, getting herself oriented, and she rehearsed three songs to the applause of the great many already there. By the time the concert started there were, according to the police, about 135,000 people there.

Since this concert was taped for television and released on disc, you can judge for yourself.
[https://www.youtube.com/watch?v=lqxEyf7JXyQ]
However, be forewarned, what was telecast and originally released on disc is about one-third of the concert. She sang more than thirty selections, so I assume they cut out those selections in which she sounded a bit hoarse. The CD and DVD re-releases contain only the tracks originally telecast. Of course, the entire concert must have been recorded. Perhaps, some day, CBS will release the full concert.

Julie Andrews

Julie Andrews is probably the only other female singer/actress/movie star who belongs in the constellation with Garland and Streisand (although fans of Liza Minelli and Doris Day may think differently). Like Streisand, British-born Julie Andrews started out on the Broadway stage, starring in *The Boy Friend*,
[https://www.youtube.com/watch?v=tVzwA4SpvUY]
then achieving stardom as the original Eliza in *My Fair Lady*, following this up with *Camelot* and then on to superstardom on the big screen with *Mary Poppins*, *The Sound of Music*, and numerous

other films, many of which were non-musicals. Like Judy and Barbra, Julie had a beautiful and unique singing voice with the added advantage of clear, crisp British enunciation.

Julie Andrews has had a tremendous career to be proud of, despite her two big professional setbacks—the first was being passed over for the lead in the movie version of *My Fair Lady*, and the second was losing her singing voice.

I will only go mildly into my usual rant about how even greater the movie version of *My Fair Lady* could have been had Jack Warner hired Julie Andrews to play Eliza Doolittle. We should probably be simply grateful for what we got because Warner wanted Cary Grant to play Henry Higgins and James Cagney to be Alfred Doolittle. But, Cagney was newly retired and declined, and Cary Grant not only declined, but allegedly told Jack Warner that, if he didn't get Rex Harrison to do the role, *he* would never do another movie for Warner Brothers. One always knew Archie Leach (Cary Grant's real name) had class! If only Audrey Hepburn had done the same thing when Julie Andrews was passed over. For one thing, Andrews could actually sing, not just better than Audrey Hepburn, but even better than Marni Nixon, who dubbed Hepburn's songs. These clips will give you an idea of how wrong-headed Jack Warner was:

Audrey Hepburn/Marni Nixon
[https://www.youtube.com/watch?v=q5fW7sERw7I];
Julie Andrews/Julie Andrews
[https://www.youtube.com/watch?v=yMNPD0MZD2I];
Audrey Hepburn/Audrey Hepburn (undubbed version)
[https://www.youtube.com/watch?v=H8zyF0ZOy3k]
Julie Andrews/Julie Andrews
[https://www.youtube.com/watch?v=yQM_KUg-YeI]
Audrey Hepburn/Marni Nixon
[https://www.youtube.com/watch?v=hA9bEKKxTNU]
Julie Andrews/Julie Andrews
[https://www.youtube.com/watch?v=TcFIbYbEEu8]

Finally, here's a recreation of a rehearsal for *My Fair Lady* with Harrison and Andrews.
[https://www.youtube.com/watch?v=HhBbYANd_8U&t=488s]

But, Andrews had the last laugh. Her movie debut in *Mary Poppins*, released the same year as the movie version of *My Fair Lady*,
[https://www.youtube.com/watch?v=UR4uLNFEauw]
won her the Academy Award over Hepburn. The very next year,

she starred in the highest grossing film of the time, *The Sound of Music* [https://www.youtube.com/watch?v=5fH2FOn1V5g], which the American Film Institute listed as the fifty-fifth greatest American film of all time, and the fourth greatest film musical. In 2001, the Library of Congress selected the film for preservation in the National Film Registry, finding it "culturally, historically, or aesthetically significant."

Andrews was now a bigger star than Hepburn, whose film career was beginning its twilight. Consider this: One year before, Jack Warner could probably have gotten Andrews for a pittance compared to what he paid for big-box-office-star Hepburn (not to mention the added expense for Marni Nixon) and I doubt *My Fair Lady* would have sold one less ticket—no doubt more. Wrong-headed? Indeed!!

Here's a terrific fun clip from Andrews short-lived TV variety show "The Julie Andrews Hour" (1972–1973) with Julie interacting with Eliza Doolittle and Mary Poppins. Too bad the picture quality is not better.

[https://www.youtube.com/watch?v=5usVahlDjv0&list=RD8h7E5rtnFH4&index=3]

Unfortunately, I did not get to see Julie in any of her three initial Broadway appearances. Even *Camelot*, in 1960, was just before I started going regularly to the theater. So, when she came back to Broadway in 1995, in a musical version of one of her hit films, *Victor/Victoria*, more than thirty years after she last appeared on Broadway, I was eager to see her live. This turned out to be easier said than done, as I had trouble getting a ticket at the reasonable prices I preferred to pay. I checked the box office every so often throughout its run, to no avail. At one point late in the run I was told at the box office that she was ill and would be out for several weeks. Finally, when she returned, I was able to get a ticket for the Friday just before she left the show

Victor/Victoria, **Marquis Theatre, June 6, 1997 (Written 6/18/97)**

Julie Andrews returned to Broadway last year, after nearly a thirty-five-year absence to star in the stage version of her 1982 hit movie, *Victor/Victoria*. This performance, given the day before she left the production for good (to be replaced by Raquel Welch) was my first chance to see Ms. Andrews in a live performance. Unfortunately, the show was somewhat beneath her talents and didn't measure up to the *My Fair Lady* and *Camelot* standards of yore. The plot pretty much follows the plot of the movie which is unique, interesting, and lots of fun. But, whereas the movie was a dramatic comedy with (very few) musical numbers, this show is supposed to be a musical, and it must be said that the musical numbers are mostly unmemorable. Henry Mancini, one of the great, recent Hollywood composers, who often worked with Blake Edwards in film and television (going from "Peter Gunn" on TV to the "Pink Panther" movies) who also did the music for the original film, was simply no Frederick Loewe. That he died before the show opened on Broadway and at least one pivotal number had to be composed after his death (by Frank Wildhorn), also didn't help. The score was not the thing in this show.

The fact is, there was no need for a stage musical version of *Victor/Victoria*, other than to try to aid the ailing film career of Blake Edwards, the erstwhile director and book author, who, of course, is Ms. Andrews husband. And, perhaps, that Ms. Andrews herself, who at sixty-one is no longer in demand in Hollywood. For those of us who have always wanted to see Ms. Andrews, this was our chance, but I, for one, wished the vehicle was a better one. She still looks good and plays a woman half her actual age with gusto. Her speaking voice remains that wonderful, deep British drawl one remembers so well from her movies. For the most part, she sang beautifully, although one must point out that, in this performance, each one of her songs had a moment when her voice nearly cracked. One hopes this was due to her recent throat illness (causing her to miss several performances which resulted in this one-week extension of her engagement) rather than any permanent problems. For the most part, Ms. Andrews carried the show like the trooper she is.

Obviously, I didn't know it at that time, but she *had* permanently lost her voice and sued the doctor who treated her during the illness. Whether malpractice was the actual cause, we don't know, as the case was settled out of court. Unlike Garland, Andrews has had the good sense to not sing in public from that point on.

The musical version of *Victor/Victoria* was taped for television. [https://www.youtube.com/watch?v=qGIxw77_YsY&t=770s]

This performance was obviously long before the one I saw. Her vocal skills are very much intact.

She was past age sixty when she lost her voice and had had a four-decade-long career as a singing actress, unlike Garland who was only forty-five when I saw her in tattered vocal state. The first decade of Julie Andrew's career was on stage, and she did not make her first movie until she was nearly thirty. By contrast, Garland's major-motion-picture career was over by the time she was thirty. However, one must consider that Garland was just a teenager when she made

her first film. Although Andrews made up for her late start in movies during the next two decades, it would be nice if we had more of a representation of her work from that earlier period. The one showing that we have of the young Julie is the 1957 premiere telecast of Rodgers and Hammerstein's, *Cinderella*, written especially for her.
  [https://www.youtube.com/watch?v=C1F4YhBOA14&t=67s]

Happy End

Earlier I mentioned how no Kurt Weill musical makes my list of great musicals because none have more than one or two great songs. Among the many Weill shows I've seen was a performance of *Happy End*, one of his early German shows (1929), given in English at Brooklyn's Academy of Music. Shirley Knight was the female star, but when we got to the theater there was a notice in the lobby that she would not appear in that performance. As my wife and I were reading the notice to find who the replacement was, I heard a couple behind us lamenting the fact that Shirley Knight was not in the performance. Having seen the actress who was replacing Knight numerous times, I resisted an urge to tell them that her replacement was likely to be *better* than Ms. Knight—although, I must admit, I had never yet seen her in a musical (but, neither had I ever seen Shirley Knight in a musical).

Happy End, **Brooklyn Academy of Music, April 14, 1977 (Written 4/16/77)**

A very enjoyable and entertaining performance of the least well-known of the Weill-Brecht collaborations. Exactly why the work is not done too frequently, isn't clear because it is an enjoyable fun-filled work and contains two of Weill's most haunting songs, *The Bilbao Song* and *Sarabaya Johnny*. Hopefully this adaptation by Michael Feingold will restore this musical play to its rightful place alongside *The Threepenny Opera* and *The Rise and Fall of the City of Mahagonny.*

  The cast was uniformly excellent, with Meryl Streep, here replacing Shirley Knight, adding to her already illustrious two year, eight play New York career, a standout as the female lead, Lt. Holiday. She also sang beautifully, especially in the aforementioned *Sarabaya Johnny*. Bill Cracker is clearly a brother of Weill/Brecht's Macheath and Christopher Lloyd played him to the hilt, though his singing voice left something to be desired.

I failed to mention in that review anything about the plot, which

I hardly remember, other than, like Shaw's *Major Barbara* and Loesser's *Guys and Dolls*, it had something to do with the Salvation Army. Interestingly, several years before Weill and Brecht found themselves to be refugees in America, this German work takes place in Chicago. Indeed, Weill/Brecht's other two great German works also take place in English-speaking countries: *The Threepenny Opera* in London and *The Rise and Fall of the City of Mahagonny* in a fictional American town.

It ended up that we needn't have trekked all the way to Brooklyn to see this production. After its Brooklyn run, it was transferred to Broadway *with* Meryl Streep. Evidently Shirley Knight left the production entirely. I don't know why. The show lasted less than two months on Broadway, but was nominated for a Tony as Best Musical. *The Bilbao Song* was chosen as the song to present at the Tony's. That was one of Christopher Lloyd's numbers.

[https://www.youtube.com/watch?v=VOuXzCnIoyU]

Meryl Streep was not yet a marquee name.

Even I, who thought very highly of Meryl Streep in those years (she and Patti LuPone were my two favorite young stage actresses of the period), have been surprised by the wealth and depth of her motion picture career which has shown her to be arguably the finest American actress of the past four decades. As Streep's popularity rose, I always wondered whether that couple still lamented missing Shirley Knight or even remembered who her replacement was.

Male Musical Theater Performers

There are some fine male musical stars out there, but none seem to come up to the level of the women—at least not insofar as their vocal attributes are concerned.

Possibly the finest male singing voice in musical theater during the mid-twentieth century was that of Alfred Drake. Drake created the male lead in three classic Broadway musicals: *Oklahoma, Kiss Me Kate,* and *Kismet.* (There was also a flop he starred in, *Kean*, to which, based on the original cast recording, I am partial.) His was a magnificent bass-baritone voice that had a lovely vocal sheen to it, setting it apart from others who also played some of these roles—like Gorden MacRae and Howard Kheel, both of whom did the movie versions of the roles that Alfred Drake created on stage.

I saw Drake several times—in the 1965 Music Theater of Lincoln

Center's revival of *Kismet*, and the first Broadway production of *Gigi*, in 1973—in which he played the Maurice Chevalier 1958 film role, Honoré, which was not quite his cup of tea. I also saw him as Claudius in *Hamlet*, as well as his appearance in *The Skin of her Teeth*, both dramatic presentations. Drake did not appear in any of the movie versions of the roles he created, but in 1958 he and his original co-star Patricia Morrison repeated their roles in a ninety-minute telecast which, luckily, has been preserved.

[https://www.youtube.com/watch?v=093myaltXAY]

His only big-screen appearance was in *Tars and Spars* in 1946.

I quote briefly from my review of the June 29, 1965 performance of *Kismet*:

> Songs such as "Rhymes Have I," "The Olive Tree," and "Sands of Time" are show-stoppers when sung by Alfred Drake.

Here is a link to a 1958 telecast of excerpts from *Kismet*. If you want to skip to Alfred Drake, go to 5:20.

[https://www.youtube.com/watch?v=1xsf_xXOqVM&list=RD1xsf_xXOqVM&start_radio=1]

Finally, twenty-three minutes of Drake, performing his most famous songs.

[https://www.youtube.com/watch?v=iCOblpkH8WE&t=597s]

The only musical performer whose voice was comparable to Drake's never appeared in a show on Broadway, but he was the one of the foremost stars of film musicals in the 1930s: Nelson Eddy. Like Drake, Eddy had a hard-to-describe, but very distinctive timbre to his voice.

[https://www.youtube.com/watch?v=i5e-iG02LhA]

Eddy began his career in opera.

[https://www.youtube.com/watch?v=rE0QcAadAKE]

While never a member of the Metropolitan Opera Company, he spent most of the 1920s singing with the Philadelphia Opera. He did, however, sing at the Met, but only while touring with the Philadelphia Orchestra and Philadelphia Civic Opera.

In the 1930s, Nelson Eddy partnered with Jeanette MacDonald to become one of the two great movie musical teams of the 1930s, the other being Fred Astaire and Ginger Rogers.

[https://www.youtube.com/watch?v=qRl6_4uWsjc]

Somehow though, while Fred and Ginger are still icons, and their movies are frequently revived, the MacDonald and Eddy films have not aged well because the type of musicals they made (closer to operetta) don't seem to speak to the present era. So too, I think, despite his magnificent singing voice and charm, Nelson Eddy's screen performances seem stilted. Here's the trailer to their first movie together *Naughty Marietta*.

[https://www.youtube.com/watch?v=33iHB45D13I]

Before she teamed with Eddy, Jeanette MacDonald made four films with Maurice Chevalier. Those films are not as well-known today, but they should be. They are light, lively, and ooze with Chevalier's infectious Gallic charm.

[https://www.youtube.com/watch?v=7PyqwP3wCUg]

Next, John Raitt. He had a wonderful singing voice, lighter than Alfred Drake or Nelson Eddy, but magnificently able to carry off songs like *Soliloquy* from *Carousel*.

[https://www.youtube.com/watch?v=CKCUapUEFkY]

As Drake did with respect to *Kismet*, Raitt recreated *Carousel*'s indelible Billy Bigelow for a 1965 Music Theater of Lincoln Center revival. Raitt got to create one other classic role on Broadway, Sid Sorokin in *The Pajama Game*, which he repeated in the big-screen version, his only major motion picture. Raitt's big solo number in in *The Pajama Game* was *Hey There*, which was a big hit for Rosemary Clooney. Here's a clip of Raitt singing it *with* Rosemary Clooney.

[https://www.youtube.com/watch?v=x02n47UUMTQ]

Another great number from that show was *There Once was a Man*. Here are Raitt and Doris Day from the movie version.

[https://www.youtube.com/watch?v=9OhCigu8zjQ]

Like Mario Lanza, Raitt appeared in only two operas early in his career, one of which was *The Barber of Seville*. Here's a clip of him singing *Largo al Factotum* (in English) from that opera.

[https://www.youtube.com/watch?v=QSv-oT7XnTw]

But, I'll end my short review of Raitt's career with him in more familiar terrain.

[https://www.youtube.com/watch?v=cHjN8CLLZI8]

As we get to the '60s, the demand for this type of male voice on Broadway had diminished. Robert Goulet, an incredibly handsome man with a beautiful baritone voice, became a star as Sir Lancelot in *Camelot* in 1960.

[https://www.youtube.com/watch?v=xL52hEArSfM]

In earlier days he would probably have appeared in lots of roles in Broadway musicals or become a movie star, but not in the last half of the twentieth century. Goulet originated only one other musical role on Broadway, the short-lived, *The Happy Time* in 1968.

[https://www.youtube.com/watch?v=en7C6cLPGsA]
He did not appear again on Broadway for twenty-five years, when, in 1993, he played the Richard Burton role (of King Arthur) in a *Camelot* revival.
[https://www.youtube.com/watch?v=FaWuMYdbKVk]
[https://www.youtube.com/watch?v=vd1nzjVD-gU]
Two years later, he replaced Philip Bosco (we will learn more about Philip Bosco later) in a non-musical comedy, *Moon Over Buffalo* and, finally, for six months, starting in late 1994, he appeared as a replacement for the character Georges, in a revival of *La Cage aux Folles* in 2005.
[https://www.youtube.com/watch?v=uXs-ge7Ay6E]
That was the total of his Broadway career. Unlike Julie Andrews or Barbra Streisand, who became movie superstars to explain their absence from Broadway, Goulet had a spotty film and TV career.

While the above four male stars of the twentieth century had voices that would be comfortable in opera, that cannot be said for most current male musical Broadway stars. Is this because of Rex Harrison's success in sing-speaking the character Henry Higgins in the 1950s? Certainly, there have always been male pop-oriented voices on Broadway, but, after *My Fair Lady*, this trend accelerated. I'm not suggesting it's a bad thing. Many male performers with untrained singing voices are wonderful because of their outsized personality. This goes back decades. Starting in the late '50s, leading male musical roles were going to actors whose personalities overshadowed their singing voices.

A year after *My Fair Lady* came Robert Preston, another actor who had never before appeared in a musical on Broadway, who absolutely, definitively sang his way through Harold Hill in *The Music Man*.
[https://www.youtube.com/watch?v=LI_Oe-jtgdI]
Recently, Hugh Jackman scored a triumph doing *The Music Man* on Broadway. Despite a better singing voice, he cannot match Preston's charismatic interpretation.
[https://www.youtube.com/watch?v=1AAdGoOcJbo]
The sixties gave us boyish Robert Morse, who equally definitively played the role of J. Pierpont Finch in 1961 in *How to Succeed in Business Without Really Trying* .
[https://www.youtube.com/watch?v=ZbAjOJwyAwc]
Then, immediately following, in 1962, there was the irrepressible Zero Mostel who triumphed in *A Funny thing Happened on the Way*

to the Forum, [https://www.youtube.com/watch?v=TjiV8wHk3Hk] only to outdo even that as Tevye in *Fiddler on the Roof.*

This trend toward less operatic sounding male voices has continued to the present day, although there are few male musical stars who can stand comparison with these icons of the past. Among those who can are Mandy Patinkin and Nathan Lane.

The trend of popular male singing voices becoming less operatic can be exemplified by the Joneses. Classically trained Allan Jones had a beautiful tenor voice that thrilled audiences in the 1937 movie version of Friml's operetta, *The Firefly,* singing *The Donkey Serenade* to Jeanette MacDonald.

https://www.youtube.com/watch?v=RyHNlfT6B9E]

You can see why very few singers covered that song. It requires an operatic voice. It stands to reason that the only subsequent recording to challenge Jones's version came from Mario Lanza.

[https://www.youtube.com/watch?v=FsWxh6eyoBU]

Allan Jones's other 1930s film appearances were in two Marx Brothers films, the classic *A Night at the Opera* and *A Day at the Races.* He also co-starred with Irene Dunn in the 1936 screen version of *Showboat.* Although he continued performing until his death in 1992, he never again achieved the popularity he had in the 1930s. Indeed, by the 1960's, most people of the younger generation of that period would probably not have heard of him. However, they probably were familiar with another Jones, Jack Jones, a popular non-classically trained crooner who sang tunes like *Lollipops and Roses.*

[https://www.youtube.com/watch?v=CRTkrMs1_yA]

Jack Jones is Allan Jones's son. Here's his uptempo and very unoperatic version of his father's signature song.

[https://www.youtube.com/watch?v=cuQwlmSzrig]

Part of the reason, too, for this trend, is that musicals calling for near-operatic male voices have become fewer. As noted earlier, the operetta form doesn't seem to speak to present-day audiences, so one doesn't see Broadway revivals of the musicals of Victor Herbert, Rudolf Friml, Sigmund Romberg, and others whose musicals in the early part of the twentieth century were the bridge between the European operettas of the late 1800s and the modern Broadway musical. Also, the age of the microphone made unnecessary the need for the unamplified voice to carry throughout a large theater.

Homage To My Favorite Musical Theater Performer

Once upon a time, years before my time, in the 1920's, among the great Broadway musical stars, was a brother/sister team. They appeared in hit musicals every season for much of that decade. The sister was thought to be the more talented one and, hearing their recordings made during that period, one might easily tend to agree with that. However, in 1931 she got married and quit show business. In 1932, her brother performed a Broadway show without her. It would be his last Broadway show.

One critic wrote of how that brother appeared to look into the wings in desperation, hoping his sister would magically appear to rescue him. That said, however, the show was pretty successful. In that same year, he married the love of his life, a divorced New York socialite, and decided to try his luck on the west coast where the talkies had just ushered in the era of movie musicals. The big studios (MGM, Warner Brothers, and Paramount) didn't seem interested in him. Ultimately, he signed a seven-year contract, standard in the Hollywood studio system, with a smaller studio that was close to bankruptcy. At this point one easily could think that he would never again reach the height of fame he had when he and his sister were the toast of Broadway and London.

The first thing the studio did was to lend him out to MGM for a short spot in a Clark Gable/Joan Crawford movie. Later, at his home studio, his first assignment was in a supporting role. Perhaps the studio didn't think he could carry a movie in a starring role, so he was cast as the best friend of the star, Gene Raymond. For his love interest in that film, they cast another refugee from Broadway, a young woman ten years his junior, whom he had actually once dated in New York, but they had not hit it off. But, onscreen, several years later, they hit it out of the ballpark.

The "suits" at the studio, even before the film was finished, let alone released, recognized what they had and bought the rights to his final Broadway musical, slating the duo to star in it. And so, the greatest dance team in movie history, Fred Astaire and Ginger Rogers, was born. It elevated them to movie stardom and helped to save RKO Radio Pictures from bankruptcy (at least for two decades). They went on to make nine films together for RKO between 1933 and 1939 (and one reunion movie a decade later for MGM) all of which are classics. Of course, you probably knew immediately who I was talking about, didn't you?

Here's the dance that catapulted Fred and Ginger to stardom, *The Carioca,* from their first film together *Flying Down to Rio* (1933).
   [https://www.youtube.com/watch?v=vOUftTHar_U&t=64s]
   From *Top Hat* (1935), The title song, *Isn't This a Lovely Day* and *Cheek to Cheek.*
   [https://www.youtube.com/watch?v=c0VeEqonEa0]
   [https://www.youtube.com/watch?v=jd_z3fpnNpc]
   From *Swing Time (1936), Pick Yourself Up, The Way You Look Tonight* and *A Fine Romance.*
   [https://www.youtube.com/watch?v=dIW_Ah0wg-w]
   [https://www.youtube.com/watch?v=sCJb5bCbnco]
   [https://www.youtube.com/watch?v=sRqK-KxNLAY]
   This is tough for me. There are too many Fred and Ginger numbers that I absolutely adore. If I included them all it might fill up the whole page, so I will just end with two from *Shall We Dance (1938). Let's Call the Whole Thing Off* and *They Can't Take that Away from Me,* the latter as sung by Fred in that film and in the same clip as danced by Fred and Ginger in their reunion and only color film *The Barkleys of Broadway* (1949).
   [https://www.youtube.com/watch?v=LOILZ_D3aRg]
   [https://www.youtube.com/watch?v=fuufFgAMkGE]
   As a bonus here's one of Fred's two numbers with Joan Crawford in his movie debut in *Dancing Lady* (1933).
   [https://www.youtube.com/watch?v=A9HOLS4g0Aw]
   I mentioned that Fred's sister, Adele, was considered to be the more-talented member of the team. There is, sadly, no documentation of her dancing, but she did make records during her Broadway career. Though already hoofing on Broadway for a half-dozen years, the first show in which they got star billing was the Gershwin brothers' *Lady Be Good* in 1926. Near the very beginning of the show there is a rather cute, though not-well-known Gershwin song, *Hang on to Me.* To show what made her such an appealing performer, listen to two versions of that song. The first is from a 2015 Encores! presentation of the show with Danny Gardner and Patti Murin.
   [https://www.youtube.com/watch?v=zbllb3umuLA].
   The second is Fred and Adele's 1926 recording with piano accompaniment.
   [https://www.youtube.com/watch?v=xqc43130tJQ]
   Note how, with a couple of interpolations, Adele takes the song to

another sphere. Incidentally, the composer must have approved—the pianist is George Gershwin!

1940 was a crossroads for Fred. He had been half of two of the most successful dance teams in show business history. Forty years old and about to try to go it alone again, he had done his seven years at RKO and was now freelance. While some might have doubted that he would succeed, between 1940 and 1946 he starred in nine filmed musicals. If none of them equaled the freshness and vitality of the earlier Astaire/Rogers films, some were fine films, most notably *Holiday Inn* and *Blue Skies* with Bing Crosby (who always had to get the girl whether his co-star was Fred Astaire or Bob Hope). There were two excellent films with Rita Hayworth (her parents were *The Dancing Cansinos*, a vaudeville dance team who Astaire knew when he and his sister, Adele, had begun in vaudeville. Fred relates in his autobiography *Steps in Time* how he was surprised to see the Cansino's one day at the studio while filming with Hayworth and was further surprised to learn Rita was their daughter.)

[https://www.youtube.com/watch?v=WUhhKELUxB0]

In 1946, after nearly thirty-five years in show business, when he was forty-six, Astaire decided to retire. He bought a racehorse and opened the Fred Astaire Dance Studios. Had his retirement stuck, his would still have been a storied show business career, but, luckily for him and for us, it didn't. Whatever his actual involvement in running the Fred Astaire Dance Studios was, it just wasn't in his blood the way show business was, so in 1948, when Gene Kelly broke an ankle and had to withdraw from *Easter Parade*, there was only one person who could replace him. One telling of the story is that Kelly personally called Astaire to ask that he replace him, others say it was MGM, but the ultimate outcome was that Fred did make *Easter Parade* with Judy Garland.

[https://www.youtube.com/watch?v=C9z9Q9KbJOg]

That led to his reunion movie with Ginger Rogers in the following year. *The Barkley's of Broadway* was supposed to be a follow-up movie with Fred and Judy, but this time Judy had to be replaced and MGM got the bright idea of reuniting the by-then legendary pairing of Astaire and Rogers!

Fred was no longer retired, and a new decade was beginning; a decade during which one might again assume that the best work of this now-fifty-year-old hoofer (as he liked to call himself) was behind him. Of course, that was not to be. In the next seven years,

Astaire was to star in eight more musicals, several of which are among his best films. In 1953, *The Bandwagon* appeared, which co-starred arguably his finest screen dance partner since Ginger, Cyd Charrisse. In supporting roles were Fred's old friend Oscar Levant, and Nanette Fabray (playing characters closely resembling the screenwriters of the movie, Betty Comden and Adolph Green). Also prominently featured was Jack Buchanan, a British actor who was a star in the U. K., but less well-known in America. *The Bandwagon* is considered by many (including me) to be among the greatest movie musicals ever made.

[https://www.youtube.com/watch?v=n2WHYXXA0a0]
[https://www.youtube.com/watch?v=jGeBU3Zr6qk]

To be fair I should add that *The Bandwagon* appeared only a year after another film considered by most to be among the greatest film musicals ever made, *Singing in the Rain,* starring Fred's friend and great screen rival Gene Kelly. I concur, and *Singing in the Rain* is my favorite Gene Kelly film.

Bandwagon aside, *Royal Wedding, Daddy Long Legs, Funny Face,* and *Silk Stockings* are other terrific movies Astaire starred in, in the 1950s. I should note that the 1956 film *Funny Face* used a bunch of songs from Gershwin's 1927 Broadway musical of the same name, which, of course, starred Fred and Adele, but the movie had a completely new screenplay.

[https://www.youtube.com/watch?v=oyJuH945H8k]

There was one song, however, that was in the stage show in 1927 but was not in the 1956 film. It was *The Babbit and the Bromide*. That song was used in the 1946 movie *Ziegfeld Follies,* sung by Fred and Gene Kelly. Here's Fred's original 1927 recording of the song with his sister Adele, again showing why she was such a delightful performer, followed by the 1946 version with Gene.

[https://www.youtube.com/watch?v=Ki-QKxhbtbs&list=RDKi-QKxhbtbs&start_radio=1]
[https://www.youtube.com/watch?v=mP7gOHJkgWs]

Similarly, *The Bandwagon* was the name of the Arthur Schwartz and Howard Dietz musical revue that was Fred and Adele's last show together in 1931, but the 1953 movie just retained the songs, with Comden and Green devising a completely original screenplay. *Silk Stockings,* in 1957, a musical remake of *Ninotchka,* a comedy that had starred Greta Garbo in 1939, was Fred's last filmed musical as a romantic lead. Fred's career as a star of movie musicals lasted a full quarter century, and *that* followed more than a decade in stage musicals on Broadway and in London. Still, his career was not over. TV and dramatic roles would follow.

In 1958, he starred in the first of four television specials that would appear over the next decade, *An Evening with Fred Astaire*,
[https://vimeo.com/261611927]
which went on to win a record nine Emmy awards. Toward the end of that year's Emmy telecast, he seemed embarrassed to accept another award!. He went on to do three more TV specials in 1959, 1960 and 1968. From his third special *Astaire Time*, here he is with his last dance partner, Barrie Chase (who appeared in all his TV specials). doing an absolutely definitive version of Cole Porter's *Miss Otis Regrets*.
[https://www.youtube.com/watch?v=zwZDt_votQc]

In 1959, Fred played his first dramatic role in *On the Beach*. Throughout the 1960s, he continued to appear in movies and on TV. For two seasons, he hosted, and occasionally appeared in, the hour-long anthology series, *Alcoa Premiere*. He also appeared several times in Robert Wagner's TV series, *It Takes a Thief* as Wagner's character's con-artist father, Alistair. He hosted and performed in several episodes of *Hollywood Palace*, a vaudeville-like variety show. Before the link to the complete Hollywood Palace shows he hosted I must highlight one short segment from one of those shows. It is four and a half minutes of pure joy for me as my two favorite musical theater performers in their only stage appearance together, humorously contrast their very different vocal styles. Watch Fred and Ethel, and if your not smiling at the end, there's no hope for you.
[https://www.youtube.com/watch?v=DgLtRLgVcQg]

Fred starred in his last big-screen musical in 1968, playing the title role in *Finian's Rainbow*. At the age of sixty-eight, he was no longer cast as the romantic lead, but he still played the lead.
[https://www.youtube.com/watch?v=v6Wp4GiCGkw]

Astaire continued working through the seventies and into the eighties in a variety of projects including, in 1971, *The Towering Inferno* for which he was nominated for a supporting-actor Academy Award. He co-hosted the first two *That's Entertainment* movie documentaries, starred in several TV movies, and in 1981, starred in his final theatrical movie, *Ghost Story*.

So why is Fred Astaire my favorite entertainer of all time? I am always able to rely on an Astaire movie to bring me joy and to lift my spirits. In every movie in which he appears, he oozes an easy-going charm that is contagious. Beyond that, everyone knows he was a sublime dancer, so I need not dwell on his dancing. However, I think Astaire is underestimated as a singer. Lacking a beautiful singing voice, and having a limited vocal range, what he did have was an innate musicality that naturally sensed the proper phrasing for a song. The great French flautist, Jean-Pierre Rampal, wrote in the liner notes for Rampal's 1985 Gershwin album: "For as long as I can remember, I revered the miracle that is Fred Astaire—both his dancing and his musicality. Like the rest of the world, we in France adore Astaire's impeccable style and grace; and as a musician, I know his timing and inflections are unsurpassed." Is it any wonder that many of the great songwriters of Astaire's era loved to write for him?

I haven't done a count, but I'm pretty certain that Astaire introduced more songs now considered a part of the "Great American Songbook" than any other singer. This would include Bing, and Frank, and Judy, and Ethel, and so on. He appeared in Broadway shows and movies in which the scores were written by Irving Berlin, George Gershwin, Cole Porter, and Jerome Kern, four of the greatest songwriters of that, or any, era. Just a few of the songs he introduced include *Lady Be Good, Fascinatin' Rhythm, Funny Face, Night and Day, Cheek to Cheek, Let's Call the Whole Thing Off, The Way You Look Tonight, They Can't Take that Away from Me, A Fine Romance, Nice Work if you Can Get It, A Foggy Day in London Town, Steppin' Out with My Baby, Dancing in the Dark, I'm Putting all My Eggs in One Basket, Isn't it a Lovely Day, Change Partners, Shall We Dance,* and (the only one of the songs *not* written by the quartet of composers listed above—this one by Harold Arlen) *One for My Baby*. And, seeing how that's just a partial list, it's more *great* songs than probably any other singer has introduced. Interestingly, Astaire never appeared in a musical by the other great songwriter of that period, Richard Rodgers.

Astaire is even closely associated with songs he *didn't* introduce. Irving Berlin's *Easter Parade* was published in 1933 and first sung in a movie by Bing Crosby in 1943's *Holiday Inn* (in which Astaire co-starred). However, it's the Astaire version of *Easter Parade* from the 1948 movie that we all remember. So, too, Astaire did not premier Irving Berlin's, *Puttin' on the Ritz*. It was introduced as the title song to a 1930 movie musical by Harry Richman. Astaire made it his own in the 1946 film, *Blue Skies*.

Astaire first recorded *Puttin' on the Ritz* not long after it was written. That 1930 recording has the original lyrics which were somewhat sanitized later by Irving Berlin for *Blue Skies*. If you've only heard Astaire's post-1946 recordings, the 1930 recording should be a revelation, showing him as a perfect jazz-age singer. There are three clips here. The first is Harry Richman from the 1930 original film, then Fred Astaire's mellower 1946 soundtrack version, then go back sixteen years to Astaire's first recording of the song that has the feel of the roaring twenties.

[https://www.youtube.com/watch?v=66km3m_UE_k]
[https://www.youtube.com/watch?v=L7y_GVkHbO4&t=96s]
[https://www.youtube.com/watch?v=2EfyYIgB-rk]

I understand that the famous statement, "Ginger did everything Fred did, but backward and in high heels" has become something of a feminist mantra. Therefore, I don't want what I write below to be taken as part of a discussion of gender politics. I personally support gender equality and firmly believe there should be an equal rights amendment in our constitution, but this is an homage to Fred Astaire and I would just like to set the record straight as to their relative contributions to the ten classic films in which they appeared together.

Let me take a step back. Why was that sentence about Fred and Ginger first created? I think it was first said (who first said it, and when, has not firmly been established) because there was a perception that Fred was given more credit than Ginger and that this was an injustice to Ginger. But it was more than that. It was that Fred was given more credit *because he was a man*! At the very least that appears to be why the Women's Movement took it up as what I call a "mantra," but, what if that premise was wrong? What if the fact that Fred was held in higher regard with respect to to those films was due, not because of his gender, but because he actually did contribute more to the films, at least with regard to the musical numbers?

Yes, it is certainly true that, *when dancing together,* Ginger did everything Fred did and, if the statement was quoted with that qualification, I would have no argument with it. But, the statement is somewhat misleading in that it might cause some to think that their contributions to their films was equal. The fact is, in those ten films, Fred did much more.

When Astaire first went to RKO, the studio assigned a young dancer to work with him. He had the unusual name of Hermes Pan (shortened from Hermes Joseph Panagiotopoulos). Among the credits for virtually all of Astaire's musical films (as well as many later TV specials), Hermes Pan is listed as either the dance director ("dances staged by") or, later, the choreographer. It's documented in many places, including Astaire's autobiography, how they worked together.

Several months before filming started, they would get together at the studio to work out the dance steps. Hermes would dance the female part as they created the full dance numbers together. Then, a week or two before filming began, Ginger (or other, later, female co-stars) came in and Hermes would teach her the steps. While Fred was co-creator of the dances (for which he never took screen credit), Ginger had no part in the creative process. It should also be noted that in most Fred and Ginger films, Fred sang about three songs, while Ginger had, at best, maybe one song or just a duet with Fred; in some she didn't even have a vocal solo. Even in dancing he almost always had at least one solo dance number in the films, while she did so rarely. If you don't believe me, watch those films again, and you should, for despite being nearly ninety years old, they remain timeless.

I do not mean to disparage Ginger by pointing out that that her contribution to their films was not as great as Fred's. She was a wonderful performer, a superb dancer, and a fine actress—and they had great onscreen chemistry that was never duplicated by any of his subsequent dance partners, even Cyd Charisse, who might have been an even-better dancer than Ginger. And it wasn't that Ginger was doing nothing while Fred and Hermes were creating the dances. While Fred made only one movie without Ginger during their partnership (1933–1939), she made *ten*.

The other famous comment about Fred and Ginger may be truer: "He gave her class; she gave him sex appeal." Indeed, it could be argued that as great as Fred was, he might not have achieved the iconic status he did without the underpinning of the Fred/Ginger partnership!

The artistic collaboration between Astaire and Hermes Pan lasted the entire span of Astaire's movie and TV career, making Pan part of and co-creator of a Fred Astaire oeuvre. Hermes bore quite a passing resemblance to Fred. He appears briefly in two movies in the early forties, dancing with Betty Grable in one, and Rita Hayworth in the other.

[https://www.youtube.com/watch?v=7nFnEsMv-Vg]
[https://www.youtube.com/watch?v=r2wCHGLAFDg]

Watching these clips, one sees dance movements that are uncannily, but unsurprisingly, like Astaire's. In 1981, the American Film Institute (AFI) gave Fred Astaire its Lifetime Achievement Award. Among the many people who paid tribute to Astaire that day was Hermes Pan (at 1:01:52).

[https://www.youtube.com/watch?v=vqGEUU27_MI]

When Fred died, at age 88 in 1987, there was a private family-only funeral. The only non-family member who was allowed to attend was Hermes Pan.

In 1999, the American Film Institute named Fred Astaire fifth on its list of top male screen legends. That seems quite an accomplishment for someone whose initial screen test is said to have stated: "Can't act. Can't sing. Balding. Can dance a little."

Returning Stars

I usually prefer to see a musical with its original cast when that is possible. In most cases, but not all, the performers who create the roles seem more ideal, perhaps because they worked with the show's creative team to flesh out their roles and were usually chosen by the show's writers. Often, the role-originators are established stars, while replacements are not as well known. As I began to attend Broadway musicals in the early 1960s, I obviously missed seeing the original cast of many of the musicals that premiered before then. Thus, the only way for me to see those earlier musicals was in revivals. Rarely are revival casts better than the original.

Sometimes, though, one or another original star returns to a role they originated in a revival. I don't know how frequently this occurred before the 1960s, but the trend seems to have been accelerated by the short-lived Music Theater of Lincoln Center (1964–1966) which gave us the return of Alfred Drake, John Raitt, and Ethel Merman to the iconic roles they originated. It must be said, unfortunately, that Merman was one of only a few female stars who got to repeat one of her most famous roles two decades after its initial triumph. In the usual double standard, producers evidently don't think the public will accept an older female performer playing a younger woman, while this doesn't appear to be as much of an obstacle for aging male stars.

Rex Harrison

Case in point—Rex Harrison. When he first performed Henry Higgins in *My Fair Lady* in 1956, he was in his late forties, perhaps even then a tad older than the character, but when he returned to the

role in the twenty-fifth anniversary production, he was in his mid-seventies, clearly way older than Shaw conceived of the character. But the audience, myself included, didn't care. His Henry Higgins was definitive. No one comes near him in sing/speaking *I've Grown Accustomed to Your Face.*
[https://www.youtube.com/watch?v=ki6GZBGcEoo]
[https://www.youtube.com/watch?v=Jbqgf4ukva4]

   I wonder if anyone considered asking Julie Andrews to reprise her Eliza? But, then again, she was busy in Hollywood. However, Cathleen Nesbitt, who had played Higgins's mother in the original production when she was sixty-seven, returned to play his mother at age nineety-two, seventy years after her first Broadway appearance!

My Fair Lady, The Uris (now Gershwin) Theatre, September 15, 1981 (Written 9/20/81)

This production had the definitive Henry Higgins, Rex Harrison. Now 73, Mr. Harrison is chronologically years too old for the role. Yet, though a mite slow of foot, and despite a lost or garbled line on occasion, he simply chews up the stage as Henry Higgins. After hearing his version of the songs so many times (he recorded it three times, twice with Julie Andrews, in the 1956 original cast album, and again in the 1958 stereo remake in London, and, of course, the movie soundtrack in 1965 with Marni Nixon) it is wonderful to hear him do it live and as good as those recordings. As Henry Higgins, Harrison is perfection. When toward the end, he exclaims: "Damn! Damn! I've Grown Accustomed to Her Face," you realize this is exactly how it should sound, and no one else doing this role will ever sound quite like that. This is not to leave out Harrison's marvelous accounts of *Why Can't the English...,* *"I'm an Ordinary Man,"* and *"A Hymn to Him."*

   [*The final part of my review reveals my take on the ending, which is not the conventional view that sees Eliza's return as her capitulation, a view that caused the producers of the most recent Broadway revival to change that ending. Admittedly, the ending used in the recent revival is closer to Shaw's original than Lerner's ending, which was taken from the revised ending of the 1938 film version of "Pygmalian."*]

   As to my thoughts on *My Fair Lady,* there isn't much I can add to what I have written about it for the five prior productions I've seen over the past twenty years. Basically, my view is that Mr. Loewe's great achievement, his music, perfectly complements Shaw's original, a possibility Shaw himself incorrectly thought impossible. I am even partial to the musical's ending, which differs from Shaw's. When Eliza enters as he is listening to those recordings of her, he is caught with his defenses down. When he calls for his slippers he is now just *posing* as that dominant, obnoxious male, and Eliza knows this and Henry knows she knows. He is responsible for his own defeat. He has created the only kind of woman he could respect and truly love, one whose mind is equal or superior to his.

Perhaps that was something of a stretch, but I am a romantic and therefore view *My Fair Lady* as a love story, so I must interpret the ending that way. *I've Grown Accustomed to Her Face* is clearly an expression of love, however much Higgins wants to deny it. However, if I were writing this today, I might change the word "created" to "brought out in Eliza", so as to not give too much credit to the chauvinistic male lead.

Zero Mostel

I had missed Zero Mostel in the original production of *Fiddler on the Roof*, finally seeing the original production with the third Broadway Tevye, Herschel Bernardi. So, when in late December, 1976, Mostel opened in a revival of that show, I had to see it.

Fiddler on the Roof, Winter Garden Theater, February 1, 1977 (Written 2/2/77)

Some time in the early 1970s, "Fiddler on the Roof" became Broadways longest running musical. After something like an eight-year run, this revival, after only a five year or so absence on Broadway, might seem to be unnecessary. Yet the show is selling as well as ever, the main reason is that back in the lead role of Tevye, is the man who created the role a dozen or so years ago, none other than Zero Mostel. Although Mr. Mostel created the role, and his name has become indelibly connected with Tevye, he actually only played the role about a year on Broadway, thus being one of Broadway's shorter-lived Tevye's and. of course, he was ridiculously passed over for the film version, so for some of us this is our only chance to see Mostel in one of his greatest roles.

Mr. Mostel's Tevye is a beautiful, bigger-than-life creation. With his great girth, wonderful facial expressions, and his amazing flair for visual and verbal comedy, Mr. Mostel's Tevye dominates the stage from start to finish. Perhaps some may sing the role better [*I was thinking then of tenor Jan Peerce, who was the last Tevye in the original production. More recently, operatic bass Bryn Terfel has essayed the role*], but Mr. Mostel makes it his by combining his comedic talents and yiddishisms, with his sense of theatrical drama making the audience eat out of his hands every moment.

I must admit I was disappointed with his singing. I recall the original cast album, plus one or two television appearances (most notably the 1971 Tony Awards show) where his voice sounded stronger and firmer. Here it was quite low and sometimes hoarse. But this is a minor quibble in an otherwise definitive performance.

As Mostel died just over seven months after this performance, I wondered whether declining health was a factor.

The first clip has Mostel singing *If I Were A Rich Man* at the 1971 Tony Awards show. Next is Bryn Terfel, vocally magnificent, turning the song into an opera aria, but ultimately failing to convey a real sense of the character. Welsh-born Terfel is clearly out of his element. Finally, highlights from the 1977 revival.

[https://www.youtube.com/watch?v=nbJEpcteKg4]
[https://www.youtube.com/watch?v=PNpsOUvEE3M&t=2s]
[https://www.youtube.com/watch?v=y9_Stu61HVg]

Mostel, being an opera lover himself, sometimes dabbled in opera. Here's a 1975 telecast of Puccini's one-act comic opera, *Gianni Schicchi*, sung in English, with Mostel in the title role!

[https://www.youtube.com/watch?v=rRsgdDUR868].

Gianni Schicchi is an Italian opera, based on an episode in one of Italy's most cherished literary creation, Dante's *Inferno*. Turning the tables on Mostel, here's a more idiomatic and more brilliantly sung fragment from the opera, sung in Italian (except at the very end) by my favorite baritone, Tito Gobbi, in another of his great impersonations.

[https://www.youtube.com/watch?v=NE0CJAswMhA&t=84s]

Yul Brynner

The King and I, The Uris (now Gershwin) Theatre, August 3, 1978 (Written 8/5/78)

The reason for this revival is the availability of Yul Brynner to repeat his definitive version of the King. Mr. Brynner, of course, created the role when the show premiered in 1951. He won an Academy Award for the film version in 1956 and then embarked on a successful career as a screen superstar. By the early 1970s, with his film career finally sagging, Mr. Brynner attempted a television series of "Anna and the King", but that was a flop. He then toured in the stage musical, "Odyssey," which, when it landed on Broadway as "Home Sweet Home," lasted a mere one performance. He then triumphantly returned to his first success as the

King in "The King and I," both on tour and now on Broadway for over a year. Mr. Brynner's dominant, exotic personality remains perfect for the role and he invests his performance with all the know-how of an assured veteran. It remains clear that he is the definitive King because he is so associated with the role, despite all the different movie roles he has done over the years, his is the face you will always see when viewing "The King and I" and his is the unique voice you will always hear saying "etcetera, etcetera, etcetera."

[https://www.youtube.com/watch?v=ElqYH2bxKtY]

If it wasn't enough that Brynner was still playing the role of the King in 1978, twenty-seven years after he first created it, he returned to Broadway as the King in 1985 for a six-month run that ended four months before his death. For much of the period between those last two Broadway appearances he toured as the King.

I noted in my review that Brynner had a successful screen career. His screen career was dwarfed by the fact that he spent the last decade or so of his life playing the King. This is rather sad because he has quite a legacy in film: from 1956 when he co-starred in *The Ten Commandments* and *Anastasia*, through *The Brothers Karamazov* and *The Buccaneer* in 1958, *The Sound and the Fury* and *Solomon and Sheba* in 1959, not to mention *The Magnificent Seven* in 1960 and its sequel *The Return of the Seven* in 1966, and his final memorable roles as the Gunslinger in *Westworld* (1973) and *Futureworld* (1976). That's just a partial list of the very varied roles he played on screen that were overshadowed by his definitive King.

Richard Kiley

Another actor who twice revived on Broadway a classic role he created was Richard Kiley.

Man of La Mancha, Palace Theatre, September 14, 1977 (Written 9/18/77)

Man of La Mancha is a dozen years old now, and not only did it become the fourth longest running musical in its initial run, but this revival is its second major New York revival. In 1972, *Man of La Mancha* played a triumphant summer engagement at the Vivian Beaumont Theater at Lincoln Center, with Richard Kiley returning as Quixote/Cervantes. This revival, just five years later, again has Kiley, the original and finest *Man of La Mancha*. It's strange to admit that I've never seen *Man of La Mancha* before.

Of course, you don't have to have seen *Man of La Mancha* before to be familiar with the music, and indeed anyone who has not heard *The Impossible Dream* must have been on Mars in the last decade. But just hearing it in context of the rest of the score and play, is a different thing entirely. And listening to it sung by Mr. Kiley, who originated it, is a moving experience.

At this performance [*the last preview*], probably getting ready for the opening, there was a pleasant surprise as the show's composer, Mitch Leigh, came out to conduct the overture."

[https://www.youtube.com/watch?v=7UBKjC4WTa8]
[https://www.youtube.com/watch?v=7RiSds2RFp4V]

There is a complete performance of *Man of La Mancha* on YouTube listed as "Original Broadway Cast." As it would be an impossible dream that the technology for such a bootleg would have existed in 1965, this is more likely the revival that I saw in 1977, although I am surprised that this technology would have existed even then.

[https://www.youtube.com/watch?v=o-PJMbCKwZ0&t=2474s]

More Returning Stars

Another actor who returned to a role he had originated earlier, in this case twenty years earlier, is Richard Burton. In 1980, he reprised King Arthur in *Camelot*. I saw it twice.

While women seem less likely to repeat their signature roles years later, Carol Channing is one female performer who has defied these odds. Carol Channing became a star as Lorelei Lee in the Jule Styne/Comden and Green musical *Gentlemen Prefer Blonds* in 1949. Twenty-five years later she reprised the role on Broadway, though for some reason they retitled the musical *Lorelei*. Even more amazingly, Channing revived her other signature stage role in *Hello Dolly!* on Broadway twice—in 1978 and 1995! I am not a Channing fan. Indeed, I don't think I could sit through an entire performance listening to her harsh, raspy, cloying voice. It is why I had to wait until she left *Hello Dolly!* to see that show.

Carol Channing in three scenes from *Hello Dolly*!. First singing *When the Parade Passes By* from the 1971 Tony Awards Show, then the title song from London in 1979, and finally an extended scene near the beginning of the show, from 1994.

[https://www.youtube.com/watch?v=mknDZ88-zfg]
[https://www.youtube.com/watch?v=iVh9zjf0Tww]

[https://www.youtube.com/watch?v=JBOz1XwyOtE]
To be honest, I had a hard time listening to these clips in their entirety. While I found her voice hard to take even in 1971, by 1994 it was excruciating. Again, I recognize that I am in a minority and many readers will love those clips. Since I need an antidote, here's my first Dolly, Ginger:
[https://www.youtube.com/watch?v=NldLf7IpI2A]
Interestingly, Carol Channing, although she did lots of TV, appeared in only two major big screen films, the hugely successful *Thoroughly Modern Millie* (1967), which starred Julie Andrews, and a dud, *The First Traveling Saleslady* (1956). The latter starred Ginger Rogers. That movie is notable for two things: It helped to finally shut down RKO Pictures, the very studio that Rogers helped save over twenty years earlier; and Carol Channing's love interest in the film was a young Clint Eastwood. That was a very odd couple, indeed.

As noted, Glenn Close did not create the role of Norma Desmond in Webber's *Sunset Boulevard*, but she did originate the role on Broadway in 1994. In 2017 she returned to the role on Broadway.
[https://www.youtube.com/watch?v=28ibjtrd21I&t=1103s]
In 1966, Angela Lansbury scored her first major success in a musical on Broadway in *Mame* in the Jerry Herman musical of that name. Of course, she previously had a successful screen career starting at age eighteen in the 1943 screen version of *The Picture of Dorian Gray*. In mid-career she turned to the stage where besides *Mame*, she created roles in Sondheim's *Antyne Can Whistle* and the much more succssseful *Sweeney Todd*. She ultimately won five Tonys. She was to subsequently have a hugely successful TV career with *Murder, She Wrote*. Although she was nominated eighteen times for an Emmy, she never won!

Mame, Gershwin Theatre, August 26, 1983 (Written 8/28/83)

This revival of Jerry Herman's mid-1960s musical hit *Mame* with a number of members of the original cast, including it's star, Angela Lansbury, did not get good reviews and is closing this week after only a month on Broadway. Strangely, I didn't have a great desire to see it eighteen years ago when it was first on Broadway. So, it surprises me that I really enjoyed it in a less well-received production. Of course, I don't think the music is in the same class as that of Stephen Sondheim, to mention the greatest of Mr. Herman's contemporaries and the other

Broadway composer with whom Lansbury has been mostly associated with (she has created leading roles in two Sondheim and two Herman musicals). Yet there is a bouncy Broadway vitality in all Jerry Herman's scores and who can deny the catchiness of the title song.

Angela Lansbury has one of the great roles of her career as Mame and after two decades she is still superb, turning her thumb on those Hollywood moguls who turned a Broadway hit into a screen flop by casting the allegedly more bankable Lucille Ball in the film version, Also recreating their original roles were Jane Connell, a splendidly hilarious Gooch and Willard Waterman, a properly staid Dwight Babcock. In all, I found much to enjoy in this production."

Here are highlights from the original 1966 production of *Mame*, followed by a complete recording of the revival. Please note that the picture and sound quality of these clips may be somewhat trying.

[https://www.youtube.com/watch?v=Fi15Nmvdb7w]
[https://www.youtube.com/watch?v=8wDq6ags8rk&t=3180s]

I have read that the other actress associated with the role of Mame, Rosalind Russell, who starred in the 1958 non-musical film version, *Auntie Mame*, was offered the role, but declined, thus missing the opportunity to have the kind of success she had when she repeated her 1942 non-musical screen role in *My Sister Eileen* in the 1950 Broadway musical *Wonderful Town*. Russell recreated her role in *Wonderful Town* in 1958 in a two-hour (including commercials) television special that can now be found on YouTube.

[https://www.youtube.com/watch?v=EsxzyqJX5wY].

This brings to mind some other performers who recreated non-musical screen roles in a Broadway musical.

Greek actress Melina Mercouri gained initial fame in America in the highly successful movie *Never On Sunday* in 1960. Seven years later she appeared in a Broadway musical version called *Illya Darling*.

[https://www.youtube.com/watch?v=OHn_vANWURg]

Unfortunately, I did not see it. But, I did see a Broadway musical version of another iconic Greek movie that starred two of the movie's stars. The explanation below is full of trivia, so bear with me.

I mentioned that I initially saw *Fiddler on the Roof* with Herschel Bernardi, the *third* Broadway Tevye.

[https://www.youtube.com/watch?v=q4k0HJcd0Ko]

Bernardi had previously gained some fame as the cop friend of the title character in the popular 1958–1961 private-eye TV series, *Peter Gunn. Fiddler* was his first Broadway show, but he was successful enough so that in 1968 he landed the title role in the Kander and Ebb musical version of the 1964 film, *Zorba the Greek*. Whether Anthony Quinn, whose acclaimed performance in the title role of the film version was approached to repeat the role onstage I don't know, but it would be difficult to believe he wasn't. At any rate, the role went to Bernardi, with his co-star being Maria Karnilova, who originated the role of Golda in *Fiddler* and was still playing it when Bernardi joined the cast. *Zorba* wasn't the smash hit Kander and Ebb had wished, but it did run for over 300 performances.

[https://www.youtube.com/watch?v=aN-wEyvlZCY]

Forward fifteen years to 1983. A revival of *Zorba* is being staged on Broadway. Who were the stars of this revival? Anthony Quinn and Lila Kedrova, the stars of the then-nearly twenty-year-old original movie. This I had to see.

Zorba the Greek, The Broadway Theatre, October 25, 1983 (Written 10/30/83)

Anthony Quinn who started out in films in the 1930s and became more popular in the 1950s, became a true star and had his best role in the 1964 motion picture *Zorba the Greek*, directed byMichael Cacoyannis, and co-starring Lila Kedrova, who won an Academy Award for her performance. Approximately five years later, Kander and Ebb turned *Zorba the Greek* into an American musical whose Broadway original cast boasted two *Fiddler on the Roof* refugees, Herschel Bernardi and Maria Karnilova. Now we have a revival of the musical with the original stars and director of the movie. All this doesn't make *Zorba* a great musical, for after all, the music is far from great, though more than serviceable. But, it does make for a more interesting theatrical experience.

Even at 68 Mr. Quinn is a broad and bigger than life performer and he wears this role like a glove. So, like Yul Brynner as the King of Siam, or Richard Burton as King Arthur, Rex Harrison as Henry Higgins, Richard Kiley as Cervantes/Quixote, he can use this role as an annuity. He even warbles the tunes adequately, though without a real singing voice. Nearly equally delightful is Lila Kedrova, a must see as Madame Hortense.
[https://www.youtube.com/watch?v=P5mErhlwQzg]

Joel Gray is another actor who reprised his signature role twenty years later. He became a star playing the emcee in the original production of Kander and Ebb's *Cabaret* in 1966, winning a Tony in the process, [https://www.youtube.com/watch?v=HAGNQwmUsqI] then repeating the success in the screen version in 1972, this time winning an Oscar. Forward to 1987 when he appeared again as the emcee in a Broadway revival of *Cabaret*.

[https://www.youtube.com/watch?v=CNGeN4lycNw&t=4945s]

This brings to mind an interesting reversal. I have lamented here how I often find the movie versions of Broadway musicals inferior to the original, especially when they replace the original Broadway stars with bigger box office names. While I loved Joel Gray in the original production and enjoyed the show, I was not overwhelmed by the show as some others seem to have been at the time. Joel Gray was the only star from the stage version retained for the movie, but I must say I *was* overwhelmed by the movie version which was vastly superior to the original stage version. Somehow, director Bob Fosse, more famous then as a Broadway director and choreographer, turned the Broadway musical into a cinematic classic and, in the process, made Liza Minelli a star. Strangely, thirty years later, another director then known only for his stage work, Rob Marshall, turned another Kander and Ebb musical, *Chicago*, into a cinematic blockbuster, also better than the original production, which I saw during the month in the summer of 1975 that Liza Minelli filled in for its regular star, Gwen Verdon.

Perhaps, someday, someone will make a *great* movie version of a Sondheim musical!

Another actor has more recently made the role of the Emcee in *Cabaret* his own. Alan Cumming did so in a 1998 Roundabout Theater Broadway revival to critical acclaim. He, too, reprised the role, again for Roundabout in 2014. I only saw his second go at it in a Broadway bootleg apparently since deleted from YouTube. Good as he was, and he was terrific, it couldn't compare to Gray's magnetic performance.

[https://www.youtube.com/watch?v=kVQFcKiShXA]

Comden and Green

The names Betty Comden and Adolph Green have appeared several times in this section about musicals. They were among the most successful Broadway lyricists of all time, working with such composers as their longtime friend Leonard Bernstein (*On the Town, Wonderful Town*), as well as Jule Styne (numerous shows including *Gentleman Prefer Blonds* and *Bells are Ringing*), Cy Coleman (*On the Twentieth Century, Will Rogers Follies*, etc.). They also wrote the book to these musicals, as well as several screenplays in the mid-twentieth century. They were quintessential New Yorkers. I remember seeing them during the intermission at several shows I attended over the years. They started out as performers, indeed playing featured roles in their first Broadway musical *On the Town*. But, after that they performed rarely, though they did do two stints on Broadway. In 1958 and 1977 they appeared together in retrospectives of their career entitled *A Party with Betty Comden and Adolph Green*. I caught their 1977 turn toward the end of its two-month run on Broadway.

A Party with Betty Comden and Adolph Green,
The Little (now Helen Hayes) Theater, April 27, 1977
(Written 4/30/77)

Well, Comden and Green are back on Broadway with a retrospective of mostly singing and sometimes clowning through some of their best songs and material of the past nearly forty years, and it's good to have them back. It should be noted that as their first big success was nearly thirty-five years ago, they are both now in their early sixties. To look at Ms. Comden one can hardly believe it as she looks magnificent. Mr. Green's hair is now silver but he still has that impish grin and when he begins to move, and dance, and jump (he does a lot of jumping) and even fall down one suspects there must be a deception somewhere because though he looks sixty he moves like a twenty-five year old.

So, these two very personable people review their career, starting with their early satiric revues at the Village Vanguard, their first Broadway success, *On the Town*, through their partnership with Jule Styne and their current work with Cy Coleman. They sing some of their best known songs and a couple of their least known songs. They both possess fine voices, and their feel for the mood and phrasing of the lyrics they wrote came through. Each of their numbers had something to offer, sometimes lesser songs being given better treatment than the more well-known songs. It was nice to see them do probably their two best sad ballads *Lonely Town* from *"On the Town* and *The Party's Over* from *Bells are Ringing.* Also, their comic classic *Carried Away* as only they can do it.

Luckily, a performance of this show was taped for television and can be found on YouTube.
[https://www.youtube.com/watch?v=8j7sO9DIXOU].
This should be required viewing for any budding lyricist or performer, or for that matter anyone who loves the American musical.

The 1971 "Tony Awards" Show

The annual Tony Award telecasts have been a television staple since 1967. Many of the clips referenced in this section come from those shows, as every year they perform at least one production number from each of the nominated musicals. The 1971 show was very special as it celebrated the twentieth-fifth anniversary of the Tony Awards, which began in 1947. In that show they highlighted one song from a Tony-winning musical in each of those twenty-five years, virtually all of them with its original star. It contained a wealth of material used for this book including the Alfred Drake and Yul Brynner clips. There was only one drawback. Doing over twenty songs, they didn't have time to do the numbers from *that* year's nominees. That was the year *Company* won Best Musical! That's why there is no clip of the original cast of *Company* in performance, but we at least have the Pennebaker documentary. But, like *A Party with Comden and Green,* viewing that 1971 Tony Awards in its entirety is a must for any lover of Broadway musicals. Here it is:

[https://www.youtube.com/watch?v=nCB_r7iSoEY]

Plays And Actors

The Summer of 1964 and Hamlet
John Barrymore

As you will see the summer of 1964 was my summer of *Hamlet*. Having become an opera lover before I began regularly going to theatrical performances, I tended to see even plays through the lens of opera. Because of that "affliction," I most enjoy classics and the traditional; leaving me less of a fan of avant garde theater. Dramatic presentations have an element I'm especially conscious of due to being an opera lover—the sound of the human voice—in this case the spoken voice. In 1961 I bought an RCA Victor LP celebrating sixty years of that label. Along with classical music highlights, it had John Barrymore's 1928 recording of "O What a Rogue and Peasant Slave Am I," the *Hamlet* soliloquy.

[https://www.youtube.com/watch?v=myUbf9rjS8w&t=6s]

To say that I was "blown away" would be an understatement. I listened, and I knew that what I was hearing was the way Shakespeare *should* sound. The passion and intensity of Barrymore's voice was monumental. I realize now that I was judging this in the same way I would judge an opera aria recording. Based on that recording, and a host of his movies, John Barrymore became my favorite actor of all time.

Obviously, I never saw Barrymore in *Hamlet* live as he died before I was born, and there is no recorded document of a complete *Hamlet* played by him. However, in 1937 he made a number of radio appearances presenting scenes from Shakespeare plays. These later appeared on recordings. While the recordings are good, they don't compare with the recording made nearer to the time he played the role on Broadway (1922–23) and in London (1925) and was proclaimed to be the greatest Hamlet of his age.

[https://www.youtube.com/watch?v=HK96YwwrfYc&t=20s]

I firmly believe that Barrymore was the Hamlet that Shakespeare would have most approved of—but, of course, that's just my opinion.

It is well known how Barrymore abandoned the stage in 1925 after his huge success as Hamlet. He turned to Hollywood, became a movie star, squandered his talents, and ultimately destroyed himself with alcohol. It is likely that, had he stayed on stage and essayed other Shakespearian roles with the same passion and commitment he did as *Richard III* (Broadway, 1920) and *Hamlet*, he would have been considered the greatest Shakespearian actor of the twentieth century. Here are some clips of Barrymore in Shakespeare:

[https://www.youtube.com/watch?v=x2jWx4IqgEM&t=10s]
[https://www.youtube.com/watch?v=0mPWndf-aXw]
[https://www.youtube.com/watch?v=dvaYL6fqFcY&t=278s]

He didn't, and the actor who is generally considered the greatest Shakespearian actor of the twentieth century, Laurence Olivier, saw Barrymore's Hamlet in London and freely admitted he borrowed much of his interpretation from Barrymore. Olivier performed dozens of Shakespeare roles over his long career, while Barrymore did only three (counting Mercutio in the 1935 Leslie Howard/Norma Shearer *Romeo and Juliet* movie), so calling Barrymore a Shakespearian actor seems a stretch.

An operatic analogy we can use here is to Mario Lanza. Lanza appeared in only two complete operas before he abandoned the opera stage for movie stardom. Therefore, calling Lanza an opera singer may be a stretch, but I have already opined that the legacy of recordings of great American songs Lanza left us might not have happened had he pursued a major operatic career.

Similarly, had Barrymore not abandoned the stage for the screen, we would not have the many movies he made with which to judge him as an actor and to keep his memory and legacy alive. Although he made a few third-rate films, especially in his last years of self indulgence, there are numerous movies, both silent and sound, that show off his genius as an actor. Orson Welles called him an "actor of genius." I agree.

In at least two swashbuckling silent films Barrymore made, *Don Juan* (1926) [https://www.youtube.com/watch?v=5zydvO0rY9Y] and *The Beloved Rogue* (1927),

[https://www.youtube.com/watch?v=tOEgvY1cjYc]

showed that he could easily rival Douglas Fairbanks (and

Barrymore's own buddy, Errol Flynn) in that genre. I will focus on his sound films, because it is his voice that was one of his major assets.

He gave wonderful performances in many films including *A Bill of Divorcement* (1932),
[https://www.youtube.com/watch?v=ph2UT_9kl-w]
Topaze (1933),
[https://www.youtube.com/watch?v=EJjj8UeXXLk&t=12s]
Grand Hotel (1933),
[https://www.youtube.com/watch?v=n9kko9FnAoc],
Twentieth Century, and, as late as 1939, *The Great Man Votes.* Also in 1939, he played a supporting role in the Claudette Colbert/Don Ameche romantic comedy, *Midnight.* He virtually steals the film from its stars with his comic antics, showing his often-overlooked comic genius.

Richard Burton

During the 1960–61 TV season, I became hooked on a documentary series: *Winston Churchill: The Valiant Years.* In twenty-seven thirty-minute episodes it told the story of Churchill's life concentrating on his leadership during the Second World War. I found it riveting. One of its assets was the actor who spoke in a voiceover taken from Churchill's memoirs. Though imitating the oratorical mannerisms of Churchill, it was clear that actor had a naturally beautiful voice. That actor was, of course, Richard Burton.

About the same time as that series was being telecast, Lerner and Loewe's *Camelot* was opening on Broadway. In it, Richard Burton played King Arthur to Julie Andrews' Guinevere. Although I didn't see the show in its original run, I heard the original cast album shortly after it was released in early 1961 (and many times thereafter). I was impressed with the natural beauty of Burton's voice. He was not a singer, but Lerner and Loewe, who previously did marvels for Rex Harrison in *My Fair Lady,* did it here, again, for Burton, writing songs that showed off the beauty of his voice without requiring him to go beyond his limited vocal range. Here are three clips from Camelot to give you idea of the magnificence of his voice. The title song from 1980, *What do the Simple Folk Do* from 1961 with Julie Andrews, from 1966 *How to Handle a Woman,* and from 1968 the final scene.

[https://www.youtube.com/watch?v=8h7E5rtnFH4&list=RD8h7E5rtnFH4&start_radio=]
[https://www.youtube.com/watch?v=BSyPiS0R0tE]
[https://www.youtube.com/watch?v=gtUgUde84EA]

I had been musing ever since first hearing Burton's voice that I would love to see him in Shakespeare when, in February of 1964, I saw a telecast of Burton's 1955 film, *Prince of Players*, in which he stars as Edwin Booth, and, in doing so, performs several scenes from Shakespeare plays. Seeing *The Prince of Players* further whetted my appetite to see Burton in roles like Hamlet.

[https://www.youtube.com/watch?v=CWTKHr8wuoA]

During this very period, when I was becoming acquainted with Burton's work, his fame was skyrocketing. Hollywood early recognized the talent of this brilliant Welsh actor and, by the mid-1950s, he was starring in major Hollywood movies such as *My Cousin Rachel* (1952), *The Robe* (1953), and *Alexander the Great* (1956). Despite this, he wasn't yet a superstar or household name. That changed in 1961 when he left *Camelot* to star opposite Elizabeth Taylor in *Cleopatra*. The ensuing scandalous romance between the two (they both were married to others at the time) made headlines and catapulted Burton to the kind of celebrity he had not achieved through his considerable acting chops. Thus, when he returned to Broadway in 1964 for the first time since *Camelot*, it was as the star of a highly publicized, all-star production of *Hamlet*. By now, he and Taylor were married (to each other), the initial scandal behind them. I always wondered whether that production would have materialized without the publicity surrounding his private life, but it did give me my chance to see Burton in *Hamlet*.

I saw two performances of Burton's *Hamlet* on Broadway; one early in its run, during June, and its final performance on August 8th. Even before then, Columbia Records had recorded the production (in audio only), having released the LP set before the Broadway premiere. I bought the recording and had listened to it well before seeing the show live.

[https://www.youtube.com/watch?v=A4uZrna_1FM&t=4s]

But hang on, I did say that this would be my "summer of Hamlet." Joseph Papp's *Shakespeare in the Park* also did *Hamlet* that summer, in Central Park; plus, it was televised! So, on June 18, exactly a week after I saw Burton's *Hamlet* on Broadway, I went to see another *Hamlet*, the one in the park. And, therein lies a story. I will let my notes written three days later tell that story:

Plays and Actors

Even before Burton's "Hamlet" was announced for Broadway, Mr. Papp announced that the first production of the 1964 New York Shakespeare Festival would be *Hamlet*. The title role was given to Alfred Ryder, who I never heard of, but Ophelia was to be played by the talented Julie Harris. Previews of this *Hamlet* were given all last week. The play opened to the critics and to television-taping cameras on Tuesday [*two days before the June 18 performance I attended and was writing about*]. Thus, two Hamlets were going on simultaneously in New York. On Wednesday evening, CBS televised the tape of the production they had made the night before.

It seems that, on that night, Alfred Ryder had laryngitis, but he went on anyway, to the consternation of the critics who couldn't say very much about it. [*They couldn't say much about it because he actually had laryngitis and they didn't want to be as mean as I, an eighteen-year-old lay reviewer whose review was not going to be published anywhere, anyway.*] I saw it on television and I can say something about it. It was simply bad. Mr. Ryder sounded atrocious and didn't act very much better. I hope Mr. Ryder just sounded like that because of the laryngitis. However, whatever the reason, he shouldn't have attempted Hamlet. His actions [*his mannerisms and movements*] reminded me of an old fuddy-duddy. He didn't even know which words to emphasize. He was just terrible. I had already made arrangements with a friend to meet on the next day to see "Hamlet" live in the park. After seeing Ryder's performance on television, I was now wondering whether I could sit through it another night. The next morning I read the news. On Wednesday, while CBS was showing Ryder's performance on television, Ryder had already been replaced in the park by Robert Burr, Richard Burton's understudy for the current Broadway production.

Evidently, Joe Papp didn't think it necessary to have an understudy for the title role, while Alexander Cohen, the producer of the Broadway production knew better, and was kind enough to let Mr. Burr perform in the park production. Luckily for Cohen, Burr never needed to stand in for Burton during Burr's run as Hamlet in the Park, so Burr was probably happy that he got to play Hamlet. This jump-started Robert Burr's career. While he never became a major star, it did help him land some meaty roles on Broadway. As for Alfred Ryder, I never heard of him after the *Hamlet* disaster.

A brief coda: During the Broadway run of Burton's *Hamlet*, a performance had been filmed with a then-new process called "Electronovision." Starting on September 23, 1964 that film was shown over a two-day period in movie theaters across the country.

I, of course, went to see it at a local movie theater. It was in black and white and very grainy, looking like something shot in the 1920s. According to the articles I read about it at the time, all prints and negatives were to be destroyed after the movie-theater run, but that thankfully didn't happen because it turned up on DVD some years ago. Of course, I bought the DVD. The booklet accompanying the DVD explains how this happened: "Prints were contractually ordered to be destroyed, but Burton sent one copy to the BFI [British Film Institute], and kept one copy at home, located by his widow in 1988." I was happy to see that the DVD's picture quality was an improvement over what I saw in the theater, so it was now almost as good as a late 1930s black and white movie! These days you don't even have to purchase the DVD to see it. It has been uploaded on YouTube and is also available for free viewing on a wonderful online theater resource, MIT Global Shakespeares

[https://www.youtube.com/watch?v=vABGEzB7T9M&t=3s].

In the summer of 1964 I saw *Hamlet* live three times; on television once, listened to an audio recording once and saw it in a movie theater once. Is it any wonder that for years afterward I could recite chunks of the play by heart?

So what did I think of Burton's Hamlet? It's pretty clear that I was already a fan of Burton by the time I saw that *Hamlet*, and his performance only enhanced my admiration of his art. Between his magnificent voice and his superb acting he made a memorable Hamlet even in a production in which the cast was dressed in rehearsal clothes. I'll just quote a little of what I wrote about Burton's performance in the second of the two performances I saw. It was written on August 9, a day after I saw the performance. These are my notes:

> Mr. Burton's performance on this occasion was slightly different from my previous viewing [*on June 11*]. He was, if anything, more anguished in his speech. He put in a good deal more laughs just by some little motion or inflection of a word. The electricity of this performance [*this being the last*] gave him more impetus, as if he needed any. He gave a reading that had power and richness of voice, as well as eloquence of language, and he didn't make one false start. [*This last comment referred to my noting in my review of the June 8 performance that he had made several false starts.*] His voice, combined with Burton's great acting, not only opened new vistas in Hamlet's justly famous soliloquies, but made such scenes as the Ophelia/Hamlet encounter, and the closet scene, come alive with

passion. Even more penetrating was the grave-digging scene and Hamlet's encounter with Leartes immediately following Ophelia's burial. What torment poured forth from Burtons lips."

Impressed as I was, I can't say I thought Burton's Hamlet outclassed Barrymore's. Even though there is no recording of a complete Hamlet by Barrymore, the little he left us, as well as the descriptions from those who saw it, make me believe I would have been even more overwhelmed by Barrymore.

[https://www.youtube.com/watch?v=uxV1SgCwruI&t=29s]

Barrymore was an intense and charismatic actor who, through sheer determination, also created a voice that could challenge the most naturally beautiful ones and whose performances have become legendary. Burton, had a naturally beautiful voice to add to his other assets as an actor. So, perhaps I should just leave it that Barrymore was the greatest Hamlet of his generation, while Burton was the greatest of his.

I should note the Burton *Hamlet* was directed by John Gielgud, himself a famous Hamlet of the 1930s, and who in this production also provided the pre-recorded voice of the Ghost of Hamlet's father which appeared as flashes of light on stage. This production had another great performance, that of Hume Cronyn's Polonius. I tended to forget how really good Cronyn was, but when I played the DVD decades later, it all came back. The scenes between Burton and Cronyn were like a lesson in great acting.

[https://www.youtube.com/watch?v=l93LR6Sw75Q]

It should also be noted that Cronyn won a Tony for his performance.

Another interesting tidbit about the production was that Eileen Herlie played Gertrude, Hamlet's mother. Herlie had previously played the same role in the 1948 Laurence Olivier movie. She was then thirty, a decade younger than her screen son. Sixteen years later she was seven years older than her stage son, Burton.

I sometimes appended "added notes" to my "reviews." On this occasion I appended:

> Since this was the last performance of this production of *Hamlet* Richard Burton made a [*somewhat humorous*] curtain speech. In part, he said, "This has been a remarkable experience, *especially for my wife*. . . . Although we've played to packed houses all week long, *we've all been fired*. . . . I've been told I'm the longest running Hamlet on Broadway; therefore

George Rose is the longest running gravedigger, Alfred Drake the longest running Claudius and Hume Cronyn the longest running Polonius. *I'd like to kill Hume Cronyn."* Nothing could have substantiated my feeling about those scenes between Cronyn and Burton more than that friendly threat."

I have to admit though, I have no idea what occurred to make it a remarkable experience for Elizabeth Taylor!

I've seen numerous actors play Hamlet live and on film since. Kevin Kline was one of the few actors who played Hamlet in New York that I missed, though I did see the PBS telecast of the production he starred in. I thought he was the best since Burton. Kline in the last few years has come to remind me of Barrymore. In the most recent play I've seen him do on Broadway, *Present Laughter*, his performance was very Barrymore-like.

[https://www.youtube.com/watch?v=JfQ5GDcHPmE]

Furthermore, in the 2013 film *The Last of Robin Hood,* Kline played Errol Flynn in his last days. Flynn was a close friend of Barrymore toward the end of Barrymore's life and actually played Barrymore in *Too Much, Too Soon*. Flynn didn't strive to look or sound much like Barrymore in that film, nor did Nicole Williamson, playing Barrymore on Broadway in *I Hate Hamlet*, nor did Christopher Plummer in his one man show *Barrymore* (I saw both on stage and the Plummer play was also telecast by PBS). Toward the end of *The Last of Robin Hood* Kline, as Flynn, for only a couple of seconds, does a dead-on recreation of Barrymore's voice and mannerisms. I'd love to see *Kline* play Barrymore.

Burton's Hamlet may have been the most memorable play I saw that year, but the summer of 1964 was a banner theater time for me, having seen several plays that I retain in my memory as particularly outstanding. Among them were: *After the Fall* by Arthur Miller, which starred Jason Robards; the Actor's Studio production of Chekhov's *The Three Sisters* with among others, Geraldine Page, Kim Stanley and Shirley Knight; and James Earl Jones in *Othello* at the Delacorte Theater in Central Park. I remember thinking that Jones showed promise as Othello, but lacked the maturity at that time to do the role justice. I saw him perform it again, this time on Broadway in 1981, seventeen years later, when he was perfect for the role, but he was entirely upstaged that year by Christopher Plummer's mesmerizing Iago.

Eugene O'Neill, Tennessee Williams, Arthur Miller, and Jason Robards

To my thinking, Eugene O'Neill, Tennessee Williams, and Arthur Miller, in that order, were the greatest American playwrights. I think it would be hard to argue against Eugene O'Neill being *the* greatest American playwright. He seems to have written more successful and great plays than any other American playwright. During the 1920s and 1930s, O'Neill won several Pulitzer's, and even a Nobel Prize.

Among the plays he wrote and had produced during that period were *The Emperor Jones* (1920), *The Hairy Ape"* (1922), *Anna Christie* (1922), *Desire Under the Elms* (1925), *Strange Interlude* (1928), *Mourning Becomes Electra* (1931), and *Ah, Wilderness!* (1933).

But, it was in his last years, when his popularity was waning, that he wrote his finest plays. Between 1939 and 1943, as his health was failing, he penned his greatest masterpieces, most notably, *A Moon for the Misbegotten, The Iceman Cometh* and *Long Day's Journey Into Night*. These are the no-holds-barred works within which he creates characters that bare their (his) soul as these plays achieve artistic greatness.

If O'Neill's career arc goes from strength to strength, both Tennessee Williams and Arthur Miller found success early in their careers, but their later plays did not come up to the level of their earlier works.

Williams emerged in 1944 with the poetically semi-autobiographical, *The Glass Menagerie*. This was only his second produced play. So too, Arthur Miller's first play *All My Sons*, had moderate success in 1947. This was followed by his masterpiece, *Death of a Salesman*, in 1949.

In Tennessee Williams's case, the mid-forties was the beginning of a fruitful period. For nearly twenty more years he wrote a string of great dramas, rightfully considered classics, starting with the masterpiece, *A Streetcar Named Desire* (1947), and going forward with *Summer and Smoke* (1948), *The Rose Tattoo* (1951), *Camino Real* (1953), *Cat on a Hot Tin Roof* (1955), *Orpheus Descending* (1957), *Suddenly, Last Summer* (1958), *Sweet Bird of Youth* (1959), and *The Night of the Iguana* (1961). He continued writing plays for the two more decades, but none come up to the standard he had set for himself with *The Glass Menagerie* in 1944. He had five more plays produced on Broadway between 1968 and 1980, but none were successful.

However, as he did throughout his career, he wrote a lot more plays that were not produced on Broadway, and in this period, some were produced Off-Broadway.

While I did attend at least one production of each of the Williams' plays mentioned above—and although his later plays pale in comparison—I also saw one of those later plays, *Small Craft Warnings*, in 1972, in its original, Off-Broadway, production. For reasons that will become obvious, I reproduce here a part of the review that I wrote at that time, on September 1, 1972.

> This is Tennessee Williams' latest play and, like most of his recent plays, it has not met with the critical or popular success of his earlier plays. But I think in years to come it will be more favorably received than it seems to be now. It is powerful, it is meaningful, and it is full of bitterness, bite, and Williams' unique grasp of people's inner feelings. Furthermore, it has Williams' language that is beautiful, even if what the characters are saying is ugly.
>
> A couple of months after this play first opened, Mr. Williams began performing in it himself, as Doc, one of the many lost souls in this play. To see him, and to hear him as the curtain opens, is a strange feeling. But, as the play progresses you realize that this is what you expected Williams to be like—and he adds a bit of authenticity to the play. He is perfect, not because he is a great actor, but because he is a *presence,* and he is not so much *playing* Doc as living one of those lost souls he created, because he knew them better than anyone else.

Like, O'Neill and Williams, Arthur Miller was prolific, but, unlike them, in the fifty-plus years he lived after his early masterpiece, *Death of a Salesman*, he waged a losing battle to create another play that comes anywhere near the scope and depth of that masterpiece. The fact that none of his later plays rose to the level of *Salesman* is both a testament to the greatness and the enduring appeal of his 1949 vision of the common man in mid-century America, as well as being a commentary on his own inability to build upon *Salesman* to create the kind of towering body of work that O'Neill produced in his final years. Miller did write some truly fine plays later on, but they were always compared to *Salesman* and found wanting. They include *The Crucible* (1953), *A View from the Bridge* (1956), *After the Fall* (1964), *The Price* (1968) and *The Ride Down Mt. Morgan* (1991). These may not be masterpieces, but they stand as a major body of fine work.

In 1976, Williams' and Miller's work came together in a double bill in a Phoenix Theater production of two of their one-act plays. Here is part of what I wrote two days after seeing the February 5 performance of that double bill at the Playhouse Theatre on West 48th Street (later renamed the Jack Lawrence Theatre).

It seems with each new production of one of Williams' earlier works, his place in American theater improves. In this case, it would be difficult to say that the short *27 Wagons Full of Cotton [first produced in 1955 and upon which the film "Baby Doll" was based in 1956]* is a major play. It hardly contains the seething drama of Mr. Williams' longer works. Its plot is a bit strange. A cotton farmer burns down a large, mechanized, rival, and the next day the superintendent of that plantation comes to him for 27 wagons of cotton. Proclaiming the good neighbor policy [*the time is early FDR*] the farmer goes off leaving his wife Flora to entertain the handsome stranger. Perhaps it's just a slice of Southern life in the hot summer, but one always suspects, even in a short play, there would be more to Williams than that. The play was terrifically done, with Meryl Streep taking top honors as the baby-faced, simple-minded wife.

At this point it doesn't seem that Arthur Miller's contribution to the American theater is on the same level as Williams, yet "A Memory of Two Mondays," nearly a half-hour longer than "27 Wagons," seems to be a better play. The story of day-to-day existence in a small northern factory during the depression, as seen through the eyes of the young helper (obviously the young Miller) takes on almost a poetic vision, as the dramatist wonders why of all those people he will be the only one to escape. Part of the success of the play is that the characters are so real, so true, and so ordinary; they are people we know and meet every day. The ensemble acting was so superb it would be difficult to pick out names, but John Lithgow as the poetic Irishman was outstanding.

I've seen two productions of *Death of a Salesman*. In 1973, the Circle in the Square produced it with one of my favorite actors as Willy Loman, George C. Scott. I thought his performance superlative, or so I wrote in my review. I must say, however, that the production I saw in 1999 at Broadway's Eugene O'Neill Theatre may have surpassed it.

Death of a Salesman, **Eugene O'Neill Theatre, June 4, 1999 (Written 6/13/99)**

Seeing "Death of a Salesman" again in this splendid rendering makes me stand in awe of Miller's supreme achievement. A tightly drawn story of a dysfunctional family as it mirrors the tragedy of post-war, mid-twentieth-century America. This is not just a gripping family tragedy (and it certainly is that), it is also a searing social commentary of American values and the American dream. It is a reality-based play that, with the use of stream-of-consciousness flashbacks, takes on a surrealistic feel as it flashes through Willy's mind portraying happier times, and as it does so, shows the seeds of Willy's tragic present until the flashback arrives that finally solves for us the mystery of Biff's apparent hatred of his father. Perhaps melodramatic and dated, that scene, and the reconciliation scene that soon follows, remains as powerful today as it must have at the play's premier fifty years ago.

The only thing I didn't like about this production was the intrusive modernistic music that didn't seem to belong. All else was perfect, starting with Brian Dennehy's big, brash, and ultimately pathetic Willy. While you feel sorry for the miserable position in life the sixty-plus Willy finds himself in, you almost understand it when you see the younger self-deluded Willy, selling his sons these same pipe dreams. Brian Dennehy in the performance of his career, gives Willy brash bluster and self-doubt so that we see all sides of this complex personality—this modern King Lear.

This production was telecast, and there is a DVD, but it is not on YouTube. Although somewhat cut, there is a 1966 telecast on YouTube with the stars of the original 1949 Broadway production, Lee J. Cobb and Mildred Dunnock.

[https://www.youtube.com/watch?v=Y7lGIUzUKOE&t=34s]

In 1964, I saw the original production of Miller's, *After the Fall*. It deeply affected me for many reasons, including a towering performance by Jason Robards, Jr. in the lead role of Quentin (Robards was then billed as junior although his namesake actor-father had recently died). This is a small part of my review of that July 25, 1964 performance written on July 26:

> Quentin is searching—searching himself for what he is; for truth, for love, for his future. It is gripping. An absorbing play by a giant playwright. The cast was absolutely superb. Jason Robards, Jr., on stage for the full three hours as the thoughtful Quentin, had an almost "tour de force." His was at times a sensitive performance, at other times a hair-raising performance, but at all times a great performance.

This was the first of many times I would see Jason Robards. To talk about Jason Robards, I must pivot back to Eugene O'Neill, as Robards was the quintessential interpreter of the works of O'Neill and played a large part in restoring O'Neill's reputation. It was in 1956 that Off-Broadway's Circle-in-the-Square theater (then still located in New York's Greenwich Village) decided to revive O'Neill's last full-length Broadway play. When *The Iceman Cometh* was first produced on Broadway in 1946, O'Neill hadn't had a successful play produced on

Broadway in over a decade and *Iceman* didn't break that cycle. It was Jose Quintero's production, ten years later, in 1956, after O'Neill's death, that began to restore O'Neill's reputation, and continued later that year in the Quintero-directed Broadway premiere of *Long Day's Journey into Night*, in which Robards played Jamie Tyrone.

Of course, being ten years old in 1956, I did not see either of these landmark productions. (And, had I at that age, I wouldn't have understood them.) But, I subsequently got to see both plays many times, as well as other O'Neill plays, some of which starred Jason Robards. Among the greatest of my theatrical experiences was the 1985 Broadway revival of *Iceman*, in which Robards returned to the role that made him a star. I am going to reproduce here a large portion of my review of that time. In that review I quote several paragraphs of an article from the *Playbill* I was given when I attended the October 1, 1985 performance. I'm pretty sure I quoted from that article because it contains the kind of romanticized rendering of how Robards won the role of Hickey in 1956 that I myself had a penchant to write.

The Iceman Cometh, Lunt:Fontanne Theatre, October 1, 1987 (Written 10/16/87)

The story of the legendary 1956 Circle in the Square production of O'Neill's "The Iceman Cometh", which single-handedly restored the reputation of O'Neill, created the reputation of Quintero as a director of rare feeling, and made a star of the young, then unknown, Jason Robards, Jr., whose bravura performance of O'Neill's agonized Hickey, made theatrical history, is well known by now. Part of this story is well-stated in an article by Robin Rief in the issue of Playbill handed out at the performance:

"Moved by O'Neill's vision that man needs dreams, no matter how shabby, in order to live, Quintero set out in the spring of 1956 to get this four-hour play on its feet. His working space was Circle In The Square, then at the forefront of the off-Broadway movement.

While he had no one in particular in mind for the role of Hickey, he certainly wasn't considering Robards. O'Neill had called for a short, beefy Irishman—a hail-fellow-well-met type in his 50s. Robards, then 34, was tall, thin and serious with a long, sort of violent face, Quintero recalls. [*This description of Hickey also perfectly describes Brian Dennehy, who played Hickey in 1990 when he was in his mid-fifties. Unfortunately, that production by Chicago's Goodman Theater did not come to New York. Twenty-five years later another Goodman Theater production, with Nathan Lane as Hickey and Brian Dennehy as Larry, played a limited run at Brooklyn Academy of Music.*]

But after auditioning for another role, Robards asked to read Hickey's last monologue, "He had it memorized," Quintero says, "and when he started—my God, it illuminated. The way he peeled away Hickey's cheerful front to get to the madness and guilt was terrifying."

Of all that's been written of Robards' now legendary performance, nothing seems so to the point as the original stage manager Michael Murray's comment that in the character of Hickey, Robards "stumbled on the actor's dream—a role which matched his own gifts so perfectly that every instinct was absolutely correct.... What he seemed to recognize at the heart of the role, underneath a jaunty, friendly...exterior was a guilt and self-loathing so intense that the spectator almost had to turn away from the man's attack on himself."

[*I will digress here to refer to something that has nothing to do with either O'Neill or Robards, but first came to my mind as I sat in the theater in 1987 reading that article. An article in* TV Guide, *three decades earlier than that, when the original* Perry Mason *TV show was on the air, purported to tell the story of how Raymond Burr had been cast in the lead role. The story I read—perhaps apocryphal—went something like this: Burr was auditioning for the role of D.A. Hamilton Burger (although I always wondered why that would have been necessary, as Burr's role in the 1951 movie,* A Place in the Sun, *wherein he played the prosecutor to perfection, should have sufficed). The story went that, after his audition, he insisted on reading for the lead Perry Mason role. This was reluctantly agreed to. During his reading, Erle Stanley Gardner, the creator of Perry Mason, who happened to be at that audition, stood up and shouted, "That's him. That's my Perry Mason." For nine seasons and decades later, across a dozen TV movies, Burr proved him right. Sorry, I just had to tell that story here. Now back to my* Iceman *review*]:

Well, it's twenty-nine years later and Robards is older than O'Neill specified Hickey's age should be. Could Quintero and Robards recreate the magic of the seminal O'Neill production? My answer is a resounding yes and some critics have even wondered whether Mr. Robards would possibly have been a better Hickey thirty years ago. The fact is that Jason Robards' Hickey is a towering creation. He has taken one of the most fascinating and complex characters of American drama and created a charismatic Everyman-Gone-Wild. He creates a character who is at once outgoing, jaunty, and finally nearly terrifying as the final layer of his own pipe dream, his love for his wife, which will not be broken. Robards is simply the definitive Hickey.

As with Robards' portrayals, Quintero's flair for directing O'Neill has never wavered, as we have seen in the past decade's combination of the two in Broadway's "A Moon for the Misbegotten" and "A Touch of the Poet." Quintero perfectly realizes O'Neill's vision of the lost souls of Harry Hope's bar, whose life is booze and pipe dreams, but to O'Neill the booze and pipe dreams are keeping them alive. We all have illusions, O'Neill is saying, and we too would die without them. The denizens of Harry Hope's bar only survive by keeping their illusions, even if their survival is, itself, rather pathetic. Quintero ruthlessly and as poetically as the author, realizes all the pathos and truth of the play."

I have seen three other productions of *The Iceman Cometh*. In two of them, Hickey was played by a well-known Black actor. This was unusual because the play has a minor Black character who is subject to racial prejudice in the plot. Thus, having a Black actor play Hickey, the character for whom everyone in the bar awaits his return and looks forward to seeing, requires further suspension of disbelief.

In my first live viewing of *Iceman* in 1974, revived by the Circle In The Square (by then a Broadway theater located in midtown), Hickey was played by James Earl Jones. It is a tribute to this great actor that long before the days when Broadway sought to diversify, Jones appeared in numerous shows, both on and off Broadway. I noted in the review I wrote of his Hickey, that I had already seen him in numerous classic roles in which one would not expect to see a Black actor. The ones I enumerated in 1974 were: Macbeth, Claudius in *Hamlet*, King Lear and Lopakhin in *The Cherry Orchard*. All of those were productions of Joseph Papp's New York Shakespeare Festival or were Public Theater productions. Papp was an early producer who sought to achieve diversity in casting.

The remaining two productions of *Iceman* that I saw starred Kevin Spacey and Denzel Washington. What I remember of Spacey's 1999 Broadway performance was that it was very athletic, which I thought took away from the seriousness of the play. Before that, Spacey was no stranger to O'Neill. Among other roles I saw him do was Jamie Tyrone in a Jack Lemmon-led production of *Long Days Journey Into Night*. Indeed, in the 1999 Tony Award show, Spacey appeared as a presenter with Jason Robards wherein they enumerated all the numerous O'Neill roles they each had played. Of Denzel Washington's 2018 stint as Hickey on Broadway, although he is another actor I admire, I found his Hickey, who should dominate the stage, underwhelming.

In my *Iceman* review, I mentioned the productions of *A Moon for the Misbegotten* and *A Touch of the Poet* that Quintero and Robards did together. In *A Moon for the Misbegotten,* Robards gave another of his great performances, abetted by Colleen Dewhurst in the first of their several stage forays together.

A Moon for the Misbegotten, **Morosco Theatre, March 25, 1974 (Written 4/5/74)**

It's not just that Robards looks perfect, it's a feeling he gives out, an electricity and aura. Every move, every line, every breath is the way one would feel that James Tyrone, Jr. would move, speak, breath, or cough, or spit, or drink. Furthermore, the sound of his voice, slightly hoarse and gruff, is just perfect. When he sits down and lays his weary head on Josie's lap, one feels as if all of mankind is getting it's first moment of relaxation in the lap of all womanhood (portrayed by the character, Josie Hogan), O'Neill's perfect version of literature's earth mother.

As if one perfect performance wasn't enough, Mr. Robards performance is equaled, if not surpassed (if that is possible), by Colleen Dewhurst's sensational Josie Hogan. Ms. Dewhurst has been one of the greatest Broadway actresses for at least a dozen years. She has played a variation of this earth mother in a number of plays, most notably Athol Fugard's *Hello and Goodbye.* She has done O'Neill before, *Desire under the Elms* (opposite her then-husband George C. Scott) [*the only production cited here that, sadly, I did not see*], *More Stately Mansions* (opposite Ingrid Bergman and Arthur Hill) and, most recently, *Mourning Becomes Elektra.* She was always superb, but, as Josie, she transcends mere greatness to give a perfect performance. The lines in the play describing Josie, really describe the Colleen Dewhurst we know from so many previous performances. And there, she is bigger than life, dominating the action as she dominates James, only to really lose herself to him by her very act of becoming his confessor instead of his lover. Ms. Dewhurst is physically Josie, tall, big, rough, but with the inner heart these earthy Irish seem to inherit. Physically, and otherwise, Colleen Dewhurst becomes Josie Hogan.

As to the play, like all late O'Neill, it bit by bit unveils layer after layer of the characters, and thus, ourselves. From Josie's hidden virginity, through James' train trip accompanying his mother's body, to Phil's knowledge of Jamie's joke, we go deeper and deeper into each character. Of course, there is the midnight to morning scene between James and Josie, as powerful, strong, poetic, and beautiful as anything O'Neill, or anyone, ever wrote, here enchantingly carried forward by performances to remember. In the final scene, the audience feels the relief James feels, and realizes, as Josie does, that she has given him more than she could have given him as his lover. For a moment there is a throwback—was it all for nothing one is almost ready to ask, when James says he doesn't remember? In that one moment all of *The Iceman Cometh* passed through my mind as I wondered if James was going to go the way of the denizens of Harry Hope's Bar. But, there is more hope in *A Moon for the Misbegotten* when James says he remembers. Everything is relieved, and James leaves Josie forever, after the only true night he's ever spent. An absolutely touching scene, played by two greats, saluting in the best fashion anyone can, America's greatest playwright.

Robards and Quintero got together again for a fine production of *A Touch of the Poet*, but it was somewhat anti-climactic after *A Moon for the Misbegotten*, a much better play. In 1988 Robards and Dewhurst did a limited run on Broadway alternating O'Neill's earlier family comedy *Ah, Wilderness!* with *Long Day's Journey into Night*. Also appearing as Robards and Dewhurst's son in both plays was Campbell Scott, Dewhurst's real-life son with her sometime husband George C. Scott (like Taylor and Burton, Dewhurst and Scott were married and divorced from each other twice).

This was the second time I saw Robards play James Tyrone, Sr. I also saw him in the role some years earlier at the Brooklyn Academy of Music. His James Tyrone, Sr. in *Long Day's Journey* was disappointing. Robards was born to play James, Sr.'s son, Jamie, as the character is known in *Long Day's Journey* and the same character years later in *A Moon for the Misbegotten*. (*Long Day's Journey* is set in the Tyrone summer home in Connecticut in August 1912. *A Moon for the Misbegotten* takes place in September, 1923 when James Tyrone, *Jr.*, who was called Jamie by his family eleven years earlier, comes back for the last time to sell the family summer home. Thus, *A Moon for the Misbegotten* is something of a sequel to *Long Day's Journey*.)

However, the role of James Tyrone, Sr., the miserly former matinee idol–sometime-Shakespearean-actor, who sold his soul for a hit show, just wasn't a natural for Robards. The elder James Tyrone in the very autobiographical *Long Day's Journey into Night* was the playwright's stage representation of his own actor-father, James O'Neill. James O'Neill came from a different generation of actors and acting tradition than Robards. I don't think James O'Neill would have felt comfortable playing most roles in his son's late plays, except, of course, playing himself in *Long Day's Journey*, any more than Robards would feel comfortable playing Shakespeare. As far as I know, Robards never performed Shakespeare on stage. This was a wise decision, because in the one foray into that realm that I know of, his Brutus in the 1970 movie version of *Julius Caesar*, Robards actually looks uncomfortable and his voice, so perfect for O'Neill, sounds out of place throughout the movie.

[https://www.youtube.com/watch?v=qjG_Huf7tZw]

If my favorite actor, John Barrymore, had not died in 1942, he would have been seventy-four years old in 1956, when *Long Day's Journey into Night* was first produced on Broadway, and would have been a perfect James, Sr. Having come from the same acting tradition as did James O'Neill, he, too, had abandoned Shakespeare for greater wealth and fame. Interestingly, the role of James, Sr. in the Broadway premiere of *Long Day's Journey into Night* went to Frederic March, who had played a version of John Barrymore in the 1930 movie version of the Ferber/Kaufman Barrymore spoof, *The Royal Family*.

I've seen *Long Days Journey* more times than any other play, except *Hamlet*, starting with an off-Broadway production during the summer of 1970 with Robert Ryan, and most recently on Broadway in the summer of 2003 with Brian Dennehy, Vanessa Redgrave, and Philip Seymour Hoffman.

Robards and Dewhurst would appear together on the Broadway stage twice more after alternating in *Long Day's Journey* and *Ah, Wilderness!* In 1983 they were in a revival of Kaufman and Hart's, *You Can't Take it with You*.

[https://www.youtube.com/watch?v=56IGjR63fjM&t=697s]

In 1989, A. R. Gurney's two-character play *Love Letters* opened on Broadway. The "gimmick" of that production was that each week a different couple would step into the roles. Robards and Dewhurst were the opening week cast.

Unlike a lot of other stage actors, Robards had a strong movie career. His breakthrough non-ONeill stage performance in *A Thousand Clowns*

[https://www.youtube.com/watch?v=zpjN97qJ0bk]

was made into a major motion picture with Robards in the lead. In the 1960's he starred in such films as *Tender is the Night, By Love Possessed,*

[https://www.youtube.com/watch?v=Eofkue3ybwk]

Any Wednesday, Hour of the Gun, The Night They Raided Minsky's (where you can catch Robards singing)

[https://www.youtube.com/watch?v=ROLgwF_Bqhs]

and, in 1970, one of my favorites of his films, *The Ballad of Cable Hogue*.

[https://www.youtube.com/watch?v=QyvbqZqQ0xI]

As the '70s progressed, he did more and more character and

supporting roles while continuing to do much television, including prestige projects such as *FDR: The Last Year,*
  [https://www.youtube.com/watch?v=NOzxnNixgkM[
Clifford Odets, *The Country Girl, The Day After,*
  [https://www.youtube.com/watch?v=utGRP9Zy1lg]
The Long Hot Summer,
  [https://www.youtube.com/watch?v=2Za-JRTQzXY&t=2s]
Inherit the Wind,
  [https://www.youtube.com/watch?v=zaqJMynKXrk]
and *Mark Twain and Me.*
  [https://www.youtube.com/watch?v=pTfZGznz70Y&t=12s]

Unfortunately, Hollywood mostly bypassed Robards' great work in O'Neill's plays. Robards recreated only his Jamie Tyrone in the wonderful 1962 big screen version of *Long Day's Journey* with Katherine Hepburn and Ralph Richardson—but, the small screen comes to the rescue.

In 1960 there was an ambitious syndicated television project called *The Play of the Week.* Each weekly, pre-taped presentation was a classic play, often having stellar casts of stage veterans. It was shown for five days, at the same time every evening during the week. (At least, that's how it aired in New York.) In its second and, lamentably, last season, they outdid themselves by taping the whole of *The Iceman Cometh* to be shown in two parts over two weeks—*with Jason Robards as Hickey.* I saw it when it was first telecast, but I can't say, at age fifteen, that I understood it. It was only later, when I got "into" O'Neill, that I realized the treasure that it was and hoped it was preserved so I could see it again. It was, and it was ultimately released on DVD and has been posted on YouTube.

Although it is in black and white, and having a set that seems somewhat claustrophobic, the play, and Jason Robards' monumental performance, come shining through. Among the supporting cast was James Broderick (Matthew's father) and the young Robert Redford (who fifteen years later was to be the star of the movie, *All the President's Men,* for which Robards won the first of his two supporting actor Academy Awards.). It was directed by Sidney Lumet, who was soon to also direct the 1962 screen version of *Long Day's Journey into Night.*

The 1974 production of *A Moon for the Misbegotten* was also videotaped and telecast on ABC in 1975. Interestingly, the time span between the 1962 movie version of *Long Day's Journey into Night* and that 1974 taping was almost the same time period that O'Neill indicates had elapsed between the two plays, so posterity can see

Robards aging as the character he is playing ages.

I recommend that anyone who has not seen Robards as Hickey in *Iceman* go to YouTube and see it.

[https://www.youtube.com/watch?v=etEFM_B9YS0&t=6785s]

For that matter, also do this for the screen version of *Long Day's Journey Into Night*

[https://www.youtube.com/watch?v=AkZ-3hBPQwQ&t=738s]

along with the 1975 *A Moon for the Misbegotten* telecast.

[https://www.youtube.com/watch?v=jNAdkbOi44o]

I think you will agree that Eugene O'Neill was America's greatest playwright.

Please note that most of the plays cited here were written during the same period in which I drew up my list of great musicals. Is there another period in American theatrical history when so many new works of such high quality appeared together? The 1940s through the 1960s was truly the golden age of Broadway.

More Great American Plays

My choice for number four on my pantheon of great American playwrights, Edward Albee, like Arthur Miller, wrote one great masterpiece, *Who's Afraid of Virginia Woolf*, that dwarfs his many other plays. Although I have seen and enjoyed several other of his plays, *Who's Afraid of Virginia Woolf* is the only play written after 1960 that, I believe, can stand alongside the masterpieces of the '40s and '50s. While I did not see the 1964 original production of *Virginia Woolf*, in 1976 I saw a fine revival with Ben Gazzara and Colleen Dewhurst. Somewhat less successful was the revival I saw in 2005 with Bill Irwin and Kathleen Turner.

In the nearly sixty years since its premiere, *Who's Afraid of Virginia Woolf* has had four Broadway revivals (although the last one, scheduled to open in March of 2020 for a limited run, was shut down after a handful of previews, due to the pandemic). Here's a portion of my review of the 1976 revival, which, like a real critic, I happened to see at its opening-night performance.

Who's Afraid of Virginia Woolf, Music Box Theater, April 1, 1976 (Written 4/3/76)

In the years since *Who's Afraid of Virginia Woolf* premiered, many analyses have appeared to show it as an allegory for a homosexual relationship (the author is gay) or an allegory of the U.S. (the main characters are called George and Martha, of Washington fame) and, while I don't know whether either Mr. Albee's sexual preference or conflicts of the union were a real influence, I probably feel that, at its most moving, the play is about a long-lasting, deeply felt relationship. George and Martha rant and rail at each other, but in one of her rare moments of honesty to Nick, Martha shocks him with the news that George is the only man that ever made her happy. That is so, she also admits, and we see clearly, because he is the only man equal to her. [*I am skipping parts of this review, as printing it would be a spoiler for those who have yet to see the play or its splendid movie version with Elizabeth Taylor and Richard Burton*].

[https://www.youtube.com/watch?v=hlVyZ6cooxc]

To say this production is marvelous is hardly doing it justice. Despite the heavy language and beginnings of raillery, the first act plays like a witty comedy moving more and more into the realm of the intense drama of the second act—and catharsis at the end of the third. Colleen Dewhurst is a theatrical treasure and her "Martha" was to the manner born; big, tough and aggressively sexy. A stunning portrayal. Ben Gazzara's "George" was aptly complementary to Dewhurst's "Martha," perfectly carrying the partly defeated look and that spark of life that he is to ignite at the end to defeat their own morbidness."

In 1973, Jason Miller (who was not related to Arthur) had a huge hit with *That Championship Season*. It may not be in the same league as *Death of a Salesman*, but it is a terrific play that won the Pulitzer Prize for Drama that year. I saw the original production in 1973, and was disappointed in the later, star-studded 1982 movie version. Jason Miller wrote a few plays after that, none produced on Broadway, but he had an extensive career as an actor, especially in movies and TV, garnering an Oscar nomination for his first screen role as a supporting actor in *The Exorcist*, the same year he won the Pulitzer.

Two well-known trivia facts about Jason Miller: He was married to Jackie Gleason's daughter, and the actor, Jason Patric, is his son. Patric appeared in the only Broadway revival (2011) of *That Championship Season*. More trivial and less-remembered is that, in 1980, Jason Miller appeared in the TV movie, *Marilyn: The Untold Story*,

[https://www.youtube.com/watch?v=5ZHAqHGc8lQ]
wherein the 1973 winner of the Pulitzer Prize for Drama portrayed the 1949 winner of the Pulitzer Prize for Drama, Arthur Miller!

Two other plays that may belong in the list are Frank D. Gilroy's

The Subject was Roses (1964) and Lorraine Hansberry's *A Raisin in the Sun* (1959). *A Raisin in the Sun* may have been the first *successful* Broadway play written by a Black playwright. Since I have seen neither on stage (only the screen adaptations), I will not discuss them in greater detail, but move on to a play by a Black playwright that I *did* see, and one that impressed me immensely. That play was Charles Gordone's, *No Place to Be Somebody*. Although it had a limited Broadway engagement at the ANTA Theater in early January, 1970, it ran for about eight months in 1969 at the Public Theater, where it was developed. After the Broadway run, it was transferred to the Promenade Theater on upper Broadway, which was not technically a Broadway Theater because it had fewer than the minimum number of seats required. It played an additional ten months at that theater. It justifiably won the 1970 Pulitzer Prize for Drama, making it the first play by a Black playwright ever to win a Pulitzer Prize.

No Place to Be Somebody belongs to that genre of plays as Saroyan's, *The Time of Your Life,* and O'Neill's, *The Iceman Cometh,* that take place entirely within a bar. At this point, more than fifty years later, I don't remember much of its content, and even re-reading my review from that time doesn't enlighten me very much either. However, I remember being deeply impressed, as the review will show.

No Place to be Somebody, **ANTA Theater, Charles Gordone, author, January 9, 1970 (Written 1/10/70)**

An absorbing, moving, and provocative modern play. There are probably another dozen adjectives I can use to praise this fine theatrical experience. The play is very complex and speaks of much in both Black and White America, and what it says isn't always easy to take. Note that, while I'm very serious about the play's dramatic content, and it should be taken seriously, the play is also an extremely hilarious comedy. This is one of the few modern works I've seen to succeed as both a drama and comedy; and, perhaps, on a third level as social commentary.

As for the performances, they were all on a high, superb level. But, above all, was the stirring, beautiful portrayal by Ron O'Neal of "Gabe." This was almost a *tour de force* portrayal, especially in his narrator-like song scenes, and particularly, the "White as Snow" number. Indeed, Ron O'Neal's performance was among the greatest I have ever seen.

Neither Charles Gordone nor Ron O'Neal built on the success of this play. Gordone never had another play produced on Broadway.

Two years later, Ron O'Neal gained instant fame starring in the Blaxploitation film, *Superfly*. Thereafter, he appeared mostly in movies and on TV, rarely playing the kind of role that would show off his dramatic talent.

I would like to see *No Place to be Somebody* again to see if my first impression was accurate and whether it stands the test of time. There was a 1969 PBS telecast that I did not see, and I don't think that Ron O'Neal was in it. I know of no DVD release, but YouTube does have a short clip.

[https://www.youtube.com/watch?v=jPZ2iSNt6wM]

It was left for August Wilson to become the first Black playwright to write a series of plays that have had successful Broadway productions and put him among the pantheon of great American playwrights.

Shaw, *Man and Superman*— Paul Sparer, Harris Laskawy, and Philip Bosco

I have heaped praise on Barrymore and Burton, but they are world famous and don't really need my adulation to add to their reputations. However, there are some performers who spend most of their careers on a stage, and although they may be as good as or better than more well-known actors, they remain almost unknown to the general public. The actors I will write about here were, perhaps, not star material as they might be better-defined as character actors, but in many of the stage performances in which I saw them, they were magnificent. I will also write about one of my all-time favorite plays, George Bernard Shaw's, *Man and Superman*, because, among other reasons, I saw these three actors play the same role in three different productions of that play.

Man and Superman is a hugely funny comedy with a wonderful plot, although some may say it has no plot at all! It's "sort of" about a man who runs away from a woman he comes to realize, perhaps too late, wants to marry him. She is anxious to procreate so as to give birth to *the Superman* (not the Superman of DC Comics, but Nietzsche's Superman!). There's also a subplot about a secret marriage. Best of all, it has a dream sequence which is also something of a philosophical treatise. Believe me, the play is much more complicated and entertaining than this weak attempt to describe it.

While Shaw often uses great plots to advance his political and philosophical agenda, his plays are so entertaining that one doesn't mind his forays into politics, philosophy, and religion, even when one doesn't agree with him. The best of his plays, more than just entertaining, are great works of literary and theatrical art.

Shaw began writing plays late, when he was in his forties. He was previously a music critic, but living to age ninety-four, he had plenty of time to write dozens of plays, many of which are classics. Among them are *Mrs. Warren's Profession* (1893), *Arms and the Man* (1893), *Candida* (1894), *Caesar and Cleopatra* (1898), *The Devil's Disciple* (1896), *Major Barbara* (1905), *The Doctor's Dilemma* (1906), *Androcles and the Lion* (1912), and, of course, *Pygmalion* (1912) which became the source for *My Fair Lady*. I think Shaw is my favorite playwright. Shakespeare may be the greater playwright, but Shaw is more fun.

Of all Shaw's plays, *Man and Superman*, written between 1901 and 1902, is his longest and most ambitious, even if it may be less well known. Uncut, it would run at least five hours. The dream sequence, called *Don Juan in Hell*, lasts about ninety minutes and has successfully been performed on Broadway, and elsewhere, by itself. This, however, does Shaw's vision an injustice, as do performances of *Man and Superman* without the *Don Juan in Hell* portion. The experience of viewing the whole of *Man and Superman*, complete with *Don Juan in Hell*, is magical. And, who but Shaw would create a central character who is famous for writing a book and then actually write the very book that the character supposedly wrote? He does this in *Man and Superman*.

All four full productions of *Man and Superman* I've seen were done by repertory companies. Because of my love for the classics, I attended many of the small repertory companies that abounded in New York in the sixties and seventies, as Broadway did not produce enough classics for me to get my fill. Indeed, of the four productions of *Man and Superman* I saw, only one was a Broadway production. I will concentrate on the first two productions I attended because they were the best—mostly because they were the least cut, and because of the performances of the first two of the actors I write about below.

The first production I saw was in 1965, produced by the now-long-defunct APA/Phoenix Repertory Company, headed by Ellis Rabb. Rabb often acted in the productions and sometimes played the male lead character, Jack Tanner (something of an anglicization of Don Juan Tenorio) in *Man and Superman*. He was not in the performance

I saw, rather, Donald Moffat played Jack. Mr. Rabb's then-wife, Rosemary Harris, played the second female lead, Violet, while Nancy Marchand played the female lead, Ann (or Donna Anna in *Don Juan in Hell*). This being a true repertory company, they often switched roles. Ms. Harris probably played Ann when her then-husband was performing Jack. She was actually the best-known performer in the cast. She may be most familiar today for playing Peter Parker's aunt in the Tobey McGuire *Spiderman* movies.

[https://www.youtube.com/watch?v=Wes8IR-yGrU]

Ms. Marchand was also to become more well-known later in her career when she played the owner of the newspaper that Lou Grant worked for in Ed Asner's *Lou Grant* series

[https://www.youtube.com/watch?v=lfuE_sOxTNI]

and even more so just before her death when she played Tony Soprano's mother.

[https://www.youtube.com/watch?v=o45oIge8RzY]
[https://www.youtube.com/watch?v=GS0DQKHMpM8]

Unfortunately, neither actor impressed me in this production of *Man and Superman*. I found Ms. Harris's raspy voice off-putting, and Ms. Marchand's acting seemed to be nothing more than a series of poses. I got to see Ms. Harris in several other stage roles, especially when APA/Phoenix moved to the Lyceum Theater, Broadway's oldest theater. In 1965 when I saw them do *Man and Superman*, they were in an Off-Broadway theater somewhere in the East 90s. Anyway, I got to appreciate Ms. Harris more in those other roles. I especially remember the APA/Phoenix production of Richard Brinsley Sheridan's, *A School for Scandal* (which included Helen Hayes in the cast) and a wonderful 1976 production of the George S. Kaufman/Edna Ferber spoof of the Barrymores, *The Royal Family* wherein she played Ethel (though of course the character in the play had a different name). That production was taped for television.

[https://www.youtube.com/watch?v=5sUM-0_hJUg&t=2s]

Several decades later, in a 2009 Broadway revival of *The Royal Family*, Ms. Harris played the elderly family matriarch, the role that the legendary Eva Le Gallienne played in the earlier production. I most recently saw Ms. Harris onstage as Henry Higgins's mother in July, 2019 at the Vivian Beaumont Theatre in Lincoln Center in a revival of *My Fair Lady*. Similarly, I appreciated Ms. Marchand more in the many later stage performances in which I saw her.

Paul Sparer

What helped to make this APA/Phoenix performance of *Man and Superman* so memorable for me was the actor who played the lovelorn Spanish/Jewish brigand, Mendoza, Paul Sparer. Mr. Sparer was just brilliant in what certainly is the most colorful role in the play. In a quote from my review of the August 1, 1965 performance written three days later, I wrote:

> The finest acting of the performance came from Paul Sparer whose Mendoza was full of authority, both from his acting and his superb voice. As the Devil (in the "Don Juan in Hell" scene) he was even better. He is a commanding actor. Even his comic lines, such as the reading of Mendoza's love poems to Luisa, were absolutely so funny that I almost split my sides laughing.

Paul Sparer and his wife, Nancy Marchand (*yes, that company had two married couples*), left APA/Phoenix not long after. But I got to see them both, especially Sparer, in many other productions. Here's what I wrote about Sparer after seeing him in a production of Ibsen's *The Lady from the Sea* at the very obscure New Repertory Company (NRC Theater) in September, 1973:

"Most worthy was Paul Sparer, a favorite of mine, and the reason for my attendance at this production. I've seen Mr. Sparer in lots of plays with every repertory group from the old APA/Phoenix, through both the New York and American Shakespeare Festivals to the Roundabout Company's production of Ibsen's, "The Master Builder," two seasons ago. I never saw him give a bad performance and his Mendoza/Devil with APA/Phoenix eight years ago and his portrayal of the title role in *In the Matter of J. Robert Oppenheimer*, a half-dozen years ago were superlatively memorable. He achieved that level again here."

I note in checking his credits on Internet Broadway Database (IBDB), which does not list Off-Broadway performances, many of his Broadway credits are as a standby. Based on the performances I saw him in, I suspect he probably was better than many of the more famous actors he was standing by for.

You may be thinking to yourself, I've never heard of Paul Sparer. He can't be that good. Unfortunately, there is little left by which to judge him. However, watch this scene from a telecast in 1983 of Euripides' *Medea* with Zoe Caldwell as Medea and Paul Sparer as Creon.

[https://www.youtube.com/watch?v=zInoTXKyOvI]
You see a classic actor, with a magnificent voice. Another bit of theater trivia. The actress playing the nurse in this clip is Judith Anderson, who in 1948 won a Best Actress Tony Award for playing the title role in *Medea* and repeated the role for a 1959 *Play of the Week* telecast.
[https://www.youtube.com/watch?v=oXu0tqkXc3g&t=724s]

Harris Laskawy

The next production I saw of *Man and Superman*, in 1969, was, this time, by an Off-Off-Broadway repertory company, the CSC (Classic Stage Company). This company was founded by Christopher Martin (not the Black actor of later fame nor the lead singer of Coldplay) and Harris Laskawy. Both acted in many of their productions. This company still exists, but not in anything like its original form as a true repertory company. I first saw the CSC when it was housed on the second floor of a building on Bleecker Street in Greenwich Village. The play was *Uncle Vanya* by Anton Chekhov.

Uncle Vanya, June 16, 1969, (Written 6/17/69)

I am grappling to replace the APA/Phoenix Repertory Company, which is no longer in existence, and this, my first viewing of a production by the Classic Stage Company was like saying hello to a new friend.

This production of *Uncle Vanya* by Chekhov, one of my favorite plays, was superb. With one set, a fairly small stage area, and with dressing rooms behind the audience, the company did a marvelous job bringing Chekhov's play to life. They almost made the play a comedy of manners, but deep within everything was the bitterness and loneliness of Chekhov's characters.

The cast was excellent. Most brilliant of all was Harris Laskawy in the title role. He played the almost-pathetic Uncle Vanya strongly so that every expression and action, as well as every line had meaning. He was simply superb."

I should note that, while APA/Phoenix Repertory Company, a combination of two separate organizations (APA stood for Association of Producing Artists), was dissolved in late 1969, the Phoenix Theater continued for another decade.

Classic Stage Company (CSC) did indeed become my "friend," as I would see most of their productions for the next decade or so. Harris

Laskawy became one of my all-time favorite actors. In 1970 he won an "Obie" for his portrayal of Uncle Vanya. It was in 1970 that I saw what I consider their finest production, a nearly four-hour rendition of my favorite play, *Man and Superman*. In it, Harris Laskawy cemented my regard for him as one of the greatest actors I've ever seen. I saw this production three times, once in 1970, and twice in 1971, after they had moved to slightly more spacious quarters on West 3rd Street.

Man and Superman, March 7, 1970, (Written 3/8/70)

When I first saw *Man and Supmeran* five years ago, as my first exposure to Shaw and the APA-Phoenix Repertory Company, I loved the play and the company. Indeed, every time I would think back to that performance, it became more memorable. Now, at last, I've gotten another chance to see what I now consider Shaw's masterpiece in a different production by another repertory group. *Man and Supmeran* is just as good, nay—even better in the second viewing, and this performance was just as memorable as the first one.

It is a basically funny play and at times I laughed hysterically. Shaw's incisive wit and philosophy come shining through in a very entertaining manner. Again, I sat enthralled through the "Don Juan in Hell" scene as the characters talked on philosophically, with only momentary comic breaks. I wasn't only enthralled, I was absorbed, enlightened, and enriched. Shaw's way of turning the tables on convention, his view of Don Juan as the captive not the captor, of men generally as the sought, not the seeker, is just a small part of what he is saying. His great ability to turn his philosophy into an exceptionally entertaining piece of theater is just part of his genius. There is so much in this play that lasted more than three and one-half hours (not counting intermission) that it would take pages to write about. Furthermore, how can one criticize or analyze Shaw, one of the greatest critic-analyzers of the century, who was his own best critic-analyzer, as the preface to the play proves. [*Shaw was famous for writing sometimes lengthy prefaces to his plays.*]

One of the most memorable aspects of the APA's *Man and Superman* was Paul Sparer's perfect Mendoza, a part I never thought could be improved upon. Harris Laskawy, though perhaps not better than Mr. Sparer, was, at least, in the same class. His voice had an all-nationality tinge to it. Moreover, his performance had a very strong bite to it, and he, too, was able to get great laughs from the "Mendoza-Luisa" poem recitation just before the end of the "Don Juan in Hell" scene.

About a year later, in April 1971, I went again to see the CSC's *Man and Superman.* I reproduce only my remarks about Mr. Laskawy from my review at the time:

> Harris Laskawy's Mendoza is a performance that ranks as one of the greatest. I have revised my estimate since last year. Mr Laskawy is better than Paul Sparer was in the same role. Indeed, this performance, and some of the others I've seen Mr. Laskawy do with CSC, indicate to me that he is one of the finest actors around today. How can I sum up his magnificent performance, employing a multi-accented voice and a great knowledge of what Mendoza and acting are all about? He did not employ a particularly Spanish accent, but there was just the tinge of an accent that seemed to include many nationalities.

I was so enthralled with the performance that I convinced a few of my friends to attend with me the CSC's final performance of that work two weeks later. I thought it to be even better (and, according to my notes, it was fifteen minutes longer—and for the first time, sold out). Unfortunately, my friends were less impressed and the event did not turn them into Shavians. I must have been really crazy in those days because my reviews reveal that the day after I saw my third *Man and Superman* with the CSC, I went back to see *Uncle Vanya* with Harris Laskawy for the second time. As I said, the CSC in those days was a true repertory company.

Over the next several years I was to see Harris Laskawy in at least a dozen leading roles at the CSC, in plays by playwrights as diverse as Shakespeare, Ibsen, and even Ugo Betti—besides the already-mentioned Chekhov and Shaw. I won't say every role was as memorable as his Vanya and Mendoza but that list gives you some idea of his range.

Harris Laskawy, never received the recognition he deserved. He left the CSC in the mid-70s. I never discovered why and I assumed that he had had a falling out with his co-director Christopher Martin, who remained the head of CSC for a decade or so more.

Laskawy continued performing with small companies in New York and I would go to see him whenever I saw he was appearing in something. The first post-CSC performance I saw was with a small, obscure repertory company, The Meat and Potatoes Company, which performed on the second floor of an office building at 38 West 39th Street. It was a contemporary play, *A Summer of Education* by Neal Weaver who, according to my notes was the founder of that company. Weaver also directed the play and designed the set! This is what I wrote of Harris's performance which I saw on September 28, 1978 and wrote about two days later:

"What made the play really come alive was the magnificent bravura performance of Harris Laskawy as Kevin. Yes, this is the same Harris Laskawy who co-founded the CSC and, for several seasons, was its finest actor, performing a wide variety of classical roles. Now, after five years, he has returned to full-time acting and the New York stage, and his performance here in a role so different from many of the roles he performed at the CSC, was nothing less than brilliant. Many times during his CSC years I had occasion to call him one of the finest actors I'd seen on any stage. This performance only confirms my feeling of the genius of this relatively unknown thespian."

Sometime in the early 1980s I saw that Harris was to appear in a production on Theater Row. I reserved tickets only to find when I got there that he was not listed in the cast. I asked why he wasn't in it and was told he'd bowed out because he was filming a movie in New Jersey. It turned out that the movie was *The World According to Garp*, in which he appears briefly with a few short lines. The scene was set in front of a mansion owned by Garp's mother (Glenn Close, in her movie debut).

On another occasion I went to see Harris in an Off- Broadway play about football called *The Guys in the Truck* by Howard Riefsnyder. It was in 1982 during a National Football League strike and there was a local TV news reporter in the lobby of the theater before the performance asking people why they had come to the show. She came up to me and I responded honestly that I was there to see Harris Laskawy. She fled from me like I had the plague. It soon became apparent that the reaction she was looking for was that people were there to get their fill of football, which they couldn't otherwise do because of the strike. (I, obviously, have no interest in football.) So, my potential fifteen seconds of fame on tape was erased. While I remember the TV incident vividly, I didn't remember anything about the play until I dug up my review and saw why.

While I praised the performances, especially that of Harris, I found the play itself inferior, closer to a sitcom. It did, however, get Harris to Broadway! Somehow, money was obtained to mount a Broadway production of this trifle. Of course, for the Broadway production they got a bigger name to star in it, Elliot Gould—Laskawy being relegated to understudy or standby. Elliot Gould did some of the previews, but he then bowed out of the production. So it opened on Broadway with

Harris Laskawy in the lead. Unfortunately it didn't do for Laskawy what similar situations did for Tom Bosley and Sutton Foster. It lasted for one performance!

I did get to see Harris on Broadway. In 1985, he played the relatively small role of the bartender in the Jason Robards revival of *The Iceman Cometh*. It was not the kind of flashy role that would get him noticed. That was the last time I saw him on stage. That year he moved to Los Angeles. IMDB shows that, between 1980 and 2005, he appeared in numerous movies and TV series, albeit, usually in small character roles—nothing that would show off the range and magnitude of his talent. In the biggest film role I saw him in, he played a gangster in one of Katherine Hepburn's last films, *Grace Quigley* from 1984. He died on July 4, 2010 in Los Angeles, at the age of 67.

When I first saw him, while he may not have had matinee-idol looks, he was tall, of medium build with strong, interesting features and dark curly hair. In the few pictures of him that I could find online, he appears to have put on weight and lost lots of hair as he got older. I could barely recognize him in those later pictures.

It's nice to see that, in the last decades of his life, Harris actually got paid for acting. In one of my early reviews of the CSC, I noted that their actors worked without compensation. A few years later,

Harris Laskawy in his CSC years and, later, in his Hollywood years.

talking to someone during an intermission of a performance (not one Harris was in), I mentioned that Harris Laskawy was one of my favorite actors. I expected he would not know that name, but he told me that Laskawy had taught at a high school in New York City that he had gone to. I was not able to verify that, as there was no mention of a teaching career in his obituary in the *Los Angeles Times*, the only obituary I could find online, but I wouldn't be surprised if that wasn't his day job for all those years when I was admiring his stage performances.

It is here that I initially ended my tribute to Harris Laskawy, but it is here that my writings become a part of the story. While preparing this section, in the fall of 2021, I did an Internet search of Laskawy, seeking to verify whether he did teach during his CSC years. I happened on a comment by his widow, Jennifer Reed, on MyHeritage.com. Further Internet searching got me her address and I wrote to her, enclosing a draft of what I had written, asking if she could confirm that Harris taught in New York City public schools in those years and whether she could tell me why he left the CSC. She graciously responded to my inquiries by e-mail. She confirmed that he taught in two New York City high schools, James Monroe High School, in the Bronx, and William Cullen Bryant High School in Queens between 1965 and 1974. As to my inquiry on why Harris left the CSC, she said his reasons were "heartfelt," but private.

I had resigned myself to never knowing why Harris left the CSC, when, in late August, 2022, out of the blue, I received a small package in the mail containing several documents from the CSC's early days, as well as a fifty-seven page document titled "Harris Laskawy," undated and unsigned, a rough draft of an interview with Laskawy in which he talks about the formation of the company, its early days and productions, and ultimately his candid and often scathing views about co-founder, Christopher Martin. Sadly, Jennifer Reed had recently died, and her brother, in going through her belongings, and finding my letter, thought I would be interested in those documents. Suffice to say, the Harris Laskawy interview did answer the question of why he left. Unfortunately, it is not easy to summarize as it was an accumulation of many things over a period of years having to do with Chris Martin's need to control every aspect of the company. That said, they had remained on friendly terms even after Harris left the CSC.

I would note two more things apropos of what I wrote. Laskawy notes that the CSC actors not only were not paid, but at some point in the very early days of the company, they actually paid "dues" ($25.00 a month) to chip in for the rent. To be fair, he also notes that Chris Martin spent a lot of his own money on lighting, sets, and various other things for the company. Indeed, there would not have been a CSC without Christopher Martin. While Laskawy was listed as a co-founder, CSC was actually Martin's brainchild.

This is the point, as I did with Paul Sparer, at which I should provide a clip demonstrating his abilities. But, unlike with Sparer, I can find no clip to show you his greatness as an actor. There are no videos of Harris in any of his great stage roles. Here are two clips, the first, an appearance on *Search for Tomorrow* in February, 1984. (He enters at 2:18.) The second is fourteen years later in *The Slums of Beverly Hills,* with Alan Arkin chewing up the scenery. Neither gives even a hint of what Harris was capable of.

[https://www.youtube.com/watch?v=qN9pT4njWFE].
[https://www.youtube.com/watch?v=VR1j_sfCdY8]

I started this lengthy overview of Harris Laskawy's career with my notes on the first time I saw him in *Uncle Vanya*, but my review did not reveal an important part of the production that Harris talks about in that interview. It reveals something of the actor that I feel is interesting enough to quote here. The punctuation is as it was in the original draft I received, appearing to be a transcription of an oral interview:

> [Unidentified interviewer to Harris]: "(I asked about the end of the play) Sonia had her big speech. Everything will be alright Uncle Vanya, don't worry about it. We're at the desk. I settle down, 'Let us go back to work,' she says. So we did. We went back to work. I was left at the desk. I wiped my tears and I went back to work, and she got up went to a case and got out a ledger book and took bills and started to enter them. The stage lights dimmed, not went out. The house lights went up, which made you know that it was over and we had applause. And the audience became aware of the fact that was it. And they would eventually get up and leave. We never left the stage until everyone was gone. We were out there working until everybody left. Well, this is on third Street. One day two couples. . . . At that time the stage was the floor of the theatre and the seats were just built up on the three sides. And the entrance was kind of down right, were [sic] the audience came in from the outer lobby. There were curtains there that led to the hallway. And these two couples lingered inside by the curtain until everyone else had gone. And they were kind of whispering to themselves. And we were still at the desk and we could see of course that they were still there. Kathryn says to me, 'I don't

know about you, but if they don't leave pretty soon, I'm going to leave the stage.' Just at that time one of the group breaks off and starts to come toward us. And I'm going Oh my God . . . . He comes tiptoeing, there was a rug on the floor, across the floor, and he leans right on the desk and I look up, And he goes, 'We just wanted to thank you for letting us come into your home tonight. .' And that's the greatest thrill of all. My greatest thrill in theatre."

Philip Bosco

After this very long tribute to Laskawy, I am going only to briefly write about Philip Bosco, partly because, although his was not quite a household name, Bosco had an extensive career in the theater and received the kind of recognition neither Sparer nor Laskawy achieved. He won a best actor Tony Award in 1989 and was voted into the American Theater Hall of Fame in 1998.

I first saw Bosco in the title role of Shakespeare's *Coriolanus* at the long-lamented American Shakespeare Festival in Stratford, Connecticut in the summer of 1965. I have seen Philip Bosco on stage more times than any other actor. This was not difficult, as IBDB lists him as having appeared in more than fifty Broadway productions between 1960 and 2006. And that's just Broadway! On the screen IMDB lists him as appearing in innumerable movies and TV series between 1963 and 2010. One of his last big screen appearances was in 2007 as Laura Linney and Philip Seymour Hoffman's father in *The Savages*.

Here's Laura Linney speaking about Bosco.
[https://www.youtube.com/watch?v=Q02x-vo7LIQ]

Strangely, Bosco's performance as Mendoza in a 1979 Circle in the Square production of *Man and Superman* was possibly my least favorite of the many performances I saw him do. He simply did not measure up to Sparer or Laskawy in that role, but he was a consummate professional who gave brilliant performances in a wide variety of roles, including many other plays by Shaw. Indeed, possibly my finest memory of him onstage was a 1986 Circle in the Square production of Shaw's *You Never Can Tell* wherein he appeared onstage for only about fifteen minutes at the end of the play during which time he stole the play from everyone else, giving the audience a lesson in great acting. Of the October 2, 1986 performance I attended, I wrote:

Philip Bosco, at his best, was the class conscious, always-deferring waiter, who helps put everything right. His was a performance to cherish and was pitch-perfect, almost as if Shaw was directing him.

The star of that production of *You Never Can Tell* was Victor Garber. Three years later they were reunited in Ken Ludwig's *Lend Me a Tenor*. For his performance in that play, Bosco won a Tony as best actor.

[https://www.youtube.com/watch?v=bbngacAVU_c]
[https://www.youtube.com/watch?v=S3QQB3mK5bU]

For a glimpse of his Shakespeare (from the following year's Tonys):
[https://www.youtube.com/watch?v=g7Gu9vWKc60]

Here is a more complete overview of Bosco's career:
[https://www.youtube.com/watch?v=jm5ZvVPbFQQ]

Back to *Man and Superman*. After a three-decade dry spell, when there was no production of *Superman* produced in New York, I finally got to see *Man and Superman* again in 2012 with the Irish Repertory Company. It was directed by David Staller.

[https://www.youtube.com/watch?v=qFrL1VLJY6E&t=58s]

The most recent live performance of *Man and Superman* I saw was on May 20, 2019, a script-in-hand reading by the Gingold Theatrical Group, a company founded by David Staller, that specializes in giving readings of Shaw's plays and occasionally stages full productions of his plays. Indeed, I have read that Staller is America's greatest authority on Shaw. Both these recent performances were cut to under three hours, but it is always great fun for me to see this play, and I always enjoy it.

I was unfamiliar with the Gingold Theatrical Group when I went to see their fully staged Off-Broadway production of one of Shaw's early plays, *Widowers' Houses*. I remember sitting in an aisle seat and, before the performance began, a man walked by, stopped, and introduced himself to me. "I'm David Staller, the director." I suppose he wanted to start a conversation, but I was so surprised that the director would approach an audience member that I was somewhat speechless. Usually quite reserved, I think I may have just muttered, "hello" —no conversation ensued. In my sixty years of theater-going, that has never happened. Subsequently, in Gingold readings I've gone to, I've noticed that Staller appears to be friendly with most of the audience; many of them by name! Evidently, others are not so reticent as I.

The only representation of a full production of *Man and Superman* that I am aware of, preserved on video, is the 2015 National Theater of Great Britain's production with Ralph Fiennes in the lead role. Part 1 [https://www.youtube.com/watch?v=ejYqJ_1m9Ho] Part 2 [https://www.youtube.com/watch?v=1J7o8udx71c]

Near the start of the pandemic, David Staller's Gingold Group did a virtual reading of *Man and Superman* on the Internet show "Stars in the House." Though not a perfect performance, and at nearly three hours, cut more than I would like, it had a talented group of actors under Staller's direction who were still a joy to see. There was one directorial bit I found really amusing. I don't know if it was Staller's idea or that of Robert Cuccioli, who played Roebuck Ramsden, but, toward the beginning, when Roebuck is railing against Jack's "little" book, he holds up a book the size of "War and Peace". If I had blinked I would have missed it, but I found it amusing.

One more thing. Some years after I had convinced several of my friends to come with me to see that last CSC performance of *Man and Superman*, some of those friends were going to see a comedian called "Brother Theodore" and they urged me to go with them.. Brother Theodore had gained some fame on David Letterman's late night show, but I was not familiar with him and I suspected it would not be my cup of tea, but I felt sort-of-obligated, having made them sit through four hours of Shaw. I wrote this at the time of the October, 1974 midnight performance in a Greenwich Village theater:

"What is a "Brother Theodore" one may ask. That's exactly what I did when some friends of mine persuaded me to go see this thing. He speaks in a German accent. (I have no idea if it's put on, in fact, I probably don't care.) He tells us he's a disciple of a new religion or spirituality. Its main tenet is that one should stop eating! He goes on and on about this and makes jokes about himself and the audience. He chooses someone in the second row and begins to insult him. He offers to make a woman in the audience "Theodora." My favorite line, came near the beginning when he said: "All our spiritual leaders are dead. Moses is dead. Jesus is dead. Mohammed is dead. And I'm not feeling so hot myself."

As you can tell, I was not very amused, except for the line I quoted. At this point you are probably wondering what has this to do with anything? David Staller would probably be able to tell you. Several years later, while perusing the bargain bins of a record store, I came across an LP containing several of Shaw's BBC radio broadcasts. Of course, I had to get it, and when I listened to it, I came across this in one of his broadcasts, circa 1940: "All the great English literary figures are dead. Milton is dead. Shakespeare is dead. Dickens is dead, And I'm not feeling so well myself."

I should have known—the best thing in Brother Theodore's performance was cribbed from Shaw!

Shakespeare in the Park

Robert Burr's *Hamlet*, in 1964, was the first play I saw at Shakespeare in the Park, but I was to see one performance of every Shakespeare play they did for the next twenty years, missing only one *non-*Shakespeare play they did during that period, Ibsen's *Peer Gynt*. In the early days of park performances, free tickets were handed out starting at six for the performance that began at eight. The line started early in the morning. My routine was to get there a little before 5:00 PM. I was always able to get a ticket. Later, when I was married, and my job made it more difficult to be there before five, my wife, Vicki, would be the one to get there before five and I would join her as soon as I could. By about 6:15, we usually had our tickets, and headed to a restaurant we liked just off Central Park West on 80th Street in one of those pre-war apartment buildings. After dinner, we would stroll back in time for the eight o'clock curtain (of course there was no actual curtain). While the quality of the performances may have varied, I remembered the many evenings I followed this routine as being some of the more delightful aspects of my theatergoing.

At its beginnings, *Shakespeare in the Park* did three productions a season; at some point it was reduced to two. Each production ran for about three weeks. In its various runs, I got to see most of Shakespeare's plays, including such rarities as *Pericles* and *Titus Andronicus*. Although those productions varied widely, there were some fine productions, as well as many fine performers who would go on to illustrious careers; these included Christopher Walken, Meryl Streep, James Earl Jones, Charles Durning, Sam Waterston, Stacy Keach, and many others.

Two of the high points of Shakespeare in the Park came in the summers of 1968 and 1970. Here are excerpts of the reviews I wrote of those performances.

Parts I and II of Shakespeare's *King Henry IV*, Saturday, July 13, 1968 (Written 7/20/68)

This marathon presentation of both parts of Shakespeare's "King Henry IV" was certainly a great theatrical experience, and one to treasure. This season, the New York Shakespeare Festival is performing the two parts of "King Henry IV" on alternate evenings, but, just this once, they presented both parts in one evening. By the time the performance drew to a close, after 3:00 A.M. Sunday morning (Part One was presented from 7:00 to 10:30, with a ten-minute break, and Part Two from 11:30 to 3:10 with a ten minute break) there was a certain rapport established, and a feeling of intimacy. After the curtain calls, Mr. Keach pointed at the about-one-half audience left from what, at 7:00, was a full house, and then the cast began applauding the audience. But, generous as the cast was, it was they who deserved the greatest applause for an amazing and moving feat.

Stacy Keach was a brilliant Falstaff, tall, padded with fat, taking in and dishing out insults with the same elan, and generally enjoying his rascally and roguish life. He really had feelings for Prince Hal and their parting scene was an etched painting of pride valiantly straining to stay alive. Sam Waterston's Prince Hal captured the essence of a Prince whose acting out the part of a good-for-nothing only so that his transformation into a good and true ruler will be more treasured. He says this in his first soliloquy and everything he does confirms this, although it is obvious he loves Sir John and it hurts him tremendously when he has to abandon [Falstaff] for his political self"

Among others in the large cast were Barry Primus, James Ray (excellent in the title role), Charlotte Rae, Stephen McHattie, Penny Fuller, George Hearn and Stephen Elliot.

Two years later, on June 27, 1970, the New York Shakespeare Festival outdid their 1968 marathon.

Parts I, II, and III of Shakespeare's *King Henry VI*, Saturday, June 27, 1970 (Written on 7/5/70)

This summer Joseph Papp's New York Shakespeare Festival has mounted its most ambitious program to date, and on this occasion probably had its finest hour. This summer, the New York Shakespeare Festival is doing Shakespeare's "King Henry VI" slightly cut in two parts, instead of three, plus "Richard III," which immediately follows "Henry VI" and caps Shakespeare's historical cycle. On Saturday, June 27, starting at 7:00 P.M. and running to 5:30 Sunday morning, the New York Shakespeare Festival held a marathon performance of all three (or, if you please, four) of these plays in chronological succession, to the delight of the packed crowd.

Thus, I got to see all of "Henry IV" in one sitting, and I was more than wide awake enough to stay for the "Richard III," but unfortunately, at 2:00 A.M. [when "Henry VI" ended] the weather was so cold I was freezing and thought I'd better leave and return on Thursday to see "Richard III" (which I did). Unlike the marathon of "Henry IV" two years ago, there were people waiting to get in when I left, so even at the end, I understand that the house was packed.

This performance was a compelling and memorable theatrical experience that had some superb high points and some beautiful performances. True, these plays can't compare with, say, the two parts of "Henry IV," or even just the last hour of "Richard III," but there are many glowing moments in them and they glowed all the more in this superb production showing the real futility of war and ambition. In these plays, battles come hard upon battles, many lives are lost, yet little is ever won, and what is won seems meaningless compared to the personal loss, yet the protagonists go on fighting for their kingdom."

I guess these were early examples of what we now call binge-watching. As I was/am usually not outdoors at 2:00 A.M., I didn't realize how cold it could get in the wee hours of the morning, even in early summer, [*Internet research tells me that the temperature was 58 degrees that night.*] so I went to the performance unprepared, without a warm jacket, and I had to leave "Richard III" for another day.

Shakespeare in the Park continues to this day. Unfortunately, I have not seen a free Shakespeare performance in the park now for nearly forty years! Just about twenty years after I began going to *Shakespeare in the Park,* I stopped. Two things happened that made it more difficult. On a happy note, our first child was born, but it was a change the festival made that altered the dynamic for me. They changed the time at which they gave out the tickets from six in the evening to noon. Working in lower Manhattan, I couldn't spend an hour or more standing on line in the middle of the day. And, even if I could, it meant going way uptown only then to go back downtown to return again in the evening. When I was not working, I would have to come to Manhattan from New Jersey, leaving early in the morning to get there in time to score tickets, and then have to kill nearly eight hours before curtain time. It was no longer the pleasant experience I had enjoyed when taking in their performances, so I went cold turkey on *Shakespeare in the Park*

I've actually seen two free Shakespeare in the Park shows at the Delacorte in the last nearly forty years, but in a reversal of my initial two decades going there, those two shows were two of their rare non-Shakespeare productions. Indeed, they were two of my favorite musicals.

In 1997, they produced Leonard Bernstein's *On the Town*, and I was eager to see it. I needed to game the system, so I tried a different method for getting a ticket. Tickets required that one be in one's seat by 7:50, else the seat was lost. At that time, the staff counts the number of no-shows and lets in the number of people equal to the number of empty seats from a line of people who have been waiting by the entrance for this count to take place. Once in the theater, you then must scurry around looking for an empty seat. The chances of getting in this way varied from night to night. I managed to get in on my second night of trying.

In 2012, it was Sondheim's *Into the Woods*.
[https://www.youtube.com/watch?v=YanlCN899bY&t=3394s]

By 2012, there was a digital lottery, so I could attempt to get tickets from the comfort of my home. Once again, I succeeded on my second try. In 1997, before getting onto the line hoping to secure entrance, I had nostalgically eaten dinner at the restaurant I had first patronized over thirty years earlier and to which I had continued to go before each of those many Shakespeare performances in the past. By 2012, that restaurant was gone.

The Two Funniest Shows I've Seen on Broadway

Heretofore I have written mostly about musicals, and serious dramas by the likes of Shakespeare, O'Neill, or Miller. Even Shaw's plays, though comedies, usually have a serious philosophical or political underpinning. What I am going to write about here are the two funniest plays I have seen on Broadway. They have no serious underpinning; just very silly plays with more laughs than any other plays I've seen. They have two things in common. They both come from Britain and they are both plays about performing a play!

The first is *Noises Off* by Michael Frayn. I saw it shortly after it opened on Broadway in December, 1983.

Noises Off, Brooks Atkinson Theatre, Dec 15, 1983 (Written 12/18/83)

Michael Frayn's *Noises Off* is a *gimmick* comedy that is often hilariously funny. Its gimmick is that each of this play's three acts are actually a different performance of the same first act of one of those dim-witted English sex-farces that seem to run forever in London, performed on tour by a troupe of second-rate players. In each act, the backstage shenanigans (mostly the romantic couplings and uncouplings of the cast) affect what is going on onstage Act I is the pre-opening run-through. Act II is a month later seen from backstage. Act III is a month after the previous act, and any resemblance to the play they are supposed to be performing that we saw in Act I is purely coincidental. The first act is reasonably funny and, of course, expository. Act II becomes a very frantic farce and, hilariously so, probably the most consistently funny of the acts. Act III, although not quite so frantic, is full of laughs, which can only be funny if you've seen Act I and know the way the play is supposed to go.

The cast was superb. Dorothy Louden did her usual broad comic turn, including her by now famous stare and pout. Brian Murray was quite likeable as the blustering, frustrated, womanizing director, whose amours cause some of the funny plot turns and laughs. Paxton Whitehead was at his best as the rather boorish actor who gets mixed up in a sort of triangle with Ms. Louden and Victor Garber. Mr. Garber, in quite a change from the other roles I've seen him in, was effective as the not very bright leading man. Deborah Rush was the "dumb blond" who keeps losing her contact lenses, and was quite delectable in her undies, in which she had to play much of her role. A perfect ensemble performance rare for the Broadway stage."

Noises Off has had two revivals on Broadway, in 2001 and 2016. I did see the first revival, which despite the presence of Patti LuPone, did not impress me as much as the original production. This, perhaps, was because that cast couldn't duplicate the perfection of the ensemble in the original production and, perhaps because I, being familiar with the play, it was no longer fresh and surprising. I had similar feelings about the 1992 movie version. Nevertheless, for nearly a quarter of a century, the original Broadway production of *Noises Off* remained in my mind as the funniest show I had ever seen on Broadway, until 2017.

The Play that Goes Wrong, by Henry Lewis, Jonathan Sayer, and Henry Shields, The Lyceum Theatre, July 20, 2017 (Written 8/2/17)

I laughed until I cried through much of the first act and only slightly less so in the second act. *The Play that Goes Wrong* is possibly the funniest thing I have seen on Broadway since the original production of *Noises Off*. The London based Mischief Theatre Company's original play, written by three of its performers, is a laugh filled mixture of slapstick, Monty

Python, and assorted other comedy genre's.

The premise is in the title. A play is being staged and everything (and I mean everything) goes wrong, including the location of the performance (they're in the wrong theater)! Indeed, the play starts before the starting time, and even the intermission is part of the play!

The cast was absolutely perfect, with flawless timing. It better be, because it looked like, if things were off even by seconds, someone really could get hurt. I gotta say it, this play really went right.

[https://www.youtube.com/watch?v=MczfOgWZ6P8]
[https://www.youtube.com/watch?v=NrY4ebngdO8]
[https://www.youtube.com/watch?v=DOWO4gq-whg&t=161s]

I recently (April, 2023) saw the Mischief Company's Broadway follow-up, *Peter Pan Goes Wrong* (in a preview performance before Neil Patrick Harris joined the cast) and though quite funny, it did not achieve the comedy heights of its predecessor.

However, between these two Broadway outings the Mischief Company has created a television show *The Goes Wrong Show*, that, so far, has had two six-episode seasons starting in 2019. I haven't seen all the episodes but what I've seen clearly put it among the funniest current television shows.

In my review I referenced *Monty Python*. Like Python, the Mischief Company is an ensemble effort. But like *Monty Python* I think there is a first among equals. This came to me when I saw the thirteen episodes of *Monty Python* that John Cleese did not appear in because he was away on another project. Without Cleese the show wasn't the same, it just wasn't as funny. That became clearer a little later when Cleese starred in *Fawlty Towers*, one of the funniest television shows ever made. As talented as the rest of the Python cast was, it was Cleese who provided extra oomph. Based on what I have seen, I think Henry Lewis (he's the heavy-set one) is to *The Goes Wrong* show what John Cleese was to *Monty Python*.

Two Seminal Solo Shows

Shows with only one performer on stage were never my favorite genre. However, I did see a few I really enjoyed. James Earl Jones as Paul Robson (1978), Emlyn Williams as Charles Dickens (1981), Victor Borge (1977), Lily Tomlin (1977 and 1986), and *Elaine Stritch at Liberty* (2002) come to mind. But one that made a great impression on me was a seminal work in the genre, Hal Holbrook's *Mark Twain Tonight!* I caught a performance during its first Broadway run in 1966.

Holbrook first performed it in New York Off- Broadway in 1959 and, along with 1966, twice more on Broadway in 1977 and 2005.

Mark Twain Tonight! **Longacre Theater, June 9, 1966 (Written 6/11/66)**

Hal Holbrook in his famous show *Mark Twain Tonight!* is simply fabulous, there's just no other word for it. Between Hal Holbrook's acting and interpretation of Mark Twain and Mr. Clemens' brilliant words, this show keeps you thinking and laughing for its entire length.

The general idea of it is that Hal Holbrook comes out dressed as, and acting as Mark Twain at 70, delivering one of Twain's famous lectures. The material is from Twain's works and Holbrook puts them together and goes about speaking and telling the stories the way he feels Twain did.

Holbrook's make-up and interpretation are superb. After a few minutes you forget it's a show and really believe you are seeing the great author himself. Mr. Holbrook has everything down to a tee. He goes much further than imitating Mark Twain, a man a good thirty years his (Holbrook's) elder in the show. In one section, Holbrook, who is forty, playing Twain as a man of seventy, proceeds to imitate Twain's famous character, Huck Finn, a boy of ten or so, then as Huck, he imitates his father, a man of fifty or so. It may seem complicated, but it was great.

I saw the show one more time during its last Broadway run in 2005. Holbrook was then eighty, and the novelty of a forty-year-old portraying a seventy year-old was gone. In each performance Holbrook may choose different material to perform. The great tour-de-force described of the '60s was not in that later performance, and, anyway, could not be duplicated by an eighty-year-old. Also, while the earlier performance ran over two hours, the eighty-year-old Holbrook pared it down to ninety minutes. Holbrook, who died in 2021 at ninety-five, last performed his most famous role on stage at the age of ninety! One version of the show was telecast in 1967
[https://www.youtube.com/watch?v=9Y-yezGRRiw&t=453s]

Another delightful, not-quite-solo show was Victor Borge's *Comedy with Music*. (A soprano, Marilyn Mulvey, joined him on stage, briefly.)

Victor Borge in *Comedy with Music,* **Imperial Theater, September 30, 1977 (First Preview) (Written 10/3/77)**

Nearly twenty-five years ago, in 1953, Victor Borge brought himself, a piano, and little else to Broadway and proceeded to make theatrical history by parlaying his original, limited run, one-man-show to a two and a half year smash. For those who don't know, Mr. Borge sits in front of the piano, stands by it, walks around it and the stage, and mainly tells stories and jokes, occasionally actually playing the instrument, which, when he is serious, he does rather well. But, Mr. Borge is not frequently serious.

To sum up, Mr. Borge is an extremely funny man. He can dart a look at a member of the audience when a cough or sneeze is heard that leaves you in stitches. Indeed, it is almost a trick of his to do so in a slow moment in his act and it never ceases to work. He will play some serious musical phrase and then juxtapose something silly like "Happy Birthday to You" and the audience will gleefully laugh along. But mostly he will just talk, tell a joke, a story, and often point out a ridiculousness in his adopted second tongue, English. Of course, the underpinning of his comedy is music and references to music abound. But, the fact is Mr. Borge's comedy has heart, and that comes through beautifully.

As with the performance I saw, Borge often had an opera singer as a guest. Knowing my favorite opera singers by now, you must realize I could not resist including this clip. Here's Borge with Danish compatriot Lauritz Melchior (how can you resist not calling them "Two Great Danes"), followed in the next link by a complete Borge show.

[https://www.youtube.com/watch?v=Z9ILp1vI70c]
[https://www.youtube.com/watch?v=3NtMbQGn31c]

Potpourri

Tony Bennett

I've stated that I am a big Tony Bennett fan. I'm writing this immediately after seeing his CBS TV special, *One Last Time*, Bennett's farewell performance at Radio City Music Hall with Lady Gaga, recorded in the summer of 2021. It was later announced that the ninety-five-year-old singer, now suffering from Alzheimer's, has retired. For his age, and condition, his performance in that concert was wonderful. [*Tony Bennett died on July 21, 2023 at the age of 96.*]

In the last years of his career, as he aged, some of Bennett's vocal agility was lost and he sometimes strained in the upper register. To cover this up, he made a number of duet albums, letting others sing those parts that would show that strain on his voice, and he also changed some phrasing by emphasizing different words to cover the lessening of his vocal flexibility. The timbre of his voice remained unchanged however, and, on occasion, he could still produce some astonishing notes that would put singers a third of his age to shame.

Such a singer might be Lady Gaga. To her credit, he *did not* put her to shame in his farewell performance. She was fabulous, and the rapport between them was real and touching, even if he had to lean on the piano for support while she romped all over the stage. He appeared to be in better voice than some earlier, but recent performances I'd seen, so this was a fitting farewell to an American icon.

[https://www.youtube.com/watch?v=7wTSu0y-TEI]
[https://www.youtube.com/watch?v=HdtEzynieTI]

Not just an icon, Tony Bennett is a great American. Reading his autobiography, *The Good Life,* some years ago, one story, having nothing to do with his career, struck me the most. Bennett, born in 1926, was drafted into the army in 1944, when he was eighteen, arriving in Germany just a few weeks before the end of the war.

Martin Luther King, Jr. Nipsy Russell and Harry Belafonte at Selma March. Tony's face is visible between Russell and Belafonte.

Collection of the Smithsonian National Museum of African American History and Culture, Gift of Monica Karales and the Estate of James Karales

He relates how, after Germany surrendered, he met there with a childhood friend from Queens. They were going to have lunch together, but his friend was not allowed into the mess hall because he was Black. Tony relates how unfathomable it was to him that American soldiers sat side-by-side *with German soldiers* in that mess hall, but this *American* soldier, could not eat there *because of the color of his skin*. Bennett's pain and anger came clearly through in print. It is no wonder that nearly twenty years later, when Harry Belafonte asked him to join him on the Selma march led by Martin Luther King, Jr., Bennett didn't hesitate.

I became a Tony Bennett fan in the 1950s, but I did not see him live until his limited Broadway concert engagement with Lena Horne in 1974. They also did a TV special together.
[https://www.youtube.com/watch?v=A5yD8PN0CQg&t=64s]

I saw him in concert several times, most recently in 2015 at the New Jersey Performing Arts Center when he was eighty-nine years old. Following is my review of the best of a half dozen concerts of his that I saw. It was, perhaps, the best concert of popular song standards I've ever seen. It's too bad CBS Records didn't record this concert for CD release. It would have been a lovely bookend to his 1962 Carnegie Hall album.

[https://www.youtube.com/watch?v=5VwKAGk_i6s]
If anyone did record it surreptitiously, I would love to hear it again. Below is my not-so-much-a-review as a tribute.

Tony Bennett, Carnegie Hall Concert, **February 18, 1997 (Written 2/22/97)**

Well, it may be a cliche, but in Tony Bennett's case it is also very true that, like fine wine, Tony Bennett's voice gets better with age. At the age of seventy, having been a recording artist for forty-seven of those years, there is simply no diminution of his vocal prowess, while his artistry simply grows. Even the sound of his voice is more mellifluous than ever. All this, together with his always-ready-to-please humbleness continue to make him my favorite living pop singer.

In the last half-dozen years, partly due to canny direction from his manager/son Danny Bennett, Tony's career has spanned the generations and he has become an idol of teens and twenty-somethings, as well as older fans like myself. Back with his original label Columbia [now CBS], his first several CD releases have won Grammy's and sold in the millions, something his records haven't done in thirty years. And you can hardly turn on the television without seeing him as a guest on "The Tonight Show", "Unplugged," or his own live Valentine's Day Special (the second annual one being just before this concert). Tony Bennett, after some lean years, is now more popular than in the 1950s, when he had a string of a dozen or so hit records.

This Carnegie Hall concert was a sort of testimony of what he has become and a summation of his recent career. The first half had just two people on stage: Tony, and his long-time music director, Ralph Sharon, at the piano. With just piano accompaniment, Tony simply sang his heart out. In just over a half hour, Tony sang a dozen or so songs magnificently. He started with the first song on the first Tony Bennett album I purchased forty years ago (simply titled "Tony," it was mono only and has long been out-of-print) "It Had to be You" and he sang it ten times better than four days before, on his televised Valentines Day Special. He went on to sing a number of other fine songs, including a short set from his new tribute to Billie Holiday CD, aptly titled "Bennett on Holiday," including a memorable "God Bless this Child" (without the Billie Holiday track on the CD).

The second part of the concert brought out the Ralph Sharon Trio with Douglas Richeson on bass and Clayton Cameron (absolutely smashing in his solo number) on drums. With this trio he likes to swing more than belt, so it took a little longer to work into the declaiming style I like so well. The set was over an hour and Tony got to do short segments from two other recent CD's, "Here's to the Ladies" with Judy Garland's signature song "Over the Rainbow" and "Steppin' Out," his tribute to my all-time favorite popular entertainer, Fred Astaire. I must mention that besides this newer material, Tony sang two or three of his older hits. His own signature song "I Left My Heart in San Francisco" hardly sounded any different from his recording of thirty-five years ago. "Rags to Riches," the only of his 1950s hits he sang here, though phrased slightly differently from his recording of forty-five years ago, sounded just as splendid. A memorable performance. Tony Bennett is a national treasure!

My Vote for the Most Overrated Popular Singer

If I were to get into trouble with Giovanni Martinelli, Richard Tucker, or Luciano Pavarotti fans for calling any of them overrated, I'm going to get in a heap of trouble with *a lot* more people for calling this singer overrated. He is almost universally regarded to be one of the greatest (many say *the* greatest) emissaries of American popular song. So why don't I appreciate Frank Sinatra as much as so many others do?

I sort of like the mid-1950s Sinatra. The 1940s Sinatra recordings are nice, showing off a pleasant, but not overwhelmingly beautiful voice. His early '50s hit recordings of *Young at Heart* is on my list of favorites from that period. Even in those days, however, I preferred Nat King Cole, Dean Martin, Frankie Laine, or Eddie Fisher. I found them to have more distinctive and beautiful voices.

During the middle 1950s, I noted a change in Sinatra. While many people thought that Sinatra's voice and personality had mellowed into the perfect vehicle for interpreting the twentieth century's great American popular song canon, I thought the opposite.

As Sinatra progressed from teen idol to worldwide icon after his Oscar-winning role in *From Here to Eternity* (1953), I noted an arrogance in his personality that crept into his singing. His singing sounded to me like he was a wise guy. (His alleged association with mafia types didn't help.) That, together with never finding his voice to be all that beautiful (which by now you know is my *most* important criterion for describing a great singer) turned me off to Sinatra. Even more bothersome to me is that his acclaim kept growing to the point of unfettered adulation. (Which was not dissimilar to how I felt about Pavarotti's growing fame.)

When I listen to Tony Bennett or Fred Astaire, their nice-guy personas permeate the material they sing, and it lifts my spirits. When I listen to late-period Sinatra, I hear a smart aleck. There are some post-1955 Sinatra recordings that I like, but, on the whole, I simply think he is way overrated.

Cole Porter's *Night and Day* was one of Sinatra's favorites. He recorded it many times. So did Fred Astaire, who introduced the song in his final Broadway show, *The Gay Divorce* in 1932. Listen to Fred's 1934 version from the film *The Gay Divorcee*

[https://www.youtube.com/watch?v=-rV1iM_3FBI]

then listen to Frank's 1962 recording, Some of Sinatra's fans consider this his best version, while others believe it's his 1957 version. I choose the 1962 version because it includes the introduction.

[https://www.youtube.com/watch?v=mGGirB4XOmI]

Obviously, Sinatra's singing chops are far superior to Astaire's more limited vocal resources, but, when it comes to Astaire, I must and do temporarily abandon my deeply held belief that the sound of the voice is the most important element a singer brings to the party. Fred's charm, utter naturalness, and impeccable phrasing simply tug at my heart and he wins me over every time. I am aware that phrasing is claimed to be one of Sinatra's great strengths, but his version seems to me contrived when compared to Astaire's. That is just *my* feeling! Speaking of singing chops, as a bonus and for contrast, I'm ending this paragraph with Mario Lanza giving *Night and Day* the full operatic treatment. Decide for yourself.

[https://www.youtube.com/watch?v=ap99Er2Zneg].

So, why do most folks love Sinatra? Bono may have provided the answer in a documentary about the making of Sinatra's first duet album. There is a scene in the back of a car in which Bono and Sinatra are talking. Bono is explaining why he likes Sinatra. One of the major reasons Bono gives is that Sinatra has—I believe the word he used was—"attitude." That's when I had my epiphany: *Others may like Sinatra for the very reason that I don't!*-Some years later in a tribute to Sinatra Bono again emphasized this view.

[https://www.youtube.com/watch?v=5y4QE7A3JXY]

The Age of the Singer/Songwriter

As is apparent, I am a lover of "The Great American Songbook," and the singers and songwriters of the early to mid-twentieth century. I have also stated that I did come to love much of the music that came after rock and roll changed the pop music business beginning in the mid-1950s. In the pre-rock days, there was a delineation between the songwriter and the singer. Irving Berlin, Cole Porter, George Gershwin, and the others, didn't sing; very few singers wrote songs, and if they did, even fewer became hits. Mel Torme's, *A Christmas Song*, is the exception and, even in that case, the hit recording was not by Torme, but Nat Cole.

[https://www.youtube.com/watch?v=8fxmh9srt1w]
[https://www.youtube.com/watch?v=c-RXKcc0sZs]

From the sixties onward, as hit songs originating from Broadway and Hollywood became rarer, the singer-songwriter took center stage.

Whether it was solo artists like Dylan and Springsteen, or artists associated with bands, like Neil Young and Eric Clapton, and rock bands whose material was written by a member or members of the group (such as Lennon/McCartney) the songwriters were the performing individuals. Generally speaking, the best renditions are those by the writer of the song causing most post-60s songs to be less covered by singers other than the writer; especially when artists like Taylor Swift write songs that are very personal to themselves. After all, in many instances, those songs grew out of the life experience of the songwriter who wrote them and, of course they are written for the vocal capabilities of that songwriter.

On occasion, well-known songs, written and performed originally by a singer-songwriter, get a complete makeover by another artist, taking it to a new level that surpasses its original . Here are three examples:

Kris Kristofferson included the song, *Me and Bobby McGee*, in his first album, *Kristofferson*, released in 1970. A year later, Janis Joplin's final album, *Pearl*, was released posthumously. Her rendition of that song became a huge hit. Going to another level, Joplin's raw, raspy, rock version took the song well beyond Kristofferson's original country version. Listening to it more than fifty years later, it hits the listener as one of the greatest rock recordings ever made. That Kristofferson and Joplin lived together for a short while adds poignancy to the recording. And, perhaps only a Rhodes Scholar (Kristofferson) could have come up with the significant line, "freedom's just another word for nothin' left to lose," but Bob Dylan came up with many more lines, equally good, having had much less schooling.

[https://www.youtube.com/watch?v=G-J7mLyD3yc]
[https://www.youtube.com/watch?v=xkgga0jywk4]

As noted earlier in the summer of 1970, I had just graduated law school and was to begin a new job in September with the Legal Aid Society in New York City. I was looking for an apartment in Manhattan. By early August I had been apartment hunting for nearly two months and was getting discouraged. I needed a break. I remembered two friends from Rutgers who had extended an open invitation to me to crash at their place if I ever came to Boston. I had never been to Boston, so I decided to hop on a train. I got to their apartment in the early evening and found that I wasn't alone. There were several others crashing there, and all of them were about to go to a concert at Harvard Stadium. As several cars were going, there was room for me. It was August 12th and the concert headliner was Janis Joplin. My friends came prepared with lots of weed (as did most everyone else in the stadium), so the stadium was filled to capacity with about 40,000 stoned fans.

We got there some time before the expected starting time of 8:00 o'clock, but the concert didn't actually begin until 8:30. This is part of what I recorded in my notebooks some days later, after getting back home:

> The concert started late and trouble began early. "The Eagle" [sic?], a rock group, came out to perform first, but it was soon obvious that the sound equipment wasn't working. The concert stopped. An announcement was made that the stadium's sound system was stolen in the afternoon and they were trying to set up the replacement equipment correctly—and were sending for more. The concert continued. The sound equipment broke down every once in a while as it went on. Sometimes you could hear the music; sometimes not. The second group on the program, "The Gas Mask," came on. I think they performed one number, but the sound system was off, so the audience shouted them down. Janis Joplin—and useful sound equipment—finally made it around 10:30 P.M., though even then it wasn't perfect. But she came out and did her thing for about fifty minutes, which was only five or six songs.

I don't remember how familiar I was with Joplin's music before that concert, but I'm pretty sure I wasn't very familiar with it. Perhaps because of my unfamiliarity with her music, the fact that I was stoned (which was never the case when I went to operas and shows), and that I was still relatively new to rock music, I did not do a critique of her performance in my review. The most notable thing I remember after so many years, was her incredible performance of *Mercedes Benz*, a song I had never heard before. (Having been written only earlier that month, it may have been the first and only time she sang it in public.)

She didn't sing "Me and Bobby McGee" at this concert. I didn't mention that she sang Gershwin's "Summertime" in my review—which, considering my preferences, is strange (except, perhaps, for being stoned). I found an audio recording of her portion of the concert on YouTube. It lasts only a little over a half hour while I calculated it to be fifty minutes. A comment on a YouTube post indicates that her comments between the songs was cut from the recording, which might explain this.

[https://www.youtube.com/watch?v=WVEKoblU5dc&t=75s]

Having not looked at what I wrote about that concert for more than fifty years, I am now intrigued to see that one of the two bands I listed as having opened for Joplin was called "The Eagle." Could they have been an early version of "The Eagles," whose first album wasn't to come out for another two years? Had I misheard the name, and could the announcer have said, "The Eagles?" An Internet search of both the concert and "The Eagles" provided no answers. All I was able to find was that her back-up band for that concert was the "Full Tilt Boogie Band." I could find no mention of the two bands that opened for her. Strangely, "Full Tilt Boogie Band" is not mentioned in my review of the concert. (A possible lapse because I was writing from memory about a week later.) At any rate, since we didn't really get to hear much of that band because of the sound equipment problems, it really doesn't matter, except as a trivia fact. What I did learn, from my internet search of this concert which in all these years I didn't realize, was that this was Joplin's last performance. I had assumed, as she lived several more weeks, that she probably had done more performances. It was only when I googled the concert that I discovered it was her last public performance.

Let's return to the focus of what this discussion is supposed to be about—original singer-songwriters who are overshadowed by another performer rendering their song. My second example is very different.

Although Rod Stewart's well-known *Maggie May* is a rock classic that demonstrates his abilities, his cover of Van Morrison's *Have I Told You Lately* is sung with restraint, in many ways not very differently from Morrison's own version, but Stewart's raspy-voiced, heartfelt version makes an even greater impression than Morrison's. At least, that's how I feel when listening to it.

[https://www.youtube.com/watch?v=iMW5c1GPoPs]
[https://www.youtube.com/watch?v=-C-YqmLtVJ4]

Dolly Parton first recorded *I Will Always Love You* in 1973. Nearly twenty years later, Whitney Houston sang it in her movie debut, *The Bodyguard* in 1992, turning it into something else. With astounding vocalizing that combines her gospel/soul roots with an uncanny pop tinge, Houston's version simply dwarfs Parton's original, revitalizing the song, and turning it into a classic.

[https://www.youtube.com/watch?v=lKsQR72HY0s]
[https://www.youtube.com/watch?v=3JWTaaS7LdU]

There have always been singer/songwriters, even before the sixties, especially among folk and country singers. Woody Guthrie and Hank Williams immediately come to mind. In the first half of the twentieth century, however, singer/songwriters did not dominate the mainstream pop airwaves as they did beginning in the late nineteen sixties, when they pushed Broadway, Hollywood, and Tin Pan Alley songwriters to the fringe as they became the dominant face of pop music.

Performing Arts on the Cheap

When I began attending theater, concerts, and the opera in the early 1960s, the lowest-priced seats were about the same price, or even cheaper, than a ticket to a movie.

A rationale I apply is that a movie will always appear in its same form, but a live performance exists for only that one time and, once a particular show closes, that's it—it's gone. At the theater, unlike a movie, you get to see famous performers perform live. It was a no-brainer that I would almost always choose to see a live performance over a movie; especially if they were a similar price. Unfortunately, nowadays, even the cheapest regular, or even discounted, ticket to a Broadway show can be three, four, ten or more times the price of a movie ticket.

Though I love the performing arts, at the rate I went to performances, especially in the first decade or two, I would have been bankrupt had I paid full price for everything I saw. More recently, just before the pandemic hit, I was not attending performances at anything like the rate I had been in those early decades. Prices had gone up so much, especially for Broadway shows, that full-price tickets put a dent in my budget. So, I will always be on the lookout for the best ticket deal.

With respect to Broadway shows, the problem isn't only that ticket prices have skyrocketed. (This becomes understandable as one suspects that the cost of mounting a production on Broadway has also skyrocketed.) In the early 1960s, every Broadway theater had a price range with several tiers, usually at least five (sometimes more). At many theaters, the last row or two of seats were budget-priced. There were different prices for, say, front orchestra, side orchestra, rear orchestra; mezzanine; and front and rear balcony—if the theater had a balcony.

As an example, in 1971, when I saw the original production of Sondheim's *A Little Night Music*, I paid $2.50 at the box office for a ticket to a seat in the very back of the theater. Orchestra seats at the time were thirty dollars, or more, and a seat just a row or two in front of mine was as high as ten or fifteen dollars, so that was a good bargain. Soon after 1971, this became a rarity.

In the fall of 1975, I probably bought the cheapest ticket to a Broadway show I ever purchased. The half-price TKTS booth had recently opened on Broadway and 47th Street. A classic play, *Trelawny of the Wells*, by Arthur Wing Pinero, was just beginning previews at the Vivian Beaumont Theatre in Lincoln Center. In those days, preview performances were priced less than the prices after the show opened (another savings practice that has been mostly abandoned). The cheapest ticket for this preview was $3.00. Bargain enough, but at the TKTS booth I bought that ticket for $1.75!

I have no memory of why I chose to go to that show that night. It was the *first* preview performance and I knew nothing about the play or who was in the cast. Indeed, after nearly fifty years, I still can't tell you much about the play; even my review doesn't refresh my recollection, except for reminding me that it is a turn-of-the-century comedy. What I *do* remember is several young cast members who held the major roles. They were Mary Beth Hurt, John Lithgow, and, in their Broadway debuts, Meryl Streep and Mandy Patinkin!

Broadway theaters now have rarely more than three layers of pricing, and the cheapest level is generally not greatly lower than the price for an orchestra ticket. Cheap balcony tickets have disappeared with the balconies themselves. No, the balconies weren't demolished, they were renamed rear mezzanine, so higher prices can be justified. Still, there are many ways of getting cheaper tickets, but the operative word here is "cheap*er*," which by my standard is not necessarily, "cheap."

Some shows still have standing room areas, something I took advantage of in my younger days. Many shows have rush tickets (a limited number of tickets, dictated by they being unsold near the moment of performance, sold only at the box office, on the day of performance, either for the general public, or for students, at a significant discount). They are sold on a first-come-first-served basis. More recently, daily lotteries have become a means of obtaining bargain priced tickets; starting with in-person lotteries and, now, online digital lotteries. In the few times I tried those lotteries, I did not succeed. Shakespeare in the Park's *Into the Woods* was the only time I actually obtained a seat through a lottery. There are several sites on the Internet that offer discounted Broadway tickets, such as TDF, TheaterMania, TodayTix, and, on occasion, Goldstar.

I did actually get to see one Broadway show for free. I was on my way home from a meeting in mid-town Manhattan one day in 1979 when I passed the TKTS booth. A random guy was standing there with a bunch of tickets who asked me if I wanted a ticket to *Beatlemania* playing on Broadway at the time. I probably said, "How much?" Upon learning they were free, I took one and saw the show; a show I hadn't been planning to see

I suppose *Beatlemania* was pretty much what I expected, which was why it was a show I had no plans to see. But, sometimes viewing a show stimulates one's thoughts and *Beatlemania* did that for me with respect to the Beatles. Thus, my review not only speaks about my view of the show, but also contains my analyses of the Beatles. I don't know if my thoughts here are original, or hold water, and I expect some of these ideas were percolating in my mind for some time before I saw *Beatlemania*, but that unexpected viewing gave me an excuse to put it into writing.

Beatlemania, **The Lunt:Fontanne Theater, May 9, 1979 (Written 5/12/79)**

The heavy advertising campaign that accompanied this show called it an "Incredible simulation!" After viewing it I could only mutter "a very poor simulation!" The show is four musicians who look somewhat like the Beatles, dressed like the Beatles, singing the Beatles songs in the style of the Beatles. Added to this were a series of projections that somewhat traced the development of the times during which the Beatles were active. At times the performers here sounded remarkably like the Beatles, but most often they sounded like what they were, imitators, not innovators.

The Beatles were creative artists as well as performing artists and part of their greatness lies in their ability (like Bob Dylan) to anticipate and perhaps even move the mood of the youth of the 1960s. To imitate the Beatles as performing artists gives us only part of the picture. The interaction between John, Paul, George, and Ringo while performing, reflected their creative synthesis. There is a reason in the nearly ten years since the Beatles split, no single former Beatle has come near reaching the artistic heights that they continually reached together between 1964 and 1970. As collaborators, each Beatle had to discipline himself to the minds, ideas and, perhaps, deficiencies of the others, and in so doing they brought out each individual Beatles' best points, while dispensing with the individual's weaknesses (or more correctly their individual excesses). After the split, as solo artists, these excesses became apparent in the most popular of each one's solo efforts. John's idealistic political activism expressed in *Imagine* and *Give Peace a Chance,* Paul's romanticism, as if answering John, in *Silly Little Love Songs* and George's ultra-spiritualism becoming *My Sweet Lord,* all excellent songs, but none with the bite, beauty and driving sound of what they produced together.

The Beatles legacy of those many recordings remains. They are now so much a part of our culture that few are unfamiliar with their songs. The sounds here just whetted one's appetite to go home and play a recording of the real thing.

Perhaps I was too harsh on this show. They were just doing their best to give the audience a taste of what the Beatles might have sounded like live. In the years since then, tribute bands have become a cottage industry—which the success of *Beatlemania* may have accelerated.

Returning to the subject of cheap tickets, a similar thing happened the year before (1978), only that time it was an Off-Broadway show. I was scanning possible shows at the TKTS booth with my wife when someone approached us offering two free tickets to Sam Shepard's *The Curse of the Starving Class*, then playing at the Public Theater. It had an earlier curtain time than Broadway shows and was only a few minutes to curtain when we got the tickets. The Public Theater is several subway stops from the TKTS booth. We took the tickets, ran to the subway, and actually made it there just a minute or two after the show had begun. I was ambivalent about the show. My wife loved it. I should note that it starred pre-Oscar-winning Olympia Dukakis.

There is a different dynamic for classical music performances, partly because they don't run for weeks or more as Broadway shows do. If you want to see an opera performance with a specific cast or singer, you may have only one or a handful of performances to choose among. With respect to orchestral concerts, the New York Philharmonic does up to four performances of a specific program during a week of its first performance, but visiting orchestras from around the world (which New York, especially Carnegie Hall, has many) do only one performance of a specific program. So, what do you do if it's sold out before you get your ticket or the tickets are exorbitantly priced?

At the opera you might still get standing room or score-desk seats at bargain prices. At the old Met, the score desks were at the end of a side of the Dress Circle where you could see the stage, although the sound might have been somewhat compromised by the overhang from the Family Circle. At Lincoln Center, score desk seats are behind the side of the Family Circle seats, *having no stage view*. To see, one must stand, or hope to find an unoccupied seat once the performance has begun. On the other hand, that area of the Family Circle has some of the best acoustics in the house.

Until the 2023–24 season, score-desk seats were not sold at the box office, but through the Metropolitan Opera Guild, a separate support organization. The prices were a real steal at $15.00 for Guild members and $20.00 for non-Guild members. There were no added fees. It was announced in the summer of 2023 that the Metropolitan Opera Guild was folding after nearly ninety years. Score desk tickets are now sold by the Met for $27.00, but there are added fees.

The Met also has digital rush tickets, at $25.00 for most performances, available on a daily basis on the Met website. A real bargain as they're in the orchestra, but, you must be quick. they sell out in minutes.

[https://www.metopera.org/season/tickets/rush-page/]

As mentioned earlier, Lois Kirschenbaum and I often sought, and obtained, free tickets just before a performance, in or near the lobby. I recall an occasion in the mid-sixties at the old Met: It was Tito Gobbi's first *Falstaff* at the Met. We were standing on Fortieth Street, not far in from Broadway. One of the people who Lois asked for an extra ticket, handed her several. They were parterre boxes, among the most expensive in the house! So, I got to see Gobbi's great Falstaff up close (the box on the side, closely overlooking the stage).

By 1990, I had been going to the Met for nearly thirty years, but I had never seen a complete, integrated Wagner *Ring* cycle, partly because in those thirty years they rarely performed an entire *Ring* cycle, and never the four operas within a week. That changed in 1989 when the new productions of the *Ring* operas conducted by James Levine, that had premiered over the prior few seasons, were given together in the spring for one cycle each week for three weeks. That has become the pattern ever since.

In the spring of 1990, seeing a *Ring* cycle was not something I was contemplating. But, one day on my way home from work, I got to the Port Authority Bus Terminal and found the lines huge as there was some tie-up at the Lincoln Tunnel. I realized it might take hours to get home, so maybe I would stay in Manhattan and catch a show. But it was Monday, a day on which most Broadway theaters are dark. Then I remembered! The Met was going to begin a *Ring* cycle that day. Perhaps I could get a ticket to *Das Rheingold*. So, I got back on the subway and went to Lincoln Center. My plan was to check the box office first, although I doubted they would still have a Family Circle seat, then call my wife to let her know what was happening, have dinner, and, if I hadn't gotten a ticket earlier, see if I could score one in the usual manner, from a patron with an extra ticket outside of the theater.

It was about six o'clock. I had just entered the area of Lincoln Center and was not quite yet at the Met, when a person walking toward me stopped to ask if I was interested in a ticket to the opera. I said, as usual, "How much?" thinking, what are the chances he will offer reasonably priced tickets? He showed me a set of four tickets; one for each opera in the cycle and asked eighty dollars for the set. They were side Family Circle, the cheapest seats in the house, which, in 1990, sold at the box office for twenty dollars each.

I, of course, grabbed them, thankful that I had just over eighty dollars in my wallet. These were probably the easiest tickets I ever got at what would now be considered bargain prices. I say that because, while eighty dollars was the face value of the tickets, in subsequent years, the Met, seeing how quickly weekly *Ring* cycles sold, put an extra charge on cycle tickets. For recent *Ring* cycles, the same seats cost around $260.00!

In the early years I was able to sneak into Carnegie Hall. It was, of course, Lois Kirschenbaum who showed me the location of the back elevator to the Carnegie Hall apartments and offices. If you got off at a certain floor, you would follow a long hallway that would bring you into the Hall. I saw a fair number of concerts that way. This loophole (as I called it) was closed by the Carnegie Hall renovation in 1986. Mostly, though, I bought tickets, because they were still reasonably priced in those days.

I remember, in 1966, getting some reasonably priced balcony tickets for a series of concerts by the Berlin Philharmonic under Herbert von

Karajan in which they performed all nine Beethoven symphonies. In later years I saw them do four Brahms symphonies and many other concerts. I remember, during another von Karajan visit to Carnegie Hall, when he was conducting Beethoven's *Missa Solemnis*, I was standing outside the entrance to Carnegie Hall looking for a ticket, when someone jumped out of a taxi, came over to me and asked if I needed a ticket. When I said, "yes," he handed me a box seat, ran back to the waiting taxi, and was immediately off. That one was certainly the easiest free ticket I ever got. All the more amazing was that there were many others standing in front of Carnegie Hall that evening, all looking for tickets to that performance.

When attempting to purchase tickets outside the venue just before a performance you invariably come into contact with ticket scalpers. Those are the people who are in the business of selling tickets at an inflated price for their own enrichment. They are truly profiting from the labor of others and preying on desperate fans who may not have earlier obtained tickets to a much-desired performance. They also compete with those of us looking for a ticket to actually *go* to the performance. Sometimes they are in your face about it with no shame. I once saw a scalper purchase a ticket from a patron who had a spare and, as the seller walked away, but still in earshot, the scalper held up the ticket shouting "anyone need an extra ticket?" You can be sure he wasn't going to sell it for what he paid for it a couple of seconds earlier.

I have never knowingly purchased a ticket from a scalper as I never pay more than the face value for a ticket, but sometimes scalpers sell at face value; usually when they obtained the ticket for free or paid much less than the face value. After a while, I could easily spot a scalper. However, these days lots of people purchase tickets on the Internet and it may be more difficult to distinguish a legitimate seller from a scammer or scalper.

What I once thought was illegal has seemingly become standard. You can now go to Ticketmaster.com and find *resale* tickets, sometimes costing hundreds of dollars or more. In my wildest imagination, I couldn't imagine paying the prices I hear some people are paying for tickets to a Taylor Swift concert.

Reflections *on* the Audience

I will briefly switch gears and look at the audience. There are two things that seem to have changed about them in the last sixty years.

When I started going to the theater, before the doors to the theater opened, ticket holders gathered in the lobby often overflowing to the street. When the doors opened, they just started going in. They were simply, "a crowd." Over the past two decades this began to change. As I now walk past Broadway theaters before performances, I almost always see people lined up in an orderly fashion. For very popular shows the line can start an hour before the doors open, and by the time the line starts moving, it could be around the block. I suppose two things made this inevitable. Many theaters began using metal detectors in the wake of 9/11 and more recent domestic mass shootings. The pandemic also made grouped crowds less inviting. I must admit I miss the easygoing atmosphere of more innocent times.

No, I'm not going to write about audience members who may rudely disrupt a performance. I'll leave that to Patti LuPone, who has rightly become very vocal about that issue. (It has been reported several times that Patti broke the fourth wall to call out an audience member for disrespectful or unruly behavior during a performance.)

[https://www.youtube.com/watch?v=WruzPfJ9Rys]
[https://www.youtube.com/watch?v=43mB4QuXGTE]

Didn't I mention earlier that Patti LuPone is fearless?

I will, however, write about the audience collectively, when they do something that disconcerts me, even though I don't know how it affects the performers. When I started going to the theater, people would applaud at the end of songs and acts and, on rare occasions, you might hear a brief cheer or, borrowed from opera, a "bravo" or two in between, depending on the quality of the performance. These days, I don't hear just applause and sometimes brief cheer, but lots of screaming, shouting and other vocal sounds of approval. Since they are sounds of approval, I don't know whether performers are as disconcerted by this. I am. And, it becomes even more jarring to me when I hear this for performances I find second rate. Another thing. Almost every show I attend these days gets a standing ovation at the end, no matter the quality. Perhaps I'm just being an old fogey in this, but I did like it better when the audience's reaction was more mannered and more meaningful.

Hamilton, Diversity, and the Future

By now you must realize that my taste in music has not changed much in the fifty years since I rejoined my generation. A lot has changed in musical styles in that half-century, but my love of the pop music and vocalists of the 1950s, opera, Broadway show music, and, finally, much of the rock and folk music of the 1960s and 1970s has not been joined by such later entries as disco, hip hop, punk rock, and so forth. Perhaps I am just a product of my time who underscores the adage that it's hard to teach old dogs new tricks.

A recent musical that has become a mega-hit is *Hamilton*. Because of the high demand, its very high ticket price, and my inability to score ten-dollar rush tickets, I have not seen it on stage. I did see a Broadway bootleg I found on YouTube long before the movie version was streamed on Disney+. I have mixed feelings about the show. I admire Lin Manuel Miranda immensely. I have seen him live twice, but never in his own works. Both times were at City Center Encores! First, a revival of Sondheim's *Merrily We Roll Along* (2012) and, later, in Jonathan Larson's *tick, tick...BOOM!* (2014), which he has since directed for the big screen. Also in the Larson revival was Miranda's soon-to-be *Hamilton* co-star, Leslie Odom, Jr. (I believe they were work-shopping *Hamilton* at the Public Theater when they appeared together in *tick, tick...BOOM!*)

While I think *Hamilton* is a terrific show and I am happy it put my favorite founding father in the spotlight (I was a fan of Alexander Hamilton long before Lin Manuel Miranda was born), it is not among my favorite musicals—because the music, as fine as it is, just doesn't move me. Although often spoken of as a rap musical, it also has some more traditional songs, but I don't find them in the same class as those found on my list of favorite musicals.

[https://www.youtube.com/watch?v=Fb4GlOabb1M]

Hamilton is a phenomenon and a musical for a different generation, a generation that grew up listening to a totally different popular music style than I did. With its welcome diversity casting, it has done much to help change the face of Broadway.

There have been virtually no new musicals in the last two decades to add to my pantheon of great musicals. This is not to say that there are no great new musicals being written. It simply says that, given my now somewhat old-fashioned perspective, most modern musicals don't achieve *my* standard-because that standard is not the standard of the current generation. The current generation is as much entitled to create its own artistic vision as was done by the generation before me who moved from big bands to solo vocalists; and then, a decade after that, when a new generation totally changed popular music with the introduction of Rock and Roll.

Lin Manuel Miranda's success may well be because he understands the Broadway musical and is as much a student of its history as he appears to be of American history. As noted, I saw him in a Sondheim and Larson musical. He did a Spanish translation for the Puerto Rican characters in the 2009 Broadway revival of *West Side Story* and, most recently, contributed additional lyrics to the Kander and Ebb musical, *New York, New York*. Miranda has combined his knowledge and admiration of the traditional musical with his love of the more modern music idiom, rap, to create something that speaks directly to the contemporary audience. As the current generation forges a new era of Broadway musicals, they should not ignore the roots of the art form. They should build upon the past, as Miranda has done.

Opera, too, appears to be entering a new era. In the 1960s, casts at the Metropolitan Opera very often changed from performance to performance, so one could go to a half dozen performances of a specific opera within the span of a few weeks and there would be a different singer in this or that role, making each performance a different experience. These days, the cast hardly changes during the run of an opera, although there is sometimes a second cast that comes in at later performances.

In my day opera was all about singers. Fans would go to see their favorite singers in different roles. Production values were secondary and brand new operas were a rarity. Indeed, on the rare occasion a new opera was presented, box office sales would fall off. We wanted to see our favorite singers in different roles in the standard repertoire, or, on occasion, in a classic opera that hadn't been seen in a long time.

Forwarding sixty years, it was recently announced that the Met will present more new operas in the coming seasons than ever before because the new operas *did better box office than many of the old standards!* Is it because contemporary opera singers don't measure up to those of the past? There were Renata Tebaldi, Birgit Nillson, Leontyne Price, Joan Sutherland, Montserrat Caballé, Marilyn Horne, Franco Corelli, Tito Gobbi, and Sherrill Milnes, to name just a few icons from my past. Are there great singers out there today of similar caliber? When I began going to the opera, old timers, bemoaning the then-current crop, would laud the singers of *their* past like Rosa Ponselle, Kirsten Flagstad, Lauritz Melchior, Beniamino Gigli, and Ezio Pinza. Am I now doing the same by suggesting that I don't find many singers comparable to those of the past? Likely— but, could it be that the current crop of opera singers, good as they may be, lack the fanatic following that previous generations had—that, instead, current audiences are clamoring for new and different operatic works, works that display greater diversity in subject matter and casting?

In regard to diversity, the Met hired its first Black principal singer in 1955. That was nearly a decade after Jackie Robinson joined the Brooklyn Dodgers and changed the face of baseball. The great contralto, Marian Anderson, was engaged for just a few performances in 1955, twenty years later than her addition to the Met roster might have occurred had she been White.

[https://www.youtube.com/watch?v=uVAjrOt_I4c]

Anderson wasn't the only great Black artist who should have been singing at the Met in the 1930s. Wouldn't it have been wonderful if the Met had given us, in the 1930s, Mussorgsky's *Boris Godunov* with Paul Robson?

[https://www.youtube.com/watch?v=iKz7TDZfeL0]

Or, how about Robson in one of the few *new* works the Met presented in that period—Louis Gruenberg's *The Emperor Jones*? Robson had performed that role to great acclaim in a 1926 Broadway revival of Eugene O'Neil's original 1920 play. He repeated the role in the 1933 movie version.

[https://www.youtube.com/watch?v=Qc7h3SWlM6I]

It would have been a stunning trifecta had Robson sung that same role in the operatic version that premiered at the Met in 1933. However, due to prejudice, the then-lily-white Met gave the audience Lawrence Tibbett instead—in blackface!

[https://www.youtube.com/watch?v=u5z5dXhCgVQ]

One last trivia digression which encompasses both the world of opera and theater. The Met has premiered two operas based on plays by Eugene O'Neill—the aforesaid, *The Emperor Jones* and *Mourning Becomes Electra* by Marvin David Levy, which was premiered in the Met's first season at Lincoln Center. The definitive biography of O'Neill, simply titled *O'Neill*, was written by Arthur and Barbara Gelb, the parents of the Met's current General Manager, Peter Gelb.

Unlike Gruenberg's *The Emperor Jones*, another opera written by a white man portraying predominantly Black characters, George Gershwin's *Porgy and Bess*, has stood the test of time. Gershwin, like Miranda after him, was noted for incorporating newer musical styles in his compositions. I believe *Porgy and Bess* is the greatest American opera so far written. It is a true opera despite the many truncated versions you may be familiar with that replaced the singing (the recitatives) between the songs (the arias) with spoken dialogue, such as the 1959 movie version and the 2012 Broadway production.

In its original opera form, *Porgy and Bess* has been performed in many opera houses throughout the world, including the Metropolitan Opera and the New York City Opera.

[https://www.youtube.com/watch?v=HdRTfqGy9TE&t=4s]

Written nearly ninety years ago, its score is an inspired one that contains an abundance of riches, including numerous songs that have become part of the Great American Songbook and been interpreted by many great (and not so great) popular singers, jazz musicians, opera singers, and classical musicians.

Two new operas presented by the Met were written by Terence Blanchard, a Black jazz trumpeter and composer. Blanchard, more than sixty years after the Met engaged its first Black singer, became the first Black composer to be showcased by the Met. While I personally find the music of *Porgy and Bess* more melodic and beautiful than Blanchard's, his opera, *Fire Shut Up in My Bones*, is a powerful work whose Black characters are not caricatures (as some of those in *Porgy* are), but are based on real-life people, which clearly resonates with today's audience.

[https://www.youtube.com/watch?v=Dk8aQVVbgEs]

It appears to me that today's audiences are looking for something different in their operatic experience than seeing yet another singer do a tired old *Tosca* or *Traviata*. This is the choice they are making and it may be for the best, as it may invigorate the art form I love so much. While I will continue to look to find in contemporary operas the equivalent of those nineteenth and early-twentieth-century operas I love so much, it's certainly not going to happen if opera houses stop commissioning and performing new works and expanding their audiences by performing works that highlight and introduce the variety of diverse cultures.

Now, if only someone would do something about those sky-high ticket prices, so that those with limited means can still afford to attend live performances.

Appendix

You may find this listing of links longer than fifteen minutes useful in planning extended listening or viewing. The timing (divided by colons) is shown in hours, seconds, and minutes. Following the timing is a description of the clip, written in a sort of shorthand.

Page 5
[https://www.youtube.com/watch?v=mTCiKVC7rBU&list=PLHWNRn9JB2ARUOrcQLGUMsWAKpd9yIo-r]
29:35 perry como chesterfield supper club

Page 9
[https://www.youtube.com/watch?v=fgHKEaGbyDo&list=PLESDrGLwFOLXT0jfvQVzzvQzEaV-3F13u]
20:42 first flash gordon serial episode 1
[https://www.youtube.com/watch?v=GLN-j5PXRbc&t=672s]]
57:44 captain video entire episode

Page 10
[https://www.youtube.com/watch?v=Yj66TCxu21I]
25:46 third flash gordon serial episode 1

Page 20
[https://www.youtube.com/watch?v=pZXd43gtYIA]
2:13:14 1949 met broadcast l'elisir d'amore tagliavini sayao

Page 21
[https://www.youtube.com/watch?v=0I1DSKeRwMs]
51:49 tagliavini voice of firestone
[https://www.youtube.com/watch?v=zAsi6bQMn7A]
2:28:00 la milanov martinelli la gioconda met 12/30/39

Page 22
[https://www.youtube.com/watch?v=RKoW84YJbEE&t=69s]
1:15:01 milanov's final gioconda highlights met 3/24/62

Page 23
[https://www.youtube.com/watch?v=pY_qx-XJ3J0&t=21s]
1:59:05 milanov final andrea chenier
[https://www.youtube.com/watch?v=Ewg1XZd-bdw&t=65s]
54:33 bergonzi concert

Page 28
[https://www.youtube.com/watch?v=rkMx0CLWeRQ]
1:48:14 tosca callas di stefano gobbi 1953 studio recording
[https://www.youtube.com/watch?v=_mkLcgZ3gXl]
1:58:42 callas hamburg and paris concerts

Page 31
[https://www.youtube.com/watch?v=PCkeF80Y-BA&t=2207s]
2:00:50 tosca tebaldi corelli gobbi met 3/23/64

Page 32
[https://www.youtube.com/watch?v=ftWYz1m4FIU&t=106s]
2:00:20 tosca callas corelli gobbi met 3/19/65
[https://www.youtube.com/watch?v=2M1McWkkKqk&t=425s]
1:54:36 tosca callas tucker gobbi met 3/23/65

Page 33
[https://www.youtube.com/watch?v=xJfTOKEJRy8]
1:41:20 gobbi rigoletto
[https://www.youtube.com/watch?v=AuubQMj4oGE]
1:28:16 gobbi tagliavini the barber of seville
[https://www.youtube.com/watch?v=yhdZeqiCuVk].
1:07:39 gobbi pagliacci
[https://www.youtube.com/watch?v=JMgwvx2CMkE]
1:19:18 gobbi l'elisir
[https://www.youtube.com/watch?v=Evj_DlJn5_8&t=3059s]
1:36:11 gobbi la forza del destino

Page 35
[https://www.youtube.com/watch?v=F9ZU0CloETU].
2:04:22 gobbi falstaff 1970 complete color video
[https://www.youtube.com/watch?v=JDZlOY-loXs]
1:59:44 gobbi falstaff 1956 studio recording
[https://www.youtube.com/watch?v=Aw5VdDCjExI]
2:00:29 gobbi tebaldi moffo falstaff 1956 chicago lyric opera
[https://www.youtube.com/watch?v=POt5FK8A6lk]
1:46:10 stabile gobbi tagliavini falstaff 1941berlin
[https://www.youtube.com/watch?v=xnFlg1z1hPc&t=412s]
44:38 callas gobbi tosca act 2 complete london 1964

Page 37
[https://www.youtube.com/watch?v=2GHCND4rTz4]
1:30:16 gobbi wozzeck

Page 38
[https://www.youtube.com/watch?v=5dzZ3YKEsIM&t=326s]
46:06 corelli

Page 42
[https://www.youtube.com/watch?v=UCm8ZdZ9cTY]
1:51:55 poliuto corelli callas bastianini

Appendix

[https://www.youtube.com/watch?v=9FTRRtBzT04]
16:35 corelli simionato gli ugonotti
[https://www.youtube.com/watch?v=W_xlg4VI8Ac]
2:46:40 gli ugonotti complete

Page 43
watch?v=O4z9LGNgWBQ&t=3900s]
2:07:49 corelli tosca 1967 parma
[https://www.youtube.com/watch?v=W_XzSVDsU0g&t=645s]
27:54 corelli telecast excerpts
[https://www.youtube.com/watch?v=xZu4jbcr-Fk]
51:31 corelli tokyo concert
[https://www.youtube.com/watch?v=CL0aDjcx2nY&t=1076s]
1:29:15 tebaldi corelli tokyo concert

Page 47
[https://www.youtube.com/watch?v=BxAU8f2PiC8]
1:01:31 zucker corelli interview part 1
[https://www.youtube.com/watch?v=hMm0sBSWaBA&t=59s]
57:44 zucker corelli interview part 2

Page 48
[https://www.youtube.com/watch?v=IKpPGocnqLQ&t=1020s]
1:14:80 corelli pagliacci
[https://www.youtube.com/watch?v=H8OtR6FkOYQ]
1:52:44 tosca 1955 corelli tagliabue
[https://www.youtube.com/watch?v=8R7BZbWQx8U&t=691s]
1:46:22 corelli tosca 1956
[https://www.youtube.com/watch?v=RnB3W9sXlCc&t=2223s]
2:22:10 corelli carmen
[https://www.youtube.com/watch?v=zCiJGYCFy90&t=85s]
1:54:24 corelli turandot
[https://www.youtube.com/watch?v=totuvUW7hJ8]
2:02:14 nilsson turandot
[https://www.youtube.com/watch?v=k9sRRKNZULE]
2:37:54 corelli la forza del destino

Page 49
[https://www.youtube.com/watch?v=EkTo4J0Q-HQ]
48:50 corelli andrea chenier act 1 color video
[https://www.youtube.com/watch?v=cNfMOe8p3Pw&t=3s]
1:02:51 andrea chenier corelli acts 2–4 color video

Page 50
[https://www.youtube.com/watch?v=OGq5Le12lr4]
15:05 böhm beethoven fidelio leonore overture no. 3

Page 53
[https://www.youtube.com/watch?v=VDDT3LgOIGQ]
2:11:31 domingo lecouvreuer met debut 9/28/68

Page 55
[https://www.youtube.com/watch?v=4q8z-s9lSSY]
2:15:39 del monaco otello 1958
[https://www.youtube.com/watch?v=f8_vhpF6YUQ&t=6s]
2:10:53 del monaco gobbi otello 1959

Page 56
[https://www.youtube.com/watch?v=Sm_Usoo7LvY],
2:19:40 domingo otello la scala
[https://www.youtube.com/watch?v=bqWzCwt2BX4]
2:19:05 domingo otello mexico city
[https://www.youtube.com/watch?v=YXRJb0vLAts].
2:22:31 domingo otello paris

Page 57
[https://www.youtube.com/watch?v=UjF8i8pTV6Y]
1:04:10 schipa farewell recital

Page 63
[https://www.youtube.com/watch?v=80R4HI_Iuuk&t=106s]
2:07:04 treigle mefistofole nyc opera

Page 64
[https://www.youtube.com/watch?v=si2ifEGW4Gs]
2:12:46 treigle caballe domingo mefistofole studio recording
[https://www.youtube.com/watch?v=5gvN4yEuWxk]
2:20:45 faust treigle sills rudel nyc opera

Page 65
[https://www.youtube.com/watch?v=CHIUjSgdF-E&t=2s]
1:42:25 mefistofole ghiaurov tebaldi full performance

Page 67
[https://www.youtube.com/watch?v=SZkKIXaIHyc&t=1464s]
2:36:13 barber of seville sills

Page 69
[https://www.youtube.com/watch?v=MVh6yeCTKm4&t=3776s]
1:23:07 ellington copenhagen

Page 71
[https://www.youtube.com/watch?v=GkcHQrlay9E&t=8s]
3:23:01 schwatzkopf don giovanni met broadcast 1/29/66
[https://www.youtube.com/watch?v=HAw4iDDWby8]
3:12:05 schwatzkopf der rosekavalier salzburg festival

Page 74
[https://ok.ru/videoembed/1346877196917]
2:04:15 stilwell la boheme

Page 76

[https://www.youtube.com/watch?v=LUK6qSmu8o0]
2:42:10 stilwell debussy pelleas et melisande
[https://www.youtube.com/watch?v=ZXHTzeCGif4&t=1463s]
1:42:30 stilwell compilation
[https://www.youtube.com/watch?v=Ca2srU8S2GQ]
2:40:00 stilwell don giovanni

Page 78

[https://www.youtube.com/watch?v=jpj2-G8G2Gw&t=1000s]
1:23:02 Mama complete 1941 movie

Page 82

[https://www.youtube.com/watch?v=esG2dm2LayU&t=11s]
2:11:22 simon boccanegra tibbet pinza martinelli met 1/31/39
[https://www.youtube.com/watch?v=qWOvo88etHo&t=673s]
2:50:44 aida cigna martinelli pinza met 2/6/37
[https://www.youtube.com/watch?v=VFjHv33exxI]
2:30:51 norma cigna martinelli pinza met 2/30/37
https://www.youtube.com/watch?v=PPDr3RFfTD0&t=101s]
3:29:59 siegfried flagstad melchior met
[https://www.youtube.com/watch?v=DwSkBywk4Io]
2:48:15 pinza don giovanni met 3/7/42
[https://www.youtube.com/watch?v=SYLCjavbph4&t=519s]
1:54:53 l'elisir gigli
[https://www.youtube.com/watch?v=0-65iDfKkqo]
1:41:23 l'amico fritz gigli
[https://www.youtube.com/watch?v=PNPaXAk5jLA]
1:53:35 boheme tebaldi lauri:volpi gobbi

Page 83

[https://www.youtube.com/watch?v=tIPuXmwwCrg]
55:14 gigli manon lescaut highlights 1950
[https://www.youtube.com/watch?v=viGxcNLPyPc]
23:40 tosca fragments gigli/tagliavini

Page 84

[https://www.youtube.com/watch?v=qWOvo88etHo]
2:5:44 martinelli pinza aida met 2/6/37
[https://www.youtube.com/watch?v=4B8nO-VvtkM]
24:05 gigli milanov aida excerpts met 2/4/39

Page 88

[https://www.youtube.com/watch?v=TdejK01vpVA]
1:01:57 lehmann melchior walkure act 1 vienna philharmonic
[https://www.youtube.com/watch?v=DV8sEecjAV8&t=37s]
2:31:20 melchior siegfried abridged

Page 89
Six complete broadcasts of Tristan und Isolde with Melchior and Flagstad, plus one with Melchior and Traubel.
[https://www.youtube.com/watch?v=0-5vJYNTdq0&t=14s]
3:16:20 met 1935
[https://www.youtube.com/watch?v=LqJjVb4u9ho&t=1s]
3:30: 22 london 1936
[https://www.youtube.com/watch?v=nxx-NBaFzoU]
3:00:02 met 1937
[https://www.youtube.com/watch?v=4YWcLaTz4lw&t=5s]
3:23:32 london 1937
[https://www.youtube.com/watch?v=iEY6E-m41Qc]
3:37:18 met 1940
[https://www.youtube.com/watch?v=TZ3yxQezbWY&t=1852s]
4:03:46 met 1941
[https://www.youtube.com/watch?v=8BYJXoQ1KTQ&t=7s]
3:13:18 traubel buenos aires 1943

Page 90
[https://www.youtube.com/watch?v=c5sNTERGzkg&t=22s]
2:55:42 tannhauser flagstad melchior met 1936
[https://www.youtube.com/watch?v=NI1cfr80sds&t=250s]
2:5:27 tannhauser flagstad melchior met 1941
[https://www.youtube.com/watch?v=H3wyiZqvFlw&t=126s]
2:42:40 tannhauser varnay melchior met 1944
[https://www.youtube.com/watch?v=mb1akz5pIWg]
2:59:54 lohengrin melchior lehmann met 1935
[https://www.youtube.com/watch?v=9xEQWhS7Te0&t=80s]
3:04:51 lohengrin melchior traubel varnay met 1950
[https://www.youtube.com/watch?v=kKnGGheAprM&t=7277s]
3:31:55 parsifal melchior flagstad met 1938
[https://www.youtube.com/watch?v=avb_RjgZ0no&t=1623s]
3:42:01 gotterdamerung lawrence melchior met 1936
[https://www.youtube.com/watch?v=ugZ-VJ-TStY&t=4966s]
3:23:42 siegfried melchior flagstad met 1937

Page 91
[https://www.youtube.com/watch?v=UB7iuH2bjnA]
1:07:24 tristan highlights leider melchior met 1933
[https://www.youtube.com/watch?v=_XSYCFnPST0]
16:40 melchior leider tristan duet studio 1929

Page 92
[https://www.youtube.com/watch?v=j3OAHSWs5-4&t=3s]
3:05:51 walkure trauble varnay melchior met 1941
[https://www.youtube.com/watch?v=RruHdPssz8U]
26:41 walkure act 1 finale melchior traubel toscanini

Appendix

Page 94
[https://www.youtube.com/watch?v=cjRqFxOw2f4&t=13s]
2:30:02 otello martinelli met 2/12/38
[https://www.youtube.com/watch?v=9_in7tPhEsk]
2:22:06 otello martinelli met 12/3/38
[https://www.youtube.com/watch?v=c5TPWBZT-EE]
2:20:42 otello martinelli met 2/24/40
[https://www.youtube.com/watch?v=uQU7ow32Px8&t=10s]
2:13:21 otello martinelli met 1/18/41
[https://www.youtube.com/watch?v=EwuyKZbm_H4&t=181s]
3:16:48 walkure melchior met 2/17/40
[https://www.youtube.com/watch?v=FHhxX77xsDI&t=71s].
3:30:02 walkure melchior met boston 3/30/40

Page 95
[https://www.youtube.com/watch?v=Uz6FLFhw_pg]
48:24 melchior kinescopes

Page 100
[https://www.youtube.com/watch?v=G923Sk1cyTQ]
2:28:25 toscanini la boheme 50th anniversary radio broadcasts (1946)
[https://www.youtube.com/watch?v=Ozyezf9dUyA&list=RDOzyezf9dUyA&start_radio=1]
2:21:33 toscanini aida 1949 telecast

Page 103
[https://www.youtube.com/watch?v=bimhicdrPUs]
19:43 lohengrin prelude toscanini vs furtwangler

Page 106
[https://www.youtube.com/watch?v=OZb2GEUmDPQ&t=644s]
36:24 talich dvorak slovanik dances op. 46
[https://www.youtube.com/watch?v=dXFR_amAZIM&t=414s]
38:49 talich slovanik dances op. 72

Page 108
[https://www.youtube.com/watch?v=-xXv55ARtsM&t=4s]
58:02 stokowski ives symphony no. 4 world premiere

Page 110
[https://www.youtube.com/watch?v=yVNDEZJPIns]
1:17:58 mahler symphony no. 2 stokowski philadelphia orch 1967

Page 112
[https://www.youtube.com/watch?v=hJv1b58QJAY]
1:07:08 bernstein walkure act 1
[https://www.youtube.com/watch?v=qldRIJsmZlc]
1:05:00 bernstein tristan highlights
[https://www.youtube.com/watch?v=-cim3B08TwY]
16:35 bernstein gotterdammerung selections duet

[https://www.youtube.com/watch?v=QYG8hkDuCHI]
20:31 bernstein farrell gotterdammerung immolation scene

Page 113

Bernstein conducts Mahler
[https://www.youtube.com/watch?v=ISBfOpztUZM]
55:21 symphony no. 1
[https://www.youtube.com/watch?v=9MNXqXXfMoM]
1:31:20 symphony 2 london
[https://www.youtube.com/watch?v=HXVueK5sjlQ]
1:45:36 symphony no. 3
[https://www.youtube.com/watch?v=UMQiATUXg00]
58:04 symphony no. 4
[https://www.youtube.com/watch?v=9KSESLJ0LWA]
1:11:48 symphony no. 5
[https://www.youtube.com/watch?v=goXH3NUhUFk]
1:23:51 symphony no. 6
[https://www.youtube.com/watch?v=_v7BmR3pPAk]
1:23:08 symphony no. 7
[https://www.youtube.com/watch?v=NSYEOLwVfU8]
1:24:08 symphony no. 8
[https://www.youtube.com/watch?v=IoNEeKJ2x44]
1:22:36 symphony no. 9
[https://www.youtube.com/watch?v=vHyV8noUXC0]
27:19 symphony no. 10 adagio

Page 116
[https://www.youtube.com/watch?v=pHdQkQ6oY8Y]
1:59:08 la traviata levine sills doningo milnes hollywood bowl 8/12/71

Page 126
[https://www.youtube.com/watch?v=tWsG2dEoUsA&t=326s]
53:00 pennebaker documentary, original cast album: company

Page 127
[https://www.youtube.com/watch?v=H4IflVde1Is&t=1944s]
36:05 company original cast reunion concert california highlights
[https://www.youtube.com/watch?v=8QRQzVvgT-A&t=110s]
1:21:32 company original cast reunion concert new york complete

Page 136
[https://www.youtube.com/watch?v=hrB8oX5lP_U]
1:31:42 merman crosby 1936 film anything goes aka tops is the limit

Page 137
[https://www.youtube.com/watch?v=7AZvqiQ63xg]
1:54:39 call me madam full movie 1953

Page 138
[https://www.youtube.com/watch?v=Lhn9rIx3y_s]
1:57:14 no business like show biz full 1954 movie

[https://www.youtube.com/watch?v=YeX2tNEFRQI]
52-37 anything goes merman sinatra lahr full colgate comedy hour telecast

Page 139
[https://www.youtube.com/watch?v=qHhjqjylP60].
1:45:43 mary martin john rait annie get your gun full telecast

Page 145
[https://www.youtube.com/watch?v=257pxUReamU]
1:55:06 lupone sunset boulevard sydmonton festival 1992 full world premiere

[https://www.youtube.com/watch?v=-BP3rWfSUt0]
2:19:15 lupone sunset boulevard london 1993 washed out black & white (glenn close comparison link page 181)

Page 146
[https://www.youtube.com/watch?v=Nfubo4hf2NM&t=3219s]
1:54:40 passion lupone macdonald cerveris
[https://www.youtube.com/watch?v=6M8pxgF2NbU&t=10s]
1:54:29 passion original broadway cast donna murphy

Page 147
[https://www.youtube.com/watch?v=gFTnBdH99Zg]
2:25:36 lupone benanti gypsy encores! full show

Page 148
[https://www.youtube.com/watch?v=v212UUWicbU&t=1672s]
1:13:26 modern milli act 1 original broadway cast
[https://www.youtube.com/watch?v=Jk1rJrb2EaQ&t=200s]
58:13 modern mille act 2
[https://www.youtube.com/watch?v=fG485DFjj5k&t=4440s]
2:31:53 anyone can whistle Encores! full show

Page 149
[https://www.youtube.com/watch?v=k0GPg1GkCvA&t=75s]
2:08:02 foster anything goes full performance

Page 151
[https://www.youtube.com/watch?v=5ftJuerpl-4&t=775s]
1:59:36 kelli o'hara brigadoon Encores! full show

Page 152
[https://www.youtube.com/watch?v=nKH4j9bh_To&t=206s]
21:22 mendez carousel (when i marry) mr. snow at 2:10

Page 155
[https://www.youtube.com/watch?v=tekrJEd2Zds]
40:31 garland at home at the palace abc paramount recording
[https://www.youtube.com/watch?v=x4dy8vcWC7c]
1:14:58 garland hartford concert 1967

[https://www.youtube.com/watch?v=HxTerOTii7c]
1:24:16 garland minelli closing night at home at the palace 1967

Page 156
[https://www.youtube.com/watch?v=Sv7a1A5AGcA]
36:32 garland lsst concert copenhgen 1969

Page 157
[https://www.youtube.com/watch?v=lqxEyf7JXyQ]
53:25 streisand a happening in central park

Page 160
[https://www.youtube.com/watch?v=qGIxw77_YsY&t=770s]
2:24:57 andrews victor/victoriacomplete musical 1995

Page 161
[https://www.youtube.com/watch?v=C1F4YhBOA14&t=67s]
1:18:19 andrews cinderella complete telecast 1957

Page 163
[https://www.youtube.com/watch?v=093myaltXAY]
1:29:03 drake morrison kiss me kate complete 1958 hallmark hall of fame telecast
[https://www.youtube.com/watch?v=iCOblpkH8WE&t=597s]
23:00 drake his famous songs

Page 171
[https://vimeo.com/261611927]
1:02:31 an evening with fred astaire
[https://www.youtube.com/watch?v=LjTzHrsnrc8]
58:58 astaire hollywood palace 10/2/65
[https://www.youtube.com/watch?v=fhO_3kyIOBI]
58:29 astaire hollywood palace 3/12/66
[https://www.youtube.com/watch?v=9pf2kMRdmhQ&t=113s]
58:22 astaire hollywood palace 4/30/66
[https://www.youtube.com/watch?v=0wwLioHbc-I]
58:59 astaire hollywood palace 10/25/69

Page 180
[https://www.youtube.com/watch?v=o-PJMbCKwZ0&t=2474s]
2:23:36 kiley man of la mancha full performance

Page 181
[https://www.youtube.com/watch?v=28ibjtrd21I&t=1103s]
2:07:56 glenn close sunset boulevard 2017 revival full performance

Page 182
[https://www.youtube.com/watch?v=Fi15Nmvdb7w]
31:08 angela lansbury mame 1966 highlights
[https://www.youtube.com/watch?v=8wDq6ags8rk&t=3180s]
2:27:07 lansbury mame 1983 revival complete

Appendix

[https://www.youtube.com/watch?v=EsxzyqJX5wY]
1:44:33 rosalind russel wonderful town 1958 telecast complete

Page 184
[https://www.youtube.com/watch?v=CNGeN41ycNw&t=4945s]
2:02:54 joel grey cabaret 1987 revival part 1
[https://www.youtube.com/watch?v=Ph5tahV0a4g]
28:21 joel grey cabaret 1987 revival part 2

Page 185
https://www.youtube.com/watch?v=8j7sO9DIXOU].
1:17:45 a party with comden and green

Page 186
[https://www.youtube.com/watch?v=nCB_r7iSoEY]
1:52:16 1971 tony awards complete telecast

Page 188
[https://www.youtube.com/watch?v=5zydvO0rY9Y]
1:52:03 barrymore don juan 1926
[https://www.youtube.com/watch?v=tOEgvY1cjYc]
1:38:22 barrymore beloved rogue 1927

Page 189
[https://www.youtube.com/watch?v=yvS1zJ0erTA&t=60s]
1:18:23 barrymore myrna loy topaz 1933
[https://www.youtube.com/watch?v=A4uZrna_lFM&t=4s]
2:58:50 burton hamlet 1954 studio lp

Page 198
[https://www.youtube.com/watch?v=Y7lGIUzUKOE&t=34s]
1:47:28 death of a salesman original cast

Page 204
[https://www.youtube.com/watch?v=qjG_Huf7tZw]
1:55:55 julius caesar robards as brutus
[https://www.youtube.com/watch?v=56IGjR63fjM&t=697s]
1:55:48 robards you cant take it with you
[https://www.youtube.com/watch?v=zpjN97qJ0bk]
1:58:04 robards a thousand clowns
[https://www.youtube.com/watch?v=Eofkue3ybwk]
1:56:02 robards lana turner by love possessed

Page 205
[https://www.youtube.com/watch?v=utGRP9Zy1lg]
2:06:50 robards the day after
[https://www.youtube.com/watch?v=2Za-JRTQzXY&t=2s]
2:22:12 robards the long hot summer
[https://www.youtube.com/watch?v=zaqJMynKXrk]
1:35:49 robards kirk douglas inherit the wind

[https://www.youtube.com/watch?v=pTfZGznz70Y&t=12s]
1:36:13 robards mark twain and me.

Page 206
[https://www.youtube.com/watch?v=etEFM_B9YS0&t=6785s]
3:20:59 robards the iceman cometh
[https://www.youtube.com/watch?v=AkZ-3hBPQwQ&t=738s]
2:50:44 hepburn richardson robards long days journey into night
[https://www.youtube.com/watch?v=jNAdkbOi44o]
2:14:07 robards dewhurst moon for misbegotten

Page 207
[https://www.youtube.com/watch?v=hlVyZ6cooxc]
2:10:59 burton taylor who's afraid of virginia woolf
[https://www.youtube.com/watch?v=5ZHAqHGc8lQ]
1:59:32 jason miller as arthur miller marilyn: the untold story

Page 211
[https://www.youtube.com/watch?v=5sUM-0_hJUg&t=2s]
1:54:09 rosemary harris the royal family 1976

Page 213
[https://www.youtube.com/watch?v=oXu0tqkXc3g&t=724s]
1:39:53 judith anderson medea 1959 play of the week complete

Page 222
[https://www.youtube.com/watch?v=ejYqJ_1m9Ho]
1:39:26 ralph fiennes man and superman national theater part 1
[https://www.youtube.com/watch?v=1J7o8udx71c]
1:31:02 ralph fiennes man and superman national theater part 2

Page 226
[https://www.youtube.com/watch?v=YanlCN899bY&t=3394s]
2:29:10 into the woods 2012 shakespeare in the park

Page 230
[https://www.youtube.com/watch?v=3NtMbQGn31c]
1:30:48 complete borge show

Page 232
[https://www.youtube.com/watch?v=A5yD8PN0CQg&t=64s]
51:00 bennett lena horne tv special

Page 233
[https://www.youtube.com/watch?v=5VwKAGk_i6s]
1:18:00 bennett at carnegie hall

Page 238
[https://www.youtube.com/watch?v=WVEKoblU5dc&t=75s]
31:34 joplin last concert

Page 249
[https://www.youtube.com/watch?v=Qc7h3SWlM6I]
1:15:15 robeson the emperor jones 1933 full movie

Page 250
[https://www.youtube.com/watch?v=HdRTfqGy9TE&t=4s]
2:32:41 porgy and bess new york city opera 2002 complete

www.ingramcontent.com/pod-product-compliance
Lightning Source LLC
Chambersburg PA
CBHW071815230426

43670CB00013B/2463